T. S. Eliot's Civilized Savage

Major Literary Authors
Volume 22

STUDIES IN MAJOR LITERARY AUTHORS

OUTSTANDING DISSERTATIONS
VOLUME 22

Edited by

William Cain
Professor of English
Wellesley College

A ROUTLEDGE SERIES

Studies in Major Literary Authors

William E. Cain, *General Editor*

T. S. Eliot's Civilized Savage

Religious Eroticism and Poetics

Laurie J. MacDiarmid

Routledge
New York & London

Published in 2003 by
Routledge
29 West 35th Street
New York, NY 10001
www.routldge-ny.com

Published in Great Britain by
Routledge
11 New Fetter Lane
London EC4P 4EE
www.routledge.co.uk

Routledge is an imprint of the Taylor & Francis Group
Printed in the United States of America on acid-free paper.

10 9 8 7 6 5 4 3 2 1

Library of Congress Cataloging-in-Publication Data
MacDiarmid, Laurie J.
    T. S. Eliot's civilized savage : religious eroticism and poetics / by Laurie J. MacDiarmid.
        p. cm. — (Studies in major literary authors ; v. 22)
    Includes bibliographical references and index
    ISBN 0-415-96636-1 (alk. paper)
    1. Eliot, T. S. (Thomas Stearns), 1888–1965—Criticism, Textual. 2. Sacrifice in literature.
3. Religion in literature. 4. Sex in literature. 5. God in literature. I. Title. II. Series.
PS3509.L43 Z698 2003
821'.912—dc21   2002153814

Contents

Acknowledgments

I WOULD LIKE TO THANK THOSE WHO HAVE PROVIDED ME WITH VALUABLE TIME, insight and support, making the completion of this project possible. In particular, I would like to thank Herbert Schneidau for his cogent criticism, editing, conversation, encouragement and cheer leading. Tenney Nathanson and Lynda Zwinger have been instrumental, as well, as careful readers and critics.

Friends and family have stood by me as I developed draft after draft of the manuscript: Debbie, Sheila and Ann pored over manuscripts at the Blue Willow; Nina and Vicki were kind enough to tell me how smart I was at crucial moments; Natalie/Nana reminded me of what was important (and what was not); Jonathan was handy with academic witticisms and appropriate role-modeling; Gordon showed me how to meditate; Mom and Dad never doubted that I would finish, and finish well; Ed and Renée generously supported my last year of research and anguish; and of course Amy was always there to make the most of every happy and triumphant moment.

I would especially like to thank my husband, David, for his keen appreciation of my project and academic potential, his patient emotional and scholarly advice, his scathing sense of humor, his sly smile, and (best of all) for the joy of Elizabeth, who puts everything into perspective.

Abbreviations

CPP	*The Complete Poems and Plays, 1909-1950*
L	*The Letters of T. S. Eliot, Volume I (1898-1922)*
PWEY	*Poems Written in Early Youth*
SE	*Selected Essays*
SP	*Selected Prose*
WL	*The Waste Land: A Facsimile and Transcript of the Original Drafts*

Introduction

CURRENT BOOK-LENGTH STUDIES OF T. S. ELIOT FOCUS ON EXPOSING AND exploring his private life, particularly his relationships with women, the development of his philosophical thinking into a social poetic, his place and importance in studies of modernism and postmodernism as genres, and his conservative politics. My project explores and links several of these areas of interest, beginning with Eliot's controversial sexuality and masculinity and ending with his religious conversion.

In fact, Eliot solves an essentially personal problem—his tortuous vision of himself in relation to others, particularly women, which has often been diagnosed as a form of male hysteria—through his public act of confirmation to the Church of England in 1927. Eliot's problem might have been endemic to young men of his generation, as they struggled to escape and yet validate Victorian sexual mores and to subscribe to a concomitant Puritan work ethic in a time characterized by social mobility and uncertainty, changing political boundaries, and increasing medical freedom. As Eliot's poetry and criticism suggests, he suffered from these contradictory dicta so peculiarly and so flamboyantly that he can never be considered an ordinary case. Eliot's actions and reactions are ever eccentric; his solution to the "problems" that concern him throughout his artistic career and life—including what he refers to, in passing, as a sexual breakdown—is necessarily left (or right) of center.

The *Oxford English Dictionary* defines hysteria as a pathological condition of the nervous system attended by "emotional disturbances and enfeeblement or perversion of the moral and intellectual faculties," and an hysteric as, from the Latin and Greek, "belonging to the womb" and/or "suffering in the womb." Indeed, Eliot seems to suffer, in private, public and poetry, from a disturbance caused by a metaphorical womb. In "The Love Song of J. Alfred Prufrock," Eliot opens with an epigraph from Dante's *Inferno,* suggesting that the domestic space his poem describes is a purgatory with no exit. The space is suffocating, like "the chambers of the sea," a room where women come and go, merging into "sea-girls wreathed with seaweed red and brown," and a dreamy space that eventually drowns the poet (CPP 7).

Eliot's legendary gynephobia makes this entrapment exquisitely unbearable. It is an exquisite sentence for the sensitive poet precisely because he enjoys the body's suffering, as evidenced in his fascination with the lives of masochistic saints, and also pleasurable because he sees his surrender to an all-consuming Other as the impulse or aim of genuine art. Thus, Eliot repeatedly welcomes the opportunity to cry out from the womb's chaotic darkness. He concludes *Ash Wednesday* with this plea: "Sister, mother / And spirit of the river, spirit of the sea, / Suffer me not to be separated // And let my cry come unto Thee" (CPP 67).

At this point, Eliot's cry is no longer a plea for release but a prayer for imprisonment, enslavement. It is a velvet prison that Eliot seeks, as he asks to be subsumed in the Other (envisioned as God) in a mystical moment of intellectual surrender akin to a celestial coupling. The issue of this "impossible union" is—in Eliot's transformed imagination—divine incarnation, witness leading to personal and cultural salvation. Eventually, Eliot converts fantastic fears of the woman (conflated with fears of death and afterlife) into a fantasy of unmediated access to phallic power. "Old men ought to be explorers," Eliot concludes "East Coker":

> Here and there does not matter
> We must be still and still moving
> Into another intensity
> For a further union, a deeper communion
> Through the dark cold and the empty desolation,
> The wave cry, the wind cry, the vast waters
> Of the petrel and the porpoise. In the end is my beginning. (CPP 129)

The "dark cold and the empty desolation" of the sea, figured throughout Eliot's work as the woman's body, is crucial to Eliot's final poetic surrender as he reinvents poetic genesis and consciousness according to the original Christian plan.

First, Eliot transforms his hellish earthly woman or "wife" into a bodiless portal to the beyond, the silent Lady of *Ash Wednesday* who honors the Virgin with her pastoral contemplation. This chivalric idealization of the heterosexual relationship lets Eliot, a nervous husband at best, off the hook; he can dispense with sexual relations altogether, that is, as a necessity of vision. In the process, as poet he identifies with the woman, her self-sacrifice, her surrender of body and voice. Eliot uses the Catholic cult of the ideal mother, signified as the Virgin Mary, to proclaim himself open to the same "Father." In short, Eliot celebrates a self-inflicted emasculation, a metaphorical castration, as a means to pleasure and power. Eliot's perfect poet turns out to be the perfect mother.

The young Eliot flees America, Harvard and family to take up residence in a Europe whose mind appears refined and historical in "Tradition and the Individual Talent." Living in England, a homesick Eliot claims he is always cognizant of "a certain sense of confinement . . . and repression," and that the weather is always "dreadful" and "the middle class localities" he finds himself in are "far uglier than anything [he] can remember in France" (L 61). Eliot wallows in his loathing and longing, and many of these fears find their focus and/or object in Eliot's sexual woman, a "perverted" vision of the mother, who turns a voracious eye and appetite on the young poet-son. In reaction, Eliot constructs a celibate masculinity for his poet, celebrating surrender to the divine as a poetic imperative, impotence as an artistic necessity, and castration as the privileged place from which to speak. Eliot's poets delight to imagine their heads brought in upon a platter.

In early poetry and criticism, Eliot attempts to project this special brand of anti-masculinity into a poetic and social imperative using his graduate studies in comparative religious consciousness and rituals. To give his poetic an intellectual or "scientific" authority, Eliot draws from anthropological and sociological studies such as Frazer's *Golden Bough*, Jessie Weston's *From Ritual to Romance*, Émile Durkheim's *Elementary Forms of the Religious Life*, Lucien Lévy-Bruhl's *How Natives Think (Les Fonctions Mentales Dans Les Sociétés Inférieures)*, and Jane Harrison's *Themis*, using them to imagine the poet as a self-sacrificing representative of the (absent) modern God. Through his performance of death, that is, the poet resurrects not only himself but also his culture, speaking with divine sanction and voice. The vegetation god's execution involves, necessarily, a ritual emasculation—whether, as in Attis' case, as the metaphorical castration of crucifixion upon the laurel tree, or, as in the case of his ecstatic celebrants, as the literal and self-inflicted act. Eliot's drowning poet gleefully, then, lops off his power with his head. Eliot's further readings in modes of religious consciousness—particularly his interest in Evelyn Underhill's *Mysticism* and William James' *Varieties of Religious Experience*—validate his own mystical moments, moments that he worries and teases apart from his earliest drafts to his final *Four Quartets*. Thus, Eliot sees his "hysteria" and nervous breakdowns not as evidence of weakness or mental instability but as the opposite—clearly, he has been chosen as divine witness.

Poems such as "The Death of Saint Narcissus," "The Love Song of Saint Sebastian," "The Love Song of J. Alfred Prufrock" and "Hysteria" reveal Eliot's mystical, masochistic fantasies. He portrays his poet as a self-sacrificing priest akin to Frazer's dying god or king, a self-flagellating savior who pits himself against a hungry female audience, as Eliot's women blend maternal and sexual demands to act as the motivating force behind the modified vegetation ritual. Instead of the sacred marriage, Eliot's poet chooses a deliberate exile, death and reunion with a "higher power" that is coded asexual or male.

This apocalyptic vision explodes in the *Waste Land,* where, ironically enough, the poet's sexual phobias result in the disintegration of not only the modern cultural apparatus, including social, political and gender roles, but of the very landscape. In this amorphous and amoral state, the androgynous Tiresias represents the poet's world-weary and sexually distressed consciousness.

Later, as I demonstrate, Eliot transforms the "horrifying" heterosexual relationship using largely Christian mythology. At the same time, he declares his own religious belief to be more practical, or actual, than theoretical. Instead of using his religious background and experience as an abstract construction on which to "pin" his more "universal" ideas about poetry, Eliot throws himself wholeheartedly into the Void, speaking, like the burning bush, in the space between human and divine. Poems such as "Gerontion" and *The Hollow Men* are painfully mundane precursors to Eliot's genuinely confessional work. *Ash Wednesday* and *Four Quartets,* in other words, bring to the surface personal pains and tensions that Eliot is careful to mask in earlier work with witty "personas" and caustic social portraits on the order of Henry James. One could argue that Eliot's poetic philosophy is always Catholic in flavor, despite his best efforts to transform that rhetoric into a series of nearly scientific certainties.

In 1921, for example, "Tradition and the Individual Talent" exposes Eliot's ambivalent relationship to masculinity, sexuality, maternity and power. A close reading of this germinal essay reveals the start of Eliot's elaborate (and yet well-worn) conversion process. Though Eliot describes the poetic genesis as essentially male, fantasizing about a process of poetic conception and reproduction which is chemical and thus fantasized as free of the mess that is the woman's body, traces of Eliot's identification with the mother and the womb linger in the essay. He sterilizes these images and desires, however, by rinsing them in vaguely Catholic rhetoric. Though his description of the poet as catalyst anticipates, in a sense, in-vitro fertilization, Eliot's three-part essay cannot separate the clinical aspects of the transfer from the romantic and religious implications of Immaculate Conception. The Holy Trinity is the best objective correlative for Eliot's poetic relationships. Father sends Holy Ghost to impregnate Virgin Mother (redeemed, after the fact, through the miracle of Immaculate Conception) with himself—the savior/son. And so the "mind that creates" is separate from, and yet synonymous with, the "body that suffers." In this poetic family romance, Eliot not only imagines an exquisite sacrifice for himself but suggests that he is torn between identification with the suffering son and his silent mother—is Eliot's poet a cultural priest or prophet? Or is he, rather, a sanctified/purified womb? As an hysteric, he must be both.

In works such as *Ash Wednesday* and *Four Quartets,* Eliot foregrounds this Christian trope of reproduction. This poetic move allows Eliot to confess and atone for events in his personal life. Eliot's 1927 conversion to the Church of England comes on the heels of his abandonment of his first wife, Vivien, and at the start of his chaste romance with a youthful love, Emily Hale.[1] Read against a backdrop of biographical criticism, studies of Christian theology, and feminist theories of pollution and the abject, *Ash Wednesday* reveals how Eliot converts his "objective" poetry into a poetry of religious witness in yet another attempt to achieve his Ideal Order. Aligning the poet with the penitent, *Ash Wednesday* converts the sexual woman into the perfect vessel; a wordless virgin, she acts as the intercessor for the repentant poet. She is the perfect mother because she teaches the poet to sit still—so that he may hear, at last, the "Word without a word, the Word within / The world and for the world" (CPP 65). In this highly abstract relationship, both male and female are bodiless, the poet little more than dissembled bones in the desert given license to sing God's praise. Thus Eliot eliminates the threat of sexual intercourse and poet is welcomed into God's womb, the Holy Ghost.

Recent critical and popular forums have revived interest in Eliot's life and work—particularly his life as it is expressed in his work. Much of this notice is negative. "There are those, of course, who think that Eliot was wrong pretty much all the time," says Anthony Lane in a March 1997 response to the publication of Eliot's juvenilia as Christopher Ricks' heavily annotated *Inventions of the March Hare*. The release of these long guarded drafts excites a fresh round of re-evaluation, apology and excoriation. "There is much in 'The Inventions of the March Hare' that will cause the poetry police to twitch their batons in anticipation," says Lane: "Poor Tom was a fogey, a bigot, a woman-hater, and an anti-Semite, [and] now it turns out that he laughed at blacks, too. How's that for a full house?" (89) Anthony Julius' *T. S. Eliot, Anti-Semitism and Literary Form* anticipates this "discovery" of Eliot's ingrained racism; mainstream readers are perhaps more intrigued by Julius' notoriety as Princess Di's divorce lawyer than by his argument, but such studies have reactivated debates about Eliot's politics and his impact on modernist aesthetics, as well as speculation about the politics of modernism as a whole. Michael Hastings' *Tom and Viv* brings to the big screen Eliot's damaged and damaging relationships with women, suggesting that Eliot's collusion with medical and religious authorities was designed to project onto Vivien Haigh-Wood his own disease, and that Eliot profited financially, socially and artistically from his marriage to her.

It seems to be a truth universally acknowledged that any critic of Eliot must, these days, chose sides. Will you be an apologist or a judge? The taint is catching. Eliot's "anti-Semitism will become the preeminent symptom in his case history: Eliot was a hater, and therefore it is meet and right that we should hate him back," Lane summarizes. "What is most depressing about [this] Eliot issue," he continues, "is the moral vanity that seems to have crept into our reading habits—the demand that authors confirm our own convictions" ("Writing" 91). This demand appears to be reciprocal. We demand that authors reflect our most proper politics, or, conversely, that the authors we read confirm our political convictions. The "fact" that we continue to write about Eliot in anything but the most scathing terms serves as the preeminent symptom in our own case histories as incipient haters.

Eliot's fall from political grace is ascribed, primarily, to his racist and sexist fantasies and his (improperly) private life. Our equally unseemly interest in Eliot's sins expresses itself in the repeated exposure of, and speculation about, his somewhat flamboyant sexual and religious masquerades—his hasty marriage, a recognition of his own sexual neuroses in the diagnosis and rejection of his wife, his clandestine conversion, his monk-like habits, and his obsessive moral self-abuse or flagellation. In a turn-of-the-century age characterized by pervasive skepticism, Eliot's intellectual (and yet eroticized) Christian mysticism strikes us as an impotent attempt to escape his own domestic horrors and perverse sexuality. A re-examination of our own reactions to Eliot's developing social poetic may show us much about our own reconstruction of such matters as sexuality, poetics, politics and spirituality. Perhaps as we recoil from what we see as Eliot's corrosive "conservatism," we safeguard our own.

Close readings of Eliot's poems and drafts, supported by discussions of those studies in religious consciousness and sociology most influential on Eliot's developing poetic and public persona, illuminate the nature of Eliot's modern man and poetic mind. Furthermore, a knowledge of current thinking in sexual psychology and the formation of subjectivity, particularly those re-readings of Freud's theories of consciousness that emphasize the role of language, provides a more complex and rewarding theoretical vocabulary for this exploration. Despite—or perhaps because of—the difficulty of this sort of metaphysical examination, it offers the most appropriate method of reviewing or rethinking Eliot's corpus, since Eliot himself traces his intuition of the "impossible union" to a fundamental problem in (or before) the acquisition of language. His Sweeney complains, in *Sweeney Agonistes*, that he can't really say more than the facts, which are "[b]irth, copulation, and death" (CPP 80), because he's "gotta use words" when he talks to anyone (CPP 83). And poetry itself, as Eliot so eloquently fails to explain in "East Coker," becomes "a different kind of failure": "each venture / is a new beginning, a raid on the inarticulate / With shabby equipment always deteriorating / In the general mess of imprecision of feeling, / Undisciplined squads of emotion" (CPP 128). If a metaphorical castration is Eliot's poet's goal, then Lacan's extended metaphor—that we are all necessarily subjugated or "castrated" by language and its elaborate social contract—best describes Eliot's lament that, ultimately, "there is only the fight to recover what has been lost / And found and lost again and again: and now, under conditions / That seem unpropitious" (CPP 128).

My first chapter, "'The Death of Saint Narcissus': A Mystic's Cautionary Tale," explores Eliot's ambivalent thinking about the male poet as a self-selecting sacrificial lamb or "dancer to God" through a reading of this early—and largely repudiated— poem. The masochistic exile's performance on the burning sands is designed to regenerate an ailing culture through a divine intervention and/or interpretation that culminates in ritual self-sacrifice. Though the poem draws from Dionysian mythology and ritual as described in Frazer's *Golden Bough* and Harrison's *Themis*, Eliot also alludes to Christ's passion—specifically forty days' temptation as he speculates about (and attempts to practice) mythological "metamorphosis and interpenetration." This might be defined as the re-investment of contemporary art and worship with ancient or primitive emotions and the recreation of the worshipper's, or reader's, relationship to the community or culture through a higher power.

This ironic portrait of a would-be mystical hero and its precursor, "The Love Song of St. Sebastian," provides us with a preliminary working out of Eliot's poetic and religious passions, as well as a partial exorcism of his personal demons: his obsession with masochistic spectacle, his desire to be the mouthpiece for an exalted or prophetic utterance, and the narcissistic and erotic dangers he sees as inherent to any self-centered sacrifice or eroticized "penetration." Eliot sets the self-denying prophet/poet (soon to be called the voice of a generation) against the palpitating narcissi he sees as misrepresenting and thus corrupting a proper relation to God, imagined here, in Durkheim's terms, as the best expression of the culture or society itself. Finally, "The Death of Saint Narcissus" acts as both a confessional and a cautionary tale, suggesting to readers that romantic mysticism is, in actuality, a sexual pathology. Eliot's readings of William James' and Evelyn Underhill's studies of mystical consciousness help to explain the dichotomy he constructs between romantic and classical mysticism, and provide insight into what he might see as Narcissus' grand failure. In addition, a look at Ovid's *Metamorphoses*, particularly his portrayal of the Narcissus myth, reveals Eliot's reliance on this classical interpretation of the figure.

Though Eliot intends his portrait as an indictment or ritual extermination of such pleasure, the poem hints at an indulgence that cannot be revised or excised from Eliot's poetic and "personality." Eliot's act of deliberate repression backfires as his poem moves from cultural critique to self-exposure. "The Death of Saint Narcissus" actually anticipates the poet's fraught role in future poems and debates, as Eliot eventually performs the same narcissistic "dance" himself, making a fetish of celibacy and impotence, and positing the suffering body/mind as somehow more "receptive" to divine penetration. Eliot's poet identifies himself with the castrated lover or husband, mirrored by such damaged women as Philomel and Ophelia, whose tongue has been cut out.

My second chapter, "The Poet-Prophet in the Mouth of Madness," takes up Eliot's further development of the dying god trope, and his use of it to create an impotent masculinity as a poetic prophylactic for his endangered or dying male poet. (In Frazer's descriptions of rituals designed to pay homage to Attis, for instance, self-elected celebrants participate in an ecstatic commemoration of the god's resurrection by castrating themselves in a dancing frenzy and throwing their bloody members on the god's altar. Thereafter, they dress as women and are seen as the god's prophets.) As with his St. Narcissus, Eliot suggests that the poet is caught between impulses of prophecy and madness, divine inspiration and damnation. More often than not, his poet is lost, as is Narcissus, to sin or perversion. Like Frazer, Eliot is fascinated and repulsed by such self-sacrifices; his poems, like Frazer's long cross-cultural "descriptions," reveal a compulsion to repeat this primitive or primal scene.

Readings of poems such as "Portrait of a Lady" and "The Love Song of J. Alfred Prufrock" reveal how Eliot casts the woman as the jealous mother/lover who demands the poet's sacrifice, portrayed in Eliot's work as the heterosexual relation. In each case, temptation and damnation is fixed in the desiring woman, whose insistent demands force the poet to become a sort of male Cassandra for his culture—a blind Tiresias punished by the woman for his sexual refusal. Eliot portrays the heterosexual relationship as a power struggle between the black widow, a disturbingly sexualized vision of the mother/lover, and her paralyzed prey. In the process, Eliot creates a troubled distinction between male and female desire and utterance—what he might see as poetic and perverse—in the effort to erect boundaries over areas of collapse, infection or penetration. A careful reading of Eliot's prose poem "Hysteria," placed against "Sweeney Agonistes" and the *Waste Land*'s "A Game of Chess," reveals this process. Eliot portrays the poet's consciousness as an attempt to "say what one means," to illuminate the divine. Even in his failure, then, Eliot's poet is aligned with God or divine prophecy, as is Tiresias, the central consciousness of the *Waste Land.* In contrast, Eliot equates female utterance with neurotic chatter, senseless repetition, epileptic laughter or hysteria. The woman's obsessive "talking cure" contaminates the *Waste Land,* drowning out the poet's weakened voice. Her voice and desire are rooted in material desires and demands: her goals are erotic, romantic, narcissistic, masturbatory. Eliot's marriage to Vivien Haigh-Wood provides an interesting comparison for his exploration of such damaged sexual relations. Clearly, he draws on personal material to develop his poetry, poetic and criticism.

Though Eliot portrays all souls in the *Waste Land* as spiritually damaged, only his poets attempt to repair the rupture between physical and metaphysical worlds through asceticism. The spiritual wound Eliot identifies is, ultimately, linked to a fundamental problem in sexual relations: modern citizens, bound to the earthly wheel, have confused Forster's plea, "Only connect," with a sexual imperative. As Eliot suggests in the *Waste Land,* this lack of transcendence results in the Father's inability to speak or mean, as in "What the Thunder Said" —which itself results in a cultural castration or death. In other words, the Word is swallowed by the *vagina dentata.* Eliot's poets attempt to "fix" the neurotic woman but their efforts are doomed, swallowed by or converted into the woman's hysteria or madness.

Eventually, the poet is driven into silence, exile, purgatory. Eliot's poet is compelled to repeat this mistake, unable to resist the woman's paralyzing presence and seductive pathology. Though he wishes to transform her hysteria into a prophetic insight, Eliot's poet discovers himself a willing participant in it. Readings of the poems suggest, in fact, that Eliot's poet seeks out these encounters and failures, finding his own pleasure in wordless submission to the woman's desires.

My third chapter, "Transformations," centers on a reading of "Tradition and the Individual Talent" in order to explore the evolution of Eliot's poetic of passive *male* incarnation. In this germinal essay, Eliot relies on an extended scientific analogy to describe the poet as "sacrificing himself" at every moment to something greater. He argues that poetry's (and, through it, tradition's) "salvation" lies not in worshipping a poet's personality—or, as he puts it, suffering body—but in, first, the poet's surrender to a fatal performance and, second, our ritual re-enactment of this transformation. Eliot proposes a poetic, then, that is masochistic and spectacular. Cultural regeneration depends upon our recognition, and mimicry, of the poet's sacrifice. In essence, Eliot conceives of his poet as a cultural or artistic savior, and the act of poetic creation as the processes of incarnation and, to a certain extent, Immaculate Conception. The extent of his analogy is ambiguous; is Eliot suggesting that the poet is a John the Baptist, Adonis, a Christ, or a Virgin Mary?

What is clear in this essay is Eliot's obsessive need to avoid the sexual relation that so plagues his poetry. Rather than employing metaphors of copulation and birth, Eliot relies on the chemistry laboratory and the abstract language of philosophy to evoke the act of conception in the service of an Ideal male Order. This revision is, like his poets' attempts at sexual intercourse, doomed to failure. Though Eliot would like to center poetic incarnation in an intellectual or metaphysical discourse, his essay dwells on ideas of homosocial genealogy and reproduction: every poet must write with his dead ancestors in his bones in order to recreate the monuments of Tradition. Thus, even Eliot's scientific analogies are charged with pathological residue.

Given that Eliot's descriptions suggest that poetic reproduction involves an intellectual reincarnation and transformation of the poet's dead forefathers, the poet's role in the act of conception remains elusive. He is clearly not the phallus/pen that dips into the material and extracts, as if from his own head, the poem whole. Eliot's fantasy of the tradition that penetrates the individual talent does not, that is, conform to the usual male fantasies of reproduction. Is Eliot's poet, indeed, the catalyst for a chemical reaction? Or is he the pure mind or receptacle for this "divine" incarnation?

Arguably, Eliot identifies himself more with the maternal space—the colonized body or virgin womb—than with the invading tradition. This identification is plagued by contradiction, appropriation and attempted transformation. A review of Eliot's own ambivalent relationship to his poetry-writing mother, investigations into the cult of ideal motherhood at the turn of the twentieth century, and a look at changing ideals of masculinity and masculine power (as well as Eliot's resistance to such paradigms), contributes to our understanding of these ambiguous currents in Eliot's poetics. A reading of "Hamlet and his Problems" fleshes out this investigation of Eliot's identification with and repudiation of the mother.

My fourth chapter, "Madness or Mysticism: Eliot's Dream-Crossed Twilight," discusses Eliot's shift from secular to religious thinking, and from an "objective" to a highly subjective poetic. Beginning with *The Hollow Men,* and in *Ash Wednesday,* Eliot changes the terms of his discourse. He abandons his reliance on anthropological and sociological investigations of classical sacrifice and resurrection narratives in favor of modern Christian—"Anglo-catholic," in his terms—analogues. His project becomes the attempt to experience one of his greatest fears: life after death. Interestingly enough, this frightening territory is inhabited by Eliot's Lady. She, too, has been killed and resurrected into a more "perfect" life and appears now as the Lady of silences—the untouchable virgin who acts as an intercessor for the penitent poet. Her self-sacrifice to this function not only eliminates the poet's fear of sexual relation but allows him to be reunited with the missing Father. Significantly, Eliot's poet no longer flees from the woman's desire but shares in it as he merges with her spirit. Perhaps Eliot's woman has come to represent pure soul, following the "archetypes" and other clichés popularized by spiritually inclined psychoanalysts such as Carl Jung.

In any case, by converting the woman to this "torn and most whole" emblem of Immaculate Conception and incarnation, Eliot is able to appropriate the maternal/feminine and to act out his own ecstatic annihilation and recuperation. Eliot comes to see the poet's role as a performance of a deliberate emasculation. His later poetry celebrates this lack, as Eliot's penitent poet plays the transvestite or hermaphrodite. The poet assumes the woman's role in order to perform for God. Eliot thus transfers the eroticism of the missing sexual relation to the penitent's relationship with the Father. Ultimately, Eliot's religious poetry describes a cultural family romance between Father and Son (Immaculate Conception, incarnation, sacrifice of the son), where women serve as passive human receptacles for this power.

This turn in Eliot's attention coincides with some of the most transitional years of his private life. In 1927, he converts to the Church of England; in 1932, he separates from Vivien while spending a year in Harvard for the Norton fellowship; in 1938, Eliot co-signs the papers for Vivien's commitment to Northumberland House. In the years between his separation, Vivien's gradual breakdown and her commitment, Eliot rekindles a chaste relationship with a youthful sweetheart, Emily Hale. Biographers such as Lyndall Gordon argue that Eliot's merciful Lady of silences and the brief moments of transcendent clarity in "Burnt Norton" are inspired by this relationship. Again, Eliot uses his poetry as a forum for private anxieties and terrors; the tone of these religious poems is more overtly confessional and emotional than "Prufrock" and the *Waste Land*. *Ash Wednesday* signals a significant change in Eliot's "objective" poetry, that is. Now, he sees the poet's cultural value in a particularly *personal* religious witness.

My final chapter, "Return of the Repressed," takes up the significance of Eliot's conversion, his self-promotion as a significant modernist poet, his confessional poetry masquerading as "objective correlatives" for poetic or transcendent emotion, and his vexed private life and desires. At the same time, I look at contemporary resurrections of this Pope of Russell Square, such as Michael Hastings' play *Tom and Viv* and the subsequent Hollywood release starring Miranda Richardson and Willem Dafoe. (A Cynthia Ozick article, "Eliot at 101," sets the stage for this popular revision of Eliot's image.) The Hollywood film suggests that Eliot used his religious conversion to eliminate Vivien—who not only provided him with the intellectual and financial means to create his most famous poetry, but who somehow represented his own uncertain sexuality and neuroses, or at the very least reminded him of them—and to avoid a latent homosexuality. Certainly, the film portrays Eliot's relationship to the Church as homoerotic. Such evidence implies that we are simultaneously fascinated with and repulsed by Eliot's life: after our voyeurism, we argue that Eliot used the "savagery" of his religious proclivities to engage in the ritualistic emotional mutilation of the women who supported him. We identify ourselves, as viewers and postmodern readers, with the women damaged by Eliot's ambitions for purity and sainthood—seeing the culture as wounded, in turn, by Eliot's disdain, sanctimonious withdrawal and implied condemnation.

Stepping back from this resurgence in Eliotic interest, I conclude that we (in the academy and outside of it) use Eliot in much the same way that we accuse him of using Viv and other women to create his purified poetry. In an age weaned on Freud and imbued with the deepest skepticism, especially regarding the issues of spirituality and the afterlife, Eliot's conversion (read as an abandonment and institutionalization of Vivien, and an apparent rejection of middle-class or bourgeois values) appears as a direct challenge to the public he rejected. It is seen as an invasive attempt to impose order on an untidy, even abject, personal life by writing a prescription for the public.

Eliot's contemporary critics use him, in turn, as the icon of a particular apocalypse, setting him up as the Guy Fawkes of the modernist era. A reawakened interest in Eliot's foibles shows how we use Eliot's personal politics to condemn him as a literary figure, poet and supposed mouthpiece of a generation. A reading of *Tom and Viv* ultimately points out, to even a casual viewer, how we cast ourselves as the happy "savages" in Eliot's apocalyptic visions, identifying with Vivien (recast in our own cultural fantasies as the all-suffering, and rather practical, amanuensis) over the stick-up-the-ass Tom.

Mary Douglas, in her *Purity and Danger,* describes such attempts to separate, purify, demarcate and punish transgressions as the imposition of "system on an inherently untidy experience" (4). So we can apply some of the same criticisms launched against Eliot to ourselves. "It is only by exaggerating the difference between within and without," Douglas reminds us, "above and below, male and female, with and against, that a semblance of order is created" (4). Somehow, Eliot's flamboyant contradictions in self-presentation—his uncertain sexuality, his "ambiguous" relations with women, his attempts to distance and purify himself from what he thought of as middle-class moral bankruptcy, and his clear ambitions as a poet and critic—trouble our own boundaries. We fight this war for the borderlands in the shaky definitions of modernism and postmodernism that plague many current discussions of Eliot's place in literary studies and mainstream culture.

The past years have seen quite a few studies of Eliot's poetry, prose and poetics, and even of the development of his philosophic and religious thinking, his misogyny and his sexuality. Few of these attempt to tackle the webbed relationships between them. That Eliot attempted to create and maintain a social order he thought lacking in the modern world is no longer an issue; he failed, even in his own estimation, to do so. We have not explored the extent of the pleasure Eliot derived from that failure, nor have we examined Eliot's concerted and continuing celebration of impotence. Despite his documented gynephobia, Eliot knit his new religious consciousness with a sexual subjectivity identified with such religious icons as the Virgin Mary, creating a masculine subject position for himself that has more to do with masquerade than mastery. Perhaps this exploration is made more difficult because we seem reluctant—particularly as members of the academy—to examine Eliot's religious thinking in any detail. Once he converts to the Church of England, we dismiss Eliot as a crackpot or a cliché, assuming that he used his conservative religion to cordon himself off from matters of modern importance.

Feminist readings of Eliot's work, sexuality and religious thinking are rare. Most are based on the premise of Eliot's will to power or mastery over the women who participated in his rise to fame and fortune. Even Jewel Spears Brooker, one of Eliot's leading female critics, sees Eliot's "escape" into religion as a form of mastery. Fewer than six book length studies focus on Eliot's sexuality, or the images of women in his work; though helpful in delineating potentially pathological aspects in his ego formation and object choice (most argue that he is gynephobic and homosexual), these explorations break no new ground. They are more interesting for what they leave out: none of these studies force us to take into consideration cultural projection or transference. They do not ask us to question or examine our own assumptions about gender roles, religious rituals and relationships. In many cases, Eliot is made the scapegoat (perhaps with good reason) for a century's tortured thoughts about gender, sexuality and God.

A re-reading of Eliot's poetics, religion and sexuality should further exhume Eliot's influential, if still negative, place in modern relationships, artistic and social.

We need, as Eliot reminds us, to move back to the close readings, since it is through "explanation" or theory that we risk losing sight of the object of our study: ourselves.

T. S. Eliot's Civilized Savage

1.

"The Death of Saint Narcissus"
A Poet's Cautionary Tale

Come under the shadow of this gray rock—
Come in under the shadow of this gray rock,
And I will show you something different from either
Your shadow sprawling over the sand at daybreak, or
Your shadow leaping behind the fire against the red rock:
I will show you his bloody cloth and limbs
And the gray shadow on his lips.

   He walked once between the sea and the high cliffs
When the wind made him aware of his limbs smoothly passing each other
And of his arms crossed over his breast.
When he walked over the meadows
He was stifled and soothed by his own rhythm.
By the river
His eyes were aware of the pointed corners of his eyes
And his hands aware of the pointed tips of his fingers.

Struck down by such knowledge
He could not live men's ways, but became a dancer before God
If he walked the city streets
He seemed to tread on faces, convulsive thighs and knees.
So he came out under the rock.

   First he was sure that he had been a tree,
Twisting its branches among each other
And tangling its roots among each other.

   Then he knew that he had been a fish
With slippery white belly held tight in his own fingers,

Writhing in his own clutch, his ancient beauty
Caught fast in the pink tips of his new beauty.

Then he had been a young girl
Caught in the woods by a drunken old man
Knowing at the end the taste of his own whiteness
The horror of his own smoothness,
And he felt drunken and old.

So he became a dancer to God.
Because his flesh was in love with the burning arrows
He danced on the hot sand
Until the arrows came.
As he embraced them his white skin surrendered itself to the redness of blood,
   and satisfied him.
Now he is green, dry and stained
With the shadow in his mouth. (PWEY 28-30)

THE DEATH OF SAINT NARCISSUS" STANDS OUT—STYLISTICALLY, THEMATICALLY and intellectually—from Eliot's earlier juvenilia. More primitive in form and polish than its highly rhetorical precursors, the playful free-verse poem describes, in detail, Narcissus' sadomasochistic sexuality, equating religious "worship" with solipsistic vampirism. Meandering, composed of longer, unmetered lines and shorter, haphazard stanzas, "The Death of Saint Narcissus" is light years from the gynephobic set pieces of "Nocturne" and "Circe's Palace," or the rhetorical preciousness of "Spleen." It provides a breath of fresh air to conclude *Poems Written in Early Youth*—if nothing else, its difference marks it as a turning point in Eliot's poetic attention and it introduces images and ideas that Eliot returns to throughout his career.

The poem previews, for instance, the characteristic tone and rhythm—the infamous "tom tom" beat—that Eliot develops in "Portrait of a Lady" and refines in his drama. "The Death of Saint Narcissus" serves as the boundary between Eliot's juvenilia and his established poetic career—even as the border between waning romanticism and what we now call modernism.

Though the poem's title and opening stanza gesture toward one of the motivating interests of Eliot's mother's poetry—the short and bloody lives of Christian martyrs—Eliot's saint surrenders in a ritual self-sacrifice more Dionysian than Christian. The poem ends with a masturbatory rather than redemptive passion. Even a casual reader of the poem will observe that Eliot's dancer does not contribute to the spiritual health of any tribe or "city." Quite the contrary: the city people and their appetites disgust the delicate Narcissus. Instead, he runs from the "knowledge" of others, unable to "live men's ways." No disciple, Narcissus ends his desert journey with sterile self-satisfaction, merging with an empty landscape. The issue of Narcissus' intercourse with "God" (who, we suspect, he has created in the image of himself) is the "dry," "stained" land, the shadow under the rock. Narcissus' dance mocks the act of communion as he consumes himself.

Eliot's Saint Narcissus promises no afterlife. In fact, Eliot's use of repetitive images of shadow, darkness, blood and mortality in the poem emphasizes its central figure's destructive effect; the "gray shadow on his lips" becomes an odd echo of Christ's bloody shroud, signaling the termination, rather than redemption, of life.

Lest we assume that Saint Narcissus' motives are altruistic or aesthetic, Eliot invents a psychic history for him that emphasizes erotic self-love (or, as the times would have it, self-abuse) over religious witness. This Saint Narcissus obviously escapes the city in order to be with his beloved: himself. His dance involves ecstatic self-caressing, voyeurism turned inward, wild self-invention, and even the hair-raising taste of his own rape.

Unlike the mechanical exercises that precede it, "The Death of Saint Narcissus" begins to develop Eliot's notion of the poet's social and cultural role as it draws overtly from his readings in comparative anthropology and sociology. The poem's evolutionary imagery describes—jokingly—the development of Eliot's poetic consciousness, and suggests that it has roots in "primitive" religious (and, by nature, sexual) violence. If Eliot intends his St. Narcissus to represent a "missing link" between savage fertility rites and Catholicism (in order to suggest, partially, that Catholicism is the missing link between classicism and Protestantism), the layered poem implies that these modes of experience are "reincarnated" in the modern mind, and that a canny reader/writer can bring them to consciousness in order to re-experience them . . . from the safety of his[1] armchair.

These mystical moments of perception or, in Levy-Bruhl's terms, collective representation, might be compared to Freud's contemporaneous descriptions of dreams and dreamwork. William Skaff shows that Eliot was aware of Freud's crucial work—though he would have been more intrigued, Skaff claims, by the thinking of some of Freud's followers, such as Jung, who investigated religious and mystical feeling using aspects of Freud's theory of the unconscious. According to Skaff, Eliot would have eventually found all psychological explanations of consciousness unsatisfactory. He would have abandoned Jung's theory of the collective unconscious, for instance, because of its emphasis on psyche over the soul. "Like natural science," Skaff concludes, "psychoanalytic theory becomes for Eliot another point of view misguidedly attempting to subsume all others, whereas he sought an explanation for religious feeling which only a synthesis of all points of view, an approximation of the Absolute, could provide" (74).

Eliot's interest in unspeakable emotions and desires, as well as their indescribable expression, informed his studies of primitive or early religious rituals. One of Eliot's professors at Harvard, James Haughton Woods, who taught Eliot Greek philosophy and introduced him to Heraclitus in 1911-12, describes one such ritual in his *Practice and Science of Religion* (1906). As he composed "The Death of Saint Narcissus," Eliot must have remembered this passage from his professor's work:

> In the forest at night the men dance in a circle around the arrow stuck tip down in the ground. There are fires to add to the festive character of the scene. There are rhythmic cries, expressions of thanks or of hope. This continues until all are worked up to almost convulsive excitement. But there is no clear concept of an arrow spirit, or of a god, or of any soul. The dance expresses what they want; but the idea is not so clear that it can be expressed in a concept or in a word or in a figure. (qtd in Crawford 74)

Certainly, Narcissus' dance imitates, in some aspects, the fertility rites that James Frazer documents in *Golden Bough*. As Robert Crawford suggests, "anthropology seeded [Eliot's] imagination, giving him a tactical weapon in his literary struggles" (75). St. Narcissus' arrow dance, characterized by "convulsive and hallucinatory violence of the most savage sort," survives in Eliot's mature work (Crawford 75). A fragment of the poem appears in the *Waste Land*'s "Burial of the Dead"—"the shadow in his mouth" becomes "shadow under this red rock," "your shadow at evening striding behind you" and "your shadow at evening rising to meet you" combined in "fear in a handful of dust" (CPP 38).

Finally, Eliot's Narcissus provides a negative example of his ideal artist, the priest-poet he envisions as a mouthpiece and savior for a moribund culture. Instead of rejuvenating the rituals and spiritual life of his "tribe" by sacrificing his body, soul and (most important) art to the social and historical "consciousness" that Eliot outlines in such essays as "Tradition and the Individual Talent," or expressing his culture's collective will or psyche through his dance as Émile Durkheim explains *Elementary Forms of the Religious Life*, St. Narcissus devours himself. William Skaff suggests, in *The Philosophy of T. S. Eliot*, that Frazer's descriptions offer Eliot a structure for his conception of the historical "unconscious"—the force that Eliot implies must motivate poetry. The primitive religious "dance," a wordless offering to the gods, comes closer, in Eliot's terms, than modern "abstractions" to expressing this racial memory, this communal experience of the divine; the poet's job must be to find a voice for this more original, culturally connected desire. In his "London Letter" of 1921, Eliot proclaims that art must attempt "interpenetration and metamorphosis," that it must offer a "revelation of that vanished mind of which our mind is a continuation" (453).

In 1923, Eliot restates this, arguing that "savage or primitive art" comes closer to capturing this raw emotional essence than tragedy or comedy. Classical forms, Eliot argues, are already abstractions and as such "require to be renewed or replaced" (11). Dance, on the other hand, is the foundation of the dramatic impulse, in Eliot's estimation. "The drama was originally ritual," Eliot comments, foreshadowing his first, religious dramas, "and ritual, consisting of a set of repeated movements, is essentially a dance" (12). Eliot bemoans the modern audience's failure to find meaning behind the drum's beating as well as its inability to find a vehicle—a proper ritual—for its expression. "We have lost the drum," Eliot concludes (12).

In *Four Quartets*, however, Eliot proposes a solution to this problem. He offers "a symbol perfected in death" as the expression of this heart or drumbeat, suggesting that it resides in prayer, or a poetry that emanates from "a single party" of the "defeated" who embraces "the constitution of silence" as he merges with the great "I am": "I think . . .," Eliot writes, "Of three men, and more, on the scaffold / . . . / Why should we celebrate / These dead men more than the dying?" After all, "We cannot revive old factions / We cannot restore old policies / Or follow an antique drum." Finally, these sacrificial men, no doubt imagined from Jesus' crucifixion, "Accept the constitution of silence" that is Paradise and are thus "folded in a single party" with God, the perfect symbol:

> Whatever we inherit from the fortunate
> We have taken from the defeated
> What they had to leave us—a symbol:
> A symbol perfected in death.

Appropriately enough, Eliot ends this pronouncement in a benediction: "And all shall be well and / All manner of thing shall be well / By the purification of the motive / In the ground of our beseeching" (CPP 143).

"The Death of Saint Narcissus" presents its readers with a puzzle. Though the poem denigrates Narcissus' self-sacrifice, it also celebrates the young man's impulse to leave the "convulsive thighs and knees" of the filthy city behind, and lingers with loving detail over Narcissus' sacrifice to God's "burning arrows." Is the poem actually an homage?

Eliot draws particularly from Sir James G. Frazer's volumes on the male vegetation god's cross-cultural death and rebirth to create Narcissus. Adonis' lynching on the laurel tree and Attis' dismemberment, ritually re-enacted each year by ecstatic penitents, provide a backdrop for the saint's brutal dance. Frazer's fascinated (and fascinating) descriptions of such ceremonies linger between Eliot's lines and Eliot borrows Frazer's ambivalent involvement in the material—Frazer's sense of shock as he describes each bloody ritual of emasculation in excruciating detail, as well as his equally powerful interest in conveying such details in a vivid manner. Like Frazer, Eliot seems bent on reviewing the "primitive" nature of such ritual expressions, as well as our ability to tap into these urges or experiences even in "civilized" or "modern" ceremonies. When he suggests that religious worship is an evolutionary process, moving from the self outward, Eliot touches on Freud's contemporaneous impression of self-satisfaction as a "primordial" or pre-social urge that develops into narcissism (Freud, "On Narcissism" 59). Freud suggests that autoerotic "instincts" are the unconscious underpinnings, or the more savage roots, of a civilized narcissism, while Eliot's poem implies that masochistic Christianity springs from (and contains) Dionysian impulses.

"If elements of primitivism were entering Eliot's poetry," says Robert Crawford, in *The Savage and the City in the Work of T. S. Eliot*, "it should not be assumed that he was simply a would-be savage. Eliot was sensitive about his interests in the primitive" (78), probably because these interests connected a few nodes of experience for him: religion, sexuality, consciousness (vs. what was coming to be known as the unconscious), and love. "His reading on Christian mysticism shows him to have been interested particularly in the physical and often sexual violence associated with extreme religious emotion," says Crawford.

> He was interested in Murisier's connections between illness and vision, reading Janet on hallucination and hysteria, and was investigating religio-sexual frenzy. He transcribed on to one of his index cards the words of Havelock Ellis in *The Psychology of Sex*, 'Love and religion are the two most volcanic emotions to which the human organism is liable.' . . . Even expressed in late romantic terms, Eliot had a hunger after and a horrified fascination with 'the voice of men in pain' and flowers whose 'petals are fanged and red / With hideous streak and stain.' Potent, bloody sexuality could furnish an escape from impotent pallor . . . (79)

"Eliot was fascinated by the idea that such intense experience might even now be available to modern man," Crawford concludes (80). Merely touching on such sensitive issues, however, compelled Eliot to deny his investment in them, even—or especially—to his closest male friends. "Eliot's attitude towards primitive man was ambivalent," Crawford explains. "The savage could seem intensely foolish, devoting great energies to inane projects. At other times he could seem a vital origin, a source to be seriously examined and tapped" (76).

On the surface, Eliot undercuts Freud's interest in the "primitive" and the unconscious that somehow retains it by assiduously condemning unconscious or pre-social urges. In fact, a cursory reading of "The Death of Saint Narcissus" yields a diatribe against the pleasure this beautiful youth derives from the violation of his own "smooth" body. Eliot portrays Narcissus' dreams of power and past incarnations as deluded fantasies for masturbation—the "green, dry and stained" corpse, laid out with the "shadow in his mouth," conjures up the evacuation of masturbation. So Narcissus' fleshy love, surrender and satisfaction are all puerile at best, and his celebratory dance offers no improvement on the race. Rather, Narcissus devolves, as his own fantasies follow the trajectory from tree to fish to girl to rock. That Narcissus justifies this breakdown and infantile satisfaction for God's sake makes it all the more horrifying.

Eliot's poem captures his anxiety about the implications of the self-sacrificing worship that he wants to posit as the method of his modern poetic. The poem suggests that Narcissus is punished, erased, because he inverts the proper principles of hierarchy: God to man. As Kaja Silverman asserts in *Male Subjectivity at the Margins*, masochism poses a challenge to the "proper" order by transgressing or blurring traditional boundaries, blending such supposed opposites as pleasure and pain, man and woman, self and other. The male masochist, like Narcissus, takes on the role designated as "feminine" in pleasure, identifying with the mother and desiring the father. As a result, he "leaves his social identity completely behind—actually abandons his 'self,' and passes over into the 'enemy terrain' of femininity" (Silverman 190).

It is this sexualized challenge to the Ideal Order and its social responsibilities that Eliot appears to reject in "The Death of Saint Narcissus." He might agree with Janine Chassequet-Smirgel's summary of the situation: "The pervert is trying to free himself from the paternal universe and the constraints of the law. He wants to create a new kind of reality and to dethrone God the father" (qtd in Silverman 187). Narcissus is a sinner—by exalting and pleasing himself rather than God, Eliot's dancer frees himself from the social and cultural constraints that Eliot claims, in his poetic, to be defending.

Freud suggests that those men who, like Narcissus, are "plainly seeking themselves as a love-object" (rather than their mothers, the proper objects of such manly affections), are those "whose libidinal development has suffered some disturbance, as in perverts and homosexuals" ("On Narcissism" 69). Eliot's Narcissus is steeped in the same air of perversion and homoeroticism. Readers such as James E. Miller, Jr. are quick to use Freud's theory of narcissism against Eliot, speculating that his rejection of Saint Narcissus is a failed attempt to cover his identification with him. Narcissus' flamboyant self-destruction is evidence of Eliot's suppressed homosexuality, Miller argues. According to this reading, Eliot does not deplore so much as explore Narcissus' perversion through poem. The harder Eliot tries to flog his poor demon, the more certain we become that Eliot takes pleasure in it for his own sake.

Eliot was, of course, aware of these speculations as he composed "The Love Song of St. Sebastian" and revised it as "The Death of Saint Narcissus." He even indulged in such speculation (anxiously and defensively) himself. In a letter to Conrad Aiken, Eliot worries that his interest in the arrow-infested portraits of St. Sebastian, the models for his Narcissus, will be seen as homosexual. Rather than putting such fears to rest, however, Eliot's defensive strategy calls attention to his sexual fascinations: " . . . I have studied S. Sebastians," Eliot writes, wondering "why should anyone paint a beautiful youth and stick him full of pins (or arrows) unless he felt a little as the hero of my verse?"

And how does the hero of Eliot's verse "feel"? Eliot implies that there *is* something erotic in such a heightened awareness of the body. "Only there's nothing homosexual about this," Eliot goes on, "—rather an important difference perhaps—but no one ever painted a female Sebastian, did they? So I give this title *faute de mieux*" (L 44).[2] Eliot's logic is a little confusing. It's as if he's arguing that the depiction of St. Sebastian's agony can't be called homosexual, or even homoerotic, because it always takes place, *faute de mieux*, between men who "feel" the same way.

Ultimately, poor Narcissus operates both as Eliot's fool and as his proxy, singled-out, ostracized and destroyed for indulging himself in the very guilty desires at the heart of Eliot's poetic philosophy. Narcissus serves as Eliot's whipping boy; it's a small leap to suggest that Eliot fills Narcissus with his own sexual guilt, and then punishes his hapless double.[3] Narcissus' death is indeed necessary for Eliot's rebirth as a poet/prophet with his finger on the culture's pulse—after all, he embodies Eliot's childish desires for self-importance and social satisfaction, his atavistic (and homoerotic) sexuality, and his murderous attitude toward the (absent) mother.

"The Death of Saint Narcissus" might be Eliot's most persistent and persuasive poetic aberration or failure. Judging from the poem's tortured history of production, publication and partial repression, its survival suggests that Eliot (and others) found more than puerile titillation or post-adolescent atonement in its various images. Incomplete revisions and censorship testify to the strangeness and difficulty that Eliot and his readers associate with the poem and its material. The poem serves as a hair-raising relic in Eliot's canon, its life mirroring the self-wounding and suicide depicted in it. Readers return to the rock, turn it over, and look with compelled (and compelling) disdain on the "bloody cloth and limbs" or the "gray shadow on his lips."[4] Eliot's brother, Henry, for example, worked with Donald Gallup to establish the Harvard Collection of Eliot's works after his death. In the process of collecting and collating Eliot's notebooks and early drafts, Henry Eliot dismissed "The Death of Saint Narcissus" out of hand, calling it "strained . . . bizarrerie" that "doesn't quite 'come off'" (Gallup 241). (Eliot's brother calls attention to the poem's erotic content even as he dismisses it from consideration—it's a poem about coming that doesn't come off.)

The poem's lengthy history is fraught with abortions, dead-ends and literary murders. In 1914, Eliot sent an initial study of the Narcissus character to Conrad Aiken, tentatively titled "The Love Song of St. Sebastian" and intended as part of a longer series, "Descent from the Cross," that he never finished (L 43-47). These drafts survived, apart from the letter to Aiken, with the original typescripts for the *Waste Land* that Eliot bequeathed, before his death, to John Quinn (L 44n). "The Death of Saint Narcissus" nearly appeared in an issue of *Poetry*—recovered galleys reveal that someone struck through entire stanzas of the poem before giving the "kill" order in the margin for the whole. Two versions of the poem appear with drafts for the *Waste Land* but they, too, have been eliminated—with the exception of a single, revised stanza—from the published version. The poem first appears in print, almost as an afterthought, at the end of *Poems Written in Early Youth*, 1967.

Likewise, "Narcissus" didn't receive much consideration during editing sessions (now famous because of Ezra Pound's midwifery) for the *Waste Land*. Eliot's two manuscript copies of the poem—scored and blurred from folding and, we might suppose, from sitting so long in his back pocket—remain untouched by Pound's acerbic commentary. In a letter to Eliot dated 24 December 1921, Pound congratulates Eliot for putting "the remaining superfluities at the end," and suggests that he "leave 'em, abolish 'em altogether for the present." If "Narcissus" remains among these "superfluities," Pound believes that it "does not advance on earlier stuff" (L 497). It could be that Saint Narcissus' dance smacks too much of retreat for Pound's taste, or that the section is too confessional to fit his "austere" vision for the poem.

On the other hand, it's equally possible that Narcissus is just one eccentric among many in Eliot's menagerie, sacrificed—in this case—for the sake of "masculine" brevity.[5] After all, as Pound comments in the half-joking occasional poem that he appends to his letter of congratulation on the *Waste Land's* finish, the final product is a landmark of male procreation. There is no place in this reproductive triumph, this "pachyderm" conception, for the flabby, fey or feminine: "These are the Poems of Eliot," he proclaims, "By the Uranian Muse begot; / A Man their Mother was, / A Muse their Sire. // How did the printed Infancies result / From Nuptuals thus doubly difficult? / If you must needs enquire / Know diligent Reader / That on each Occasion / Ezra performed the caesarean Operation" (L 498).

Pound walks the same fine line as Eliot does in "The Death of Saint Narcissus," at once dismissing and enlarging the homoerotic nature of the poetic act—what Eliot calls a dance. For a man to become a mother, as Pound suggests, the Uranian muse must visit . . . everything, that is, depends on Uranus.

Pound's rhapsodic introduction emphasizes Eliot's feminine role in the transaction: "Complimenti, you bitch," he writes, then celebrates his own vigorous contribution to the transaction, his "deformative secretions": "His foaming and abundant cream / Has coated his world. The coat of a dream; / Or say that the upjut of his sperm / Has rendered his senses pachyderm" (L 499). In short, though Pound feels that "The Death of Saint Narcissus" doesn't, as Henry Eliot puts it, quite "come off," with a little help from Uranus and friends the *Waste Land* certainly does.

Critics agree. "Narcissus" should be faulted for excesses and missteps rather than examined for its relevance to the development of Eliot's mature poetic. The general impulse is to cite the poem as a lapse—at best a fortunate fall—in Eliot's elaborate personal defenses, or to use it as an unguarded autobiographical moment in a body of work renowned for deliberate indirection. "Narcissus" brings to the surface, critical readers claim, Eliot's off-center sexual impulses and agonies, and so affords us a glimpse of manuscripts and papers now zealously guarded from review by Eliot's estate. Like Tom Matthews, James E. Miller, Jr. and others, Lyndall

Gordon—one of Eliot's most established and respected biographers—reads in "Narcissus" Eliot's struggle with, among other things, heterosexuality and a Puritanical upbringing. Gordon argues that Eliot draws from his mother's studies of the saints in order to explore his own spiritual and poetic ambitions. At the same time, she says, he is able to touch on his developing ideas about sexuality.

Gordon attributes the poem's difficulty and repression to Eliot's ongoing ambivalence about such matters as spirituality, ambition and sexuality, as well as his relationship to—and potential identification with—his mother and her Puritanical social ties and imperatives. Eliot's early attempts to reconcile "the medieval Christian inferno," Gordon claims, with the demands or problems of "modern life" as exemplified by his Eastern and Unitarian upbringing, result in a wild mixture of ecstatic atonement: first "The Love Song of St. Sebastian " and then "The Death of Saint Narcissus" (*Eliot's Early Years* 57, 59)[6]. These poems are typical of Eliot's adolescent poetry, Gordon says, most of which are obsessed with martyrdom and religious ecstasy. As far as Gordon is concerned, Eliot's Narcissus is simply an "arresting personality" who "deliberately cuts himself off from his kind, but to his dismay sees no divine light, only his own flaws—his self enthrallment, his indifference to others, his masochistic delight in the burning arrows" (EEY 91). Further, Narcissus is the embryonic incarnation of Eliot's tortured medieval modern (or modern medieval), Dante (EEY 57). Narcissus arrests us, according to this reading, because his fantasies are undone, at once so condemnatory and confessional. He proves, in this instance, the early Eliot's undoing. According to Gordon and others, Narcissus' dance allows Eliot to explore his own uncertain moral motives, at once celebrating and punishing himself for them (EEY 91, 92). Though "The Death of St. Narcissus" concludes with a gesture toward Christian orthodoxy, "the taste of death in [Narcissus'] mouth" serves as "the sense of God's abandonment," Gordon says (EEY 92, 93).

Indeed, "The Love Song of St. Sebastian," precursor to "The Death of Saint Narcissus," reveals the medieval mysticism and masochism behind this classical representation of Eliot's artist. The unfinished poem concerns itself with images of Christian masochism and sadism, representing the saint's torture and physical pain as "inversions" of misogynist rage and homoerotic desire. Briefly, "The Love Song of St. Sebastian" presents a two-part (point-counterpoint) vision of the saint: first, as a masochist who flogs himself to death for his lover's sake, dying between her breasts, then as the sadist who strangles the beloved so that no one else will have her. The poem reveals the savagery and masochism Eliot attributed to heterosexual urges— even or especially those tinged with religious import—and the potentially solipsistic nature of the saint's (and, by implication, the social poet's) self-sacrifice in such rituals. As in "The Death of Saint Narcissus," it is unclear whether Eliot wants to suggest that all martyrdom is sexually masochistic, masturbatory, sadistic, narcissistic, or all of the above, or whether he just wants to reveal and revel in the pitfalls of ascetic "self" abuse.

The poem opens with St. Sebastian's awareness of his body and its sensations, clad in its "shirt of hair." Eliot sets the "neophyte's" passion against a perverse sexual scene; the penitent participates in a vague encounter, suggestive of copulation, that fetishizes the woman's hair and feet and ends in the sufferer's ecstatic, and literal, *petit mort*: "I would come in a shirt of hair / . . . / And sit at the foot of your stair," says the speaker (L 46). " I would flog myself until I bled / And after hour on hour of prayer / And torture and delight / Until my blood should ring the ~~light~~ lamp[7] / And glisten in the light." This turns the speaker into the passive participant in the sexualized relationship. "I should arise your neophyte / And then put out the light / To ~~And~~ follow where you lead / . . . / In the darkness toward your bed." The imagined other is glorified for her blank femininity, a white gown and feet and braided hair, while the speaker abases himself and describes the bed as a sacrificial altar, the sexual act as ending in death. "Then you would take me in / Because I was hideous in your sight / You would take me in to your bed without shame / Because I should be dead / And when the morning came / Between your breasts should lie my head."

The second stanza shifts in point of view and aim. Now the "saint" becomes satyr, sinner and sadist. Sebastian inverts his masochistic desires as he strangles his hapless lover and so claims unlimited power over her: "I would come with a towel in my hand / And bend your head ~~between~~ below my knees," the speaker says. He looks at the woman's ears, how they "curl back in a certain way / Like no ones else in all the world" and thinks how, at the end of time, when the world "melts or freezes in the sun," he will remember this curl. This image of the other's willing sacrifice becomes a fetish as the speaker imagines the last minutes when he "should for a moment linger / And follow the curve with my finger / And your head between my knees." This conclusion to the sexual encounter ensures its immortality, as well as its meaning. "I think that at last you would understand / There would not be one word to say / You would love me because I should have strangled you / And because of my infam~~my~~. . . . / And I should love you the more because I had mangled you / And because you were no longer beautiful / To anyone but me" (L 46-47). Indeed, the poem presents a mangled view of the love relationship, as is mingles violence with sexual and religious ecstasy.

In both stanzas, it's difficult to see where Eliot's sympathies lie. Though there is something compelling about the saint's adoration of the beloved, who in the first stanza seems somehow synonymous with God, when that desire is projected away from the ego, as in the second stanza, it becomes vile. Further, it appears obvious that Eliot is covering "perverse" sexual activity with vague religious symbolism. The woman's hair and feet evoke not only Mary Magdalene's offering of herself to Christ but also her genitalia (as is often the case in "standard" fetishists' imaginations); the dead man's head, lying between her breasts, conjures up not only John the Baptist, brought in on his silver platter, but the flaccid penis after lovemaking. In the second stanza, Eliot hints at oral copulation (as evidenced by his change of preposition—putting the woman's head below, rather than between, the man's knees), and he substitutes the woman's curled ear for her vagina. The world's melting or freezing serves to hint at sexual sensation or pleasure. In both stanzas, Eliot substitutes a literal death, by suffocation and then strangling, for the *petit morte* of orgasm. Finally, a reader can't help but note the homoerotic implications of this poem, given its intended audience. With Conrad Aiken (and other friends like him) in mind as his primary reader, Eliot must have been aware of the poem's sexual innuendo, just as Pound gloried in the bawdy nature of his "complimenti" poem.

Harvey Gross identifies Eliot's conflation of sexual and religious passions, calling Eliot's vision of St. Sebastian "an unhappy spirit tormented by unresolved religious and sexual urgings" inspired by Eliot's viewing of Mantegna's Ca' d'Oro St. Sebastian (104). According to Gross, Mantegna's St. Sebastian caught Eliot's eye not only for its vivid and realistic mix of eroticism, pain and homoerotic pleasure but because Mantegna captured a sense of St. Sebastian as the civilized martyr *and* "*primitif,*" a view Gross deems "odd enough" to be Eliot's own (106). Gross notes Eliot's interest in the Dionysian underpinnings of such violently erotic rituals as St. Sebastian's martyrdom and Christ's passion. Eliot places St. Sebastian's ambiguous passions against "the gestures of a Dionysian ritual with its acts of maiming and dismemberment," Gross claims, just as he sees "behind the decaying civilization of modern Europe . . . a savage landscape" (110-111).

Gross advocates an additional source for Eliot's Sebastian, a source with further implications for Eliot's Narcissus: Gabriele d'Annunzio's *Le Martyre de Saint Sébastien* (1911), "meant to rival Wilde's *Salomé* in its exploitation of a phony Orientalism, exaggerated religious sentiment, and perverse sexuality" (108). D'Annunzio wrote the play for Ida Rubenstein, a celebrated dancer known for her "boyish figure," who had recited and danced the role in the past. D'Annunzio thought her, as "Androgyne," the ideal St. Sebastian (Gross 108). Given the play's hyperbole, and the sexually androgynous nature of its hero/ine, Eliot could have had Rubenstein in mind himself as one of the models for his Narcissus, and might have hoped to capture some of d'Annunzio's titillation, speculation and even revolutionary intent in his new poems. Eliot was in Paris when *Le Martyre de Saint Sébastien* was produced, as Gross argues, and even if he failed to attend the spectacle, he could not have been unaware of the public furor it provoked.

Certainly, Eliot hoped to uncover or recover, and explore, the savagery inherent in any religious ritual or relic. In later poems with ostensibly Christian, even Catholic, subject matter—"Geronion," *Ash Wednesday* and *Four Quartets,* for instance—Eliot celebrates a "devouring" submission to the Other, privileging "the backward half-look / Over the shoulder, towards the primitive terror" (CPP 133). The saint appears as the focal point for this backward look in Eliot's work, an ambiguous and ambivalent pivot in Eliot's poetic consciousness. Eliot's saints, that is, satisfy both modern and "primitive" or primal desires. In "The Dry Salvages," Eliot claims that " . . . to apprehend / The point of intersection of the timeless / With time, is an occupation for the saint— / . . . something given / And taken, in a lifetime's death in love, / Ardour and selflessness and self-surrender" (CPP 136).

Read in context, it's clear that Eliot conflates this generic saint with his social poet, the cultural "priest" he describes in "Tradition and the Individual Talent." Gross identifies Eliot's Sebastian, in fact, as representative of the artist and his "desire to hold himself open to all experience. He stands, naked and vulnerable, while the arrows inflict their terrible wounds" (114). But Sebastian and Narcissus share the same failure: their pain stands out not as sacrifice for rebirth, a Dionysian spilling of blood for the regeneration of Spring, but as self pleasure: passion rather than Passion. In both poems, sacrifice leads to no issue, no lilacs bred from reluctant land, no white flowers floating on a still pool.

It is likely that Eliot means us to see Ovid's Narcissus behind his own saint— the beautiful youth who sacrifices himself out of self-love—and Ovid's end (Hell) in that of St. Narcissus. Ovid's Narcissus is, like Eliot's, identified with an emptied landscape, a pastoral paradise he uses to escape human (and particularly sexual) contact. Ovid's Narcissus is tied to the still, green pool where he first catches sight of himself; at the end of the narrative, this Narcissus has been absorbed by the pool and converted into a flower. Likewise, Eliot's Narcissus is transformed into shadow and rock: "Now he is green, dry and stained / With the shadow in his mouth."

Eliot uses one of Ovid's repeated images in his own poem—shadow indicates, in both poems, the sterile nature of Narcissus' attempt to find immortality in his own image, body or dance. This might be read as a sign of Narcissus' attempt to short-circuit the system of human exchange and reproduction, his need to circumvent social and religious laws of procreation. Ovid's Narcissus is repulsed by the attentions paid to him by covetous countrymen and women: " . . . in that slender stripling / Was pride so fierce no boy, no girl, could touch him" (III, 356-57). Similarly, Eliot's Narcissus finds he cannot "live men's ways" because their touch is repulsive. In no uncertain terms, both Narcissi reject human intercourse. "Keep your hands off," Ovid's Narcissus cries, when Echo attempts to embrace him, "and do not touch me! / I would die before I give you a chance at me" (III, 391-92). Narcissus falls in love, instead, with shadow: " . . . he saw / An image in the pool, and fell in love / With that unbodied hope, and found a substance / In what was only shadow," writes Ovid (III, 419-22). Narcissus' "love" becomes an attempt to consume himself in this shadow, this reflection of surface and inner emptiness; Eliot's Narcissus eats and is eaten by shadow, ending with the shadow in his dead mouth.

Eliot clearly alludes to Ovid's Narcissus (and "the strangeness / Of his infatuation") as he locates St. Narcissus' budding self-worship in a tour through the land: "He walked once between the sea and the high cliffs" and "he walked over the mead-

ows." It is by water, as in the case of Ovid's hero, that Eliot's saint develops his fatal
self-awareness and is "struck down": "By the river / His eyes were aware of the pointed corners of his eyes / And his hands aware of the pointed tips of his fingers."

In Ovid's narrative, Tiresias foretells Narcissus' death by self-knowledge. At
Narcissus' birth, his mother, Lirope, asks Tiresias if her son will live to old age.
Tiresias answers: "Yes, if he never knows himself" (III, 349).[8] This comment illuminates one of the more enigmatic lines in "The Death of Saint Narcissus," suggesting a gloss for "such knowledge." In one of the drafts, the line is more didactic:
" . . . because he was struck down/mad by the knowledge of his own beauty," Eliot
writes (WL 91). In short, Eliot's Narcissus, like Ovid's, "burn[s] with love" for his
"own self": "I start the fire I suffer," Ovid's hero proclaims (III, 464-65).

Both Ovid and Eliot suggest that Narcissus' rejection of the city and social
intercourse results in a revenge plot. In a sense, the slighted city rises up to strike
down those who cannot "live men's ways." In Ovid's text, it is Nemesis, the Goddess
of Vengeance, who hears the prayers of one of Narcissus' rejected suitors: " . . . May
Narcissus / Love one day, so, himself, and not win over / The creature whom he
loves!" (III, 405-7) And so Narcissus' doomed passion withers him into a trace of
himself, "only a flower with a yellow center / Surrounded with white petals" (III,
509-10), just as Eliot's hero is reduced to a green and dry stain on the rock. While
Eliot's Narcissus is pleasured by the friction of his own body caressing itself as he
walks the cliffs by the sea, and by the feel of the arrows penetrating his body, Ovid's
Narcissus' passion is a burning that compels him to pray for "escape from my own
body" (III, 469). His dissolution is described, appropriately, as a melting:

> As yellow wax dissolves with warmth around it
> As the white frost is gone in morning sunshine,
> Narcissus, in the hidden fire of passion,
> Wanes slowly, with the ruddy color going,
> The strength and hardihood and comeliness,
> Fading away, and even the very body
> Echo had loved. (III, 490-496)

Like Eliot's Narcissus, Ovid's hero not only demands but tears at his own body, beating it in his passion until it takes on a "glow, a rosy color." In both poems, Narcissus'
demand for self-knowledge is answered with blood: rape fantasies are rewarded with
self-sacrifice, love is conflated with grief. "In his grief," Ovid writes, "He tore his gar-
ment from the upper margin, / Beat his bare breast with hands as pale as marble, /
And the breast took on a glow, a rosy color . . ." (III, 483-86). Eliot's Narcissus
"danced on the hot sand / Until the arrows came. / As he embraced them his white
skin surrendered itself to the redness of blood, and satisfied him."

Both Ovid and Eliot scorn Narcissus' misguided love, his masochistic passion or "burning." It is, by nature, an unrequited lust. In the following passage, Ovid draws attention to Narcissus' "delusion":

> . . . Foolish boy,
> He wants himself; the loved becomes the lover,
> The seeker sought, the kindler burns. How often
> He tries to kiss the image in the water,
> Dips in his arms to embrace the boy he sees there,
> And finds the boy, himself, elusive always,
> Not knowing what he sees, but burning for it,
> The same delusion mocking his eyes and teasing.
> Why try to catch an always fleeting image,
> Poor credulous youngster? What you seek is nowhere,
> And if you turn away, you will take with you
> The boy you love. The vision is only shadow,
> Only reflection, lacking any substance.
> It comes with you, it stays with you, it goes
> Away with you, if you can go away. (III, 430-445)

Eliot and Ovid seem to be commenting on the same problem: Narcissus' delusional love, the self-worship he confuses with (a proper) devotion. This misapprehension concludes, as in "The Death of Saint Narcissus," with death. In the *Waste Land*, this death extends beyond the individual and the landscape to the spiritual, the empty Chapel Perilous. Ovid's Narcissus finds himself, at last in Hell. "What you seek is nowhere," says Ovid, "the vision is only shadow." This could be said, ironically (or not) of Eliot's vision of God, both in "The Death of Saint Narcissus" and, later, the *Waste Land*. Like Ovid's Narcissus, Eliot's personae look for the missing beloved at the bottom of the still(ed) pool, watching "all unsatisfied" for "that image / Vain and illusive"—they, too, drown "in [their] own watching eyes" (Ovid III, 447-49). Here, again, Eliot's vision or version of the modern religious delusion is debatable. Is there a God to see the legitimate dance? And, if so, what is the dancer's reward? Deluded or not, Eliot's dancer is rewarded with pain, oblivion, silence. Ovid's Narcissus seems to speak with Eliot's voice:

> . . . He rises, just a little,
> Enough to lift his arms in supplication
> To the trees around him, crying to the forest:
> "What love, whose love, has ever been more cruel?" (III, 449-52)

Good question—and one that, it seems, Eliot asks over and again throughout his work, mingling issues of spirituality with issues of poetics, confusing (or cohering) the two realms of experience.

Ovid's bitter condemnation of Narcissus' passion lingers in Eliot's description of his hero's body: "I will show you his bloody cloth and limbs / And the gray shadow on his lips." Narcissus is no Christ, Eliot seems to say, since his sacrifice leads nowhere. Ovid's and Eliot's Narcissus leave the city in order to find themselves, and like Milton's Satan, find themselves in Hell (or find Hell in themselves). Their desertion, their rebellion, their refusal to participate in the social (and sexual) contract is punished, as might be any garden-variety treason.

And yet: could we see in (Eliot's vision of) Christ a Narcissus? After all, Narcissus' bloody dance in the desert, and his satisfaction in penetration and the taste of his (or the horror of his) own whiteness—as well as St. Sebastian's masochistic and then sadistic intercourse—were intended, at first, to form part of a sequence called "Descent from the Cross." As Gordon suggests, Eliot concerned himself, at least on the surface of his most characteristic poetry, with Christian imagery and ideas, seeking to reconcile his somewhat medieval fantasies of poetic grandeur (in, strangely enough, a monumental insignificance) and social status with his "enlightened" Protestant background. Dante, Gordon says, provides Eliot with the perfect figure of identification, the modern mind in the medieval setting. But Dante seems, like Tiresias in the *Waste Land*, to be a convenient alibi for a confession or vision that might be—to Eliot's "modern" audience—more condemning. What was a good boy of Unitarian stock, from Boston via St. Louis, doing with the Papists?

In "The Death of Saint Narcissus," Eliot begins to explore some of the ideas he studied in Frazer's extensive volumes, such as the vegetation rites he claims (in his Notes) as the heart of his *Waste Land*. Frazer's comparative or, as Eliot put it, descriptive method of social and cultural analysis emphasizes similarity across time and place, and thus argues (indirectly) for a process of cultural evolution.[9] Thus, Frazer implies by sheer repetition and proximity of evidence, primitive rituals of human sacrifice designed to ensure the health and welfare of a given tribe, for instance, survive underneath the most "civilized" (or sublimated) of Christian communion liturgies.

Frazer links dying god rituals and their motifs to early questions about the cyclical nature of seasons. In his introduction to the rites of Adonis, Frazer claims that early civilizations attached animistic wishes to observations of inclement weather and natural disaster: "At a certain state of development men seem to have imagined that the means of averting the threatened calamity were in their own hands," Frazer says, "and that they could hasten or retard the flight of the seasons by magical art" (3). Dying god rituals record a development in this thinking: "They now pictured to themselves the growth and decay of vegetation, the birth and death of living creatures, as effects of the waxing or waning strength of divine beings, of gods and goddesses, who were born and died, who married and begot children, on the pattern of human life" (3). Frazer suggests that this change in thinking is narcissistic or egotistical; though these more sophisticated worshippers no longer see themselves as capable of directly influencing their environment, that is, they observe their landscape and conceive of their gods according to their own likenesses. Frazer points out that vegetation rituals developed to "aid the god, who was the principle of life, in his struggle with the opposing principle of death" and "were in substance a dramatic representation of the natural processes which they wished to facilitate" (4). As such, these dramas must follow a specific format: "They set forth the fruitful union of the powers of fertility, the sad death of one at least of the divine partners, and his joyful resurrection" (Frazer 4).

"The Death of Saint Narcissus" draws on Frazer's description of the Eastern Mediterranean Adonis for its "ritual" power. In a draft for the poem, included with the *Waste Land* drafts, Eliot identifies Narcissus' "city" as Carthage. The stark desert landscape for Narcissus' dance is reminiscent of the Sumerian "homeland" that Frazer accuses the original people of Adonis of abandoning. Frazer says of them: "An ingenious, but unproved hypothesis would represent them as immigrants driven from central Asia by that gradual desiccation which for ages seems to have been con-verting once fruitful lands into a waste and burying the seats of ancient civilization under a sea of shifting sand" (7). He cites L. W. King's *History of Sumer and Akkad* for this "hypothesis," and his further commentary on this passage is quite evocative of passages in Eliot's *Waste Land,* particularly Frazer's description of driving hordes tumbling over cracked desert to escape falling cities: "The gradual desiccation of Central Asia, which is conjectured to have caused the Sumerian migration, has been similarly invoked to explain the downfall of the Roman empire; for by rendering great regions uninhabitable it was supposed to have driven hordes of fierce barbar-ians to find new homes in Europe" (Frazer 7*n*).

Compare this to Eliot's passage in "What the Thunder Said":

> Who are those hooded hordes swarming
> Over endless plains, stumbling in cracked earth
> . . .
> Falling towers
> Jerusalem Athens Alexandria
> Vienna London
> Unreal (CPP 48)

Eliot's chain of desiccation, or disintegration, follows the same migratory route as Frazer's. Clearly, Frazer's descriptions of the dying god rituals, particularly those cen-tered on worship of Adonis, provided Eliot with fertile poetic ground—as he admits in the Notes for the *Waste Land.*

Frazer provides a genealogy for Adonis, tracing the classical figure back to a Sumerian god called "Tammuz," whose name, Frazer claims, means "true son" or "true son of the deep water," and whose lover, Ishtar—the great mother goddess, representing all reproductive energies—yearly follows her dead son/spouse to "the gloomy subterranean world" (8). (This "true son of the deep water" is perhaps one of the models for Eliot's Phelbas, the drowned Phoenician Sailor "who was once handsome and tall as you" [CPP 47].) Their cyclical death and rebirth are held responsible for the seasons, as in most dying god myths and rituals. Frazer connects this particular version of the myth and its rituals to "a comely youth beloved by Aphrodite" (11). As Frazer tells it, Aphrodite and Persephone fight over possession of the youth when he's an infant; Zeus settles the score when he decrees that Adonis live with Persephone for part of the year and with Aphrodite for the other, creating the seasons of winter and spring. In short, the dying god ritual repeats this annual death and rebirth, demanded by the mother/lover goddess of fecundity, usually as a human representative of the fertility god (often a "son") submits to sacrifice so that, through him, his people and their city or land can be rejuvenated.

"The Death of Saint Narcissus" borrows aspects of the dying god motif as described by Frazer, leaving some significant details out—the goddesses of love and death do not battle for possession of Narcissus, nor does he pose as the youthful lover of either. Instead, the hero is struck mad with self-knowledge. As such, however, he represents reproductive desire, natural and human, albeit thwarted or short-circuited. Narcissus remembers being a fish, a tree, a young woman raped in the woods by an old man, and is enchanted with the experience of feeling himself in each of these guises. These recalled (or reincarnated) desires impel him to his course as a "dancer to God."

If Eliot's poem mimics the dying god schema, then, Narcissus poses as an anti-redeemer, a dancer whose ill-fated offering cannot regenerate a languishing land and its people. As a self-appointed prince or "son" of God who cannot live men's ways, and who abandons his city to find pleasure in his own arms, Narcissus fails to represent the spirit/life of his people—and so his blood can't rejuvenate or fecundate the parched land, itself a reflection of the people or "city" who depend upon it for sustenance. It's as if he visits the underworld, plunging his land into winter, and never returns. Aphrodite is cheated out of her turn.

The dying god myths and rituals that Frazer compares, as well as the Christian tradition that Eliot conflates with these classical narratives, share the principle of communal witness. The tribe or a person itself participates in the priest's or king's (the "true son's") death, replacement and resurrection. In the same *Adonis* volume, for example, Frazer describes the dancing of the "Tshi-speaking peoples of the Gold Coast" as prophetic for their sacred intercourse:

> They work themselves up to a necessary pitch of excitement by dancing to the music of drums; each god has his special hymn, sung to a special beat of the drum, and accompanied by a special dance. It is while thus dancing to the drums that the priest or priestess lets fall the oracular words in a croaking or guttural voice which the hearers take to be the voice of the god . . . These

mouthpieces of the deity are consulted in almost every concern of life and are handsomely paid for their services. (69)

Eliot suggests that the proper poet be like this priest; his poetry, like the priest's dying utterance, is deemed to be the god's word. In contrast, Narcissus dances on the hot sand by his lonesome; the arrows come at him divorced from any human agency. He has the chance—which he blows—to express an inchoate social desire, to converse with God.

As a "dancer before God," Eliot's Narcissus puts himself before God, replaces God. Frazer describes dying god rituals as attempts to preserve or re-energize the health of a tribe or people through the demanded self-sacrifice of a youthful stand-in for the godhead or king, and these rituals depend upon a communal response for their effect. In contrast, St. Narcissus rejects the city in order to have god to himself. Thus, Eliot implies that Narcissus is doomed to extinction. He will not contribute to cultural reproduction; he will never reproduce. He is not the oracular artist, preaching in the desert, that the times demand. If St. Narcissus is a figure meant to represent the poet, then he serves as Eliot's scapegoat (or, as in *The Hollow Men*, the Guy Fawkes), the poet of bad faith who Eliot condemns to blue books and blue-stockings in "Tradition and the Individual Talent."

And yet "The Death of Saint Narcissus" introduces a prophetic poetic voice that will appear in future poems: "The Love Song of J. Alfred Prufrock," for instance, "Gerontion," Tiresias in the *Waste Land*, and *Ash Wednesday*. These all seem to be warm-up acts for the real poetic coup de grâce, Eliot's *Four Quartets*. In each, Eliot explores what he sees as the sexual, spiritual, cultural and political state of affairs—in Europe and elsewhere. His increasingly stern pronouncements, intoned as if from the height of a pulpit, imply that these realms of experience and knowledge are, in effect, inseparable. The sacrificial son cannot appoint himself; he must be chosen, *demanded*, by the powers that be—and he must submit to his fate, or glory, with a cognizance of his own insignificance, of the irrelevance of his own words in the face of God's Word. In this sense, poor Prufrock is a more Eliotic hero than the bleeding Narcissus. Prufrock's stigmata and public execution are metaphorical and, better, he denies them—no Prince Hamlet, he.

Eliot suggests that it is the idea of Narcissus' failed sacrifice that should interest us. But it is the particular, bloody detail in the poem that seduces us . . . or, at the very least, catches and holds our interest. Narcissus' dance paints a vivid picture in the mind—just as Christ's Passion is rendered, at least in Eliot's imagination, in the wide-screen colors of the Old Testament rather than the transparent wash of the New, where every utterance and image must be, by definition, interpreted by the proper pastor. "The Death of Saint Narcissus" is ostensibly a gospel reading, an allegorical sermon about the poet's job as mouthpiece, as the spiritual representative of a time and place. There is no escape for the true poet, Eliot suggests is the moral of this often-repeated story—and no passion but that of his people for God. But the reader is struck by the details of Eliot's story that refuse to be incorporated, the bloody Old Testament issues—like Abraham's near-sacrifice of his only son, Isaac, on God's pyre and at God's (joking, if not passive aggressive) request—that characterize Eliot's Trinity. In this sense, Eliot's poetic and religious schema is much nearer to Catholicism than it is to the (very rational) brand of Protestantism he was weaned on.

Frazer's work provides Eliot with an intellectual alibi for his interest in Catholic dogma by presenting him with the evolutionary model. In his first volume of the *Adonis Attis and Osiris* study, Frazer connects the "sacred dramas" of the Catholic church to the rites of Adonis, suggesting that the Catholic preference for a "visible form" reveals the survival of the religion's Dionysian roots: "the Catholic Church has been accustomed to bring before its followers in visible form the death and resurrection of the Redeemer."

> Such sacred dramas are well fitted to impress the lively imagination and to stir the warm feelings of a susceptible southern race, to whom the pomp and pageantry of Catholicism are more congenial than to the colder temperament of the Teutonic peoples. (255)

The very language that Frazer uses to describe the transmutation of classical into Catholic borrows from the vegetation ceremonies he describes. "Seeds" of the new Catholicism, that is, are "planted" into the soil provided by the traditions of Adonis, and Christian liturgy is "grafted" onto "the old stock of paganism." "When we reflect how often the Church has skilfully contrived to plant the seeds of the new faith on the old stock of paganism," Frazer muses,

> we may surmise that the Easter celebration of the dead and risen Christ was grafted upon a similar celebration of the dead and risen Adonis, which, as we have seen reason to believe, was celebrated in Syria at the same season. The type, created by Greek artists, of the sorrowful goddess with her dying lover in her arms, resembles and may have been the model of the *Pietà* of Christian art, the Virgin with the dead body of her divine Son in her lap, of which the most celebrated example is the one by Michael Angelo in St. Peter's. That noble group, in which the living sorrow of the mother contrasts so wonderfully with the languor of death in the son, is one of the finest compositions in marble. (256-57)

Glib as it is, Frazer's passage connects many of Eliot's primary (and primal) images: the suffering/dead Son and the Virgin mother are "modern" analogies for the vengeful goddess (Frazer substitutes sorrow for vengeance; in this case, Eliot accepts no substitutes . . .) who demands the death of her son/lover, just as the careless women in "The Love Song of J. Alfred Prufrock"—who talk so much of

Michelangelo—would like to see his head brought in upon the teatime platter give way to the Lady of Silences in *Ash Wednesday*'s garden.

Frazer implies, as might Eliot's kin, that Catholic worshippers—with their "warm" feelings and susceptible southern minds—are more "primitive" than their Puritan successors. On the surface, Eliot participates in this light scorn for the childish consciousness and religious expression of an "inferior" race. However, we might consider whether Eliot's own preference for the visible form indicates a "surviving" interest in his religion's roots in Catholicism, and thus whether his "Death of Saint Narcissus" might serve as a confessional poem in all senses of the word. Perhaps Eliot's poetic indeterminacy, the caginess of his images and the vagueness of his most characteristic refrains, is due in part to his Grandfather Greenleaf Eliot's Unitarian legacy and his increasing feelings of rebellion against this inheritance, his developing interests in more erotic forms of religion (and/or more religious forms of sexuality). Robert Crawford suggests that Eliot uses Narcissus to "burn off the page the polite saintliness of an exhausted way of life," the life embodied (in his mind) by his mother's poetry and her acts of social reform, "replacing it with a savage rite" (80). Eliot's "reaction" against his childhood "was to set against this world a fascination with hidden depths of emotion and revelation of such emotion in ways far alien to, and more potent than, the Bostonian world around him."

> He wished to move beyond gentility and genteel religion, both of which he analysed bitingly; at least philosophy other than that 'taught by retired nonconformist ministers' had the virtue of being 'on the whole anti-religious, which was refreshing.' Refreshed, Eliot became not antireligous, but stayed at once both scientifically distant from and passionately fascinated with religion's visionary violence. (Crawford 74)

And so "sex and religion break out with a developing savagery" in Eliot's poetry "that is like a shock treatment which Eliot wishes to administer to himself and the quiet, respectable society of which he is a part" (Crawford 79). According to this reading, Narcissus serves not only as Eliot's scapegoat but as his alter ego: a mask for a scholar tired of his polite, disaffected Unitarian background, an alibi for a virginal fop who craves the blood and guts of an Indian dance, the ecstatic oblivion of a masochistic intercourse with "god."

2.

The Poet-Prophet in the Mouth of Madness

IN *ELIOT'S EARLY YEARS*, LYNDALL GORDON ARGUES THAT A SERIES OF INEXPLICABLE metaphysical moments, beginning in 1910 as Eliot graduates from Harvard with a bachelor's degree, impel him on a lifelong quest for religious order. Gordon uncovers these visions in the Berg Collection manuscripts, specifically in "2nd Debate between the Body and Soul," where a "ring of silence . . . closes round him and seals him off, in a state of beatific security, from the floods of life that threaten to break like a wave against his skull. . . . Contained there, he contemplates the power of some unverbalized, elusive truth, taking command of it, and then bursting out, ingenuous and pure" (39). This moment serves as an oasis in the "clatter of graduation, the exhortation of practical men, the questions of parents, the frivolity of millinery and strawberries" (34–5).

The "clatter of graduation" is indeed worrisome as it infringes on Eliot's artistic ambitions, but he seems most disturbed by social expectations he connects with female relatives. Prufrock and the narrator of "Portrait of a Lady," for example, confront older women obsessed with fashion and social "graces." Their obsessive talk forces the poet inward, where he "drowns" in self-reflection. The female voice undermines the mystical nature of the poet's soul-searching: "That is not what I meant," she says, when he asks his overwhelming question, implying that she desires to hear herself echoed through his mouth. Later, "what are you thinking?" transforms itself into the command: "Tell me what *I'm* thinking."

Eliot's earliest poetry portrays the enemy of his Absolute as this self-interested woman who bleeds into devouring seas and bitter moons. Motivated by frustrated maternal and sexual ambitions, Eliot's Lady expresses herself in sadistic sociality, forcing the would-be poet to play her "easy tool": "Deferential, glad to be of use, / Politic, cautious, and meticulous; / Full of high sentence, but a bit obtuse" (CPP 7).

Eliot's Lady comes to embody his Unreal City,[1] a savage place where civilization provides a thin veneer over primitive appetites.[2] In "Rhapsody on a Windy Night," for example, "The worlds revolve like ancient women / Gathering fuel in vacant lots" (CPP 13). The poet is helpless against this world, embodying as he does "[t]he notion of some infinitely gentle / Infinitely suffering thing" (CPP 13). "Wipe your hand across your mouth, and laugh," the poet admonishes his reader.

The battle of will and wits deteriorates to an elemental level as Eliot's woman merges with the Great Mother. Dowagers, lovers and wives convert sexual desire and neurosis into hysterical talk, talk that subjects Eliot's poet to an obliterating sea change. This "darkness on the face of the deep" that *is* Eliot's lady portends a return to pre-Genesis chaos: "In the beginning God created the heaven and the earth. And the earth was without form, and void; and darkness was upon the face of the deep. And the Spirit of God moved upon the face of the waters" (Gen 1:1–2). Eliot's death by water, then, signals a return to the Mother's body, to the womb, suffocation and dissolution in female matter, an abrogation of God's light, order and salvation. This fatal confrontation, Eliot suggests, results in heavy casualties—the Unreal City, like Sodom and Gomorrah, explodes and falls.

In his introduction to the *Selected Prose of T. S. Eliot,* Frank Kermode describes Eliot's "poetic genius" as the ability to at once possess and surrender to the object of his inquiry. This possession and surrender is both erotic and religious. Eliot's poet stages a passive-aggressive investigation of the woman that degenerates into a possession *by* her—he derives pleasure-pain from converting voyeuristic control into masochistic failure as he turns impotence into prayer. Kermode suggests, in fact, that Eliot's approach "celebrates a peculiar blend of fascination and disgust, a mortuary eroticism balancing on the moment of simultaneous enchantment and loss, the sexual surrender" (13). As Eliot's poet rejects, faces and then submits to temptation— ambition, masturbatory fantasies, narcissism, sexual desire, fornication—he must metamorphose these "sinful" energies into poetry. This, finally, is his portal to the divine.

Though Eliot uses his "loving" ladies to embody an avaricious, disconnected and doomed society, that is, their tea parties set the stage for a painful initiation into the patriarchal mysteries. After all, fractured revelations are wrung from these destructive relationships. The flower-twisting Lady in Eliot's "Portrait" evokes a "tobacco trance" in the young poet; the sirens in "Prufrock" make him hear "human voices"; a series of Medusan wives, jaded lovers and prostitutes in the *Waste Land* lead Eliot/Tiresias to consider his ruin.

Eliot borrows from Harrison and other "scientific" sources to compose a poetic mythology for an Unreal City he finds lacking in spiritual, cultural and historical consciousness. Conflating dying god rituals with initiation rites, like Harrison, Eliot develops a poet whose fate is to submit to the lover/mother's deadly seduction in a totemic ritual designed to save the Father's world. The poet's decomposition mimics the death and resurrection of vegetation gods such as Attis, Adonis, Osiris, and Christ. "Portrait of a Lady," "The Love Song of J. Alfred Prufrock," *The Waste Land,* "Gerontion" and other poems allude to incarnation, crucifixion and communion as mythological touchstones in the process of spiritual healing.

Finally, Eliot implies that the poet's dissolution and resurrection ordinates him as God's chosen vessel or voice, the word within the Word. Though Eliot's anti-heroes seem ill suited as initiates to the Masculine Mysteries, their very impotence assures their entry. Prufrock's ritual unmanning destroys his value for the domestic circles that consume him and his death promises an escape into the Absolute. Prufrock's inability to force the moment to its crisis and his subsequent drowning ironically multiply his power.

If Eliot's poets are "easy tools," his Ladies are ambitious Eves, Circes, Lamias, sirens, Herodias, Salomés, Medeas, Medusas, aunts, sisters, mothers, wives. To set the stage for the poet's fatal seduction, Eliot recreates the atmospheres of Juliet's tomb and Cleopatra's throne, where images of narcissism, decapitation, sexual inter-course, prostitution, poverty, cannibalism, savagery, and drowning "lean in" from stone walls to wither his poet.

And despite attempts to expose and exorcise her, Eliot's Lady reproduces her-self—and further paralyzes—her captive male audience. It is a process that Eliot confesses himself helpless to prevent. In a letter to Ezra Pound, dated 2 February 1915, Eliot says of this process: "I enclose a copy of the Lady, which seems cruder and awkwarder and more juvenile every time I copy it" (L 86).

In a certain sense, Eliot's early and most "definitive," poetry takes as its master plot Hawthorne's *Scarlet Letter,* where a tortured and self-doubting poet-cleric finds himself locked in archetypal struggle with a ravenous temptress determined to pluck him from the path to Heaven. In "Prufrock" and other skirmishes, the poet fails to "penetrate" the overwhelming female question. Instead, Eliot's Lady uses a flood of conversation to "wreck" the hero, her chatter laced with fears (and fantasies) of oral copulation, as the poet's unspoken wish for the woman's destruction turns inward, converted into a suicidal wish, as in "Prufrock." The Lady's desire—overgrown, aligned with "nature," perverse, uncivilized, carnivorous—swallows the poet's voice, and thus takes it on, as Vivien and her proxy do in "A Game of Chess."[3]

In a letter dated 15 April 1915, Eliot rants against the "evil influence" of pro-liferating dowagers. Borrowing the spirit of Pound's "manifesto,"[4] Eliot raves against the crass "monopolisation of literature" by women in the American university sys-tem, which has replaced "facts" with mere "words." The "Evil Influence of Virginity on American Civilization" is, Eliot says, responsible for converting serious male scholarship into Uplift and Recreation.[5] "The Germans have at least a few facts, and we have only words; they have Archaeologie and we have How to Appreciate the Hundred Best Paintings, the Maiden Aunt and the Social Worker," Eliot writes. "Of course it is imprudent to sneer at the monopolisation of literature by women," he confesses (L 96).

Eliot suggests that the Lady's intellectual "monopolisation," stems, primarily, from her "Degradation in Society"—an ambiguous social position, that is. She must express her ambitions covertly and so is limited by the interior and artificial space she is forced to inhabit: "The Chair she sat in, like a burnished throne, / Glowed on the marble, where the glass / Held up by standards wrought with fruited vines / . . . / Doubled the flames of the sevenbranched candelabra" (CPP 40). An impaired Venus de Milo, the sterile Lady appears surrounded by narcotic odors and fires, and "withered stumps of time," her wrath spoken through the fire in her snaky hair. Her menace can be traced, obliquely, to the crimes mutely witnessed on her walls, to Philomel's "change":

> Above the antique mantel was displayed
> As though a window gave upon the sylvan scene
> The change of Philomel, by the barbarous king
> So rudely forced; yet there the nightingale
> Filled all the desert with inviolable voice
> And still she cried, and still the world pursues,
> "Jug Jug" to dirty ears.
> And other withered stumps of time
> Were told upon the walls; staring forms
> Leaned out, leaning, hushing the room enclosed.
> Footsteps shuffled on the stair.
> Under the firelight, under the brush, her hair
> Spread out in fiery points
> Glowed into words, then would be savagely still. (CPP 40)

Bound to dressing and drawing rooms, Eliot's Ladies discover ways to "confuse and trouble" the poet's mind with a kind of savage stillness. They use sex and sexuality to exchange men like commodities, to fight for dominance amongst themselves. "He's been in the army four years, he wants a good time," says the scheming woman. "And if you don't give it him, there's others will, I said" (CPP 41).

Prufrock and the rest of Eliot's poets who listen to the Lady discover that they must struggle to divide inspiration from insanity, truth from hysteria or delusion in her talk.[6] And while the poet is paralyzed, unable to say just what he means, Eliot's women come and go, surviving with "inviolable voice."[7] In fact, Eliot identifies women with mouths, eating, and appetites of all kinds. The fanged flowers in "Circe's Palace" and the Lamia in "Portrait" blend into the singing sirens in "Prufrock," whose rejection of the narrator implies a disappointed sexual appetite:

> [They will say: "How his hair is growing thin!"]
> My morning coat, my collar mounting firmly to the chin,
> My necktie rich and modest, but asserted by a simple pin—
> [They will say: "But how his arms and legs are thin!"] (CPP 4)

If not overtly cannibalistic, Eliot's women employ social intercourse with destructive intensity. They use their eyes as daggers, "eyes that fix you in a formulated phrase, / . . . sprawling on a pin, / . . . pinned and wriggling on the wall" (CPP 5), and their hands as the hangman's rope.

In "Portrait of a Lady," the woman works out her aggression toward the young narrator on a lilac that she

> . . . twists . . . in her fingers while she talks.
> "Ah, my friend, you do not know, you do not know
> What life is, you who hold it in your hands";
> (Slowly twisting the lilac stalks)
> "You let it flow from you, you let it flow,
> And youth is cruel, and has no remorse
> And smiles at situations which it cannot see." (CPP 9)

The narrator is "strangled" by the woman's expression of thwarted desire. He cannot answer. "I smile," he says, "of course, / And go on drinking tea" (9).

Eliot's women are emotional executioners, the modern equivalents of Salomé and her mother, Herodia.[8] Prufrock is as helpless as blind John the Baptist to resist the power of their appetite:

> . . . though I have wept and fasted, wept and prayed,
> Though I have seen my head [grown slightly bald] brought in upon a platter,
> I am no prophet—and here's no great matter;
> I have seen the moment of my greatness flicker,
> And I have seen the eternal Footman hold my coat, and snicker,
> And in short, I was afraid. (CPP 6)

Prufrock is unable to bite the matter off (as his ladies seem so capable of doing) with a smile. Nor is he able to roll the universe into his ball, like Marvell. The Lady's unspeakable desire frightens Eliot's poet into silence—the novels, teacups and skirts, the arms braceleted and bare, the whiff of perfume from the dress, make it "impossible" for him to "say just what [he] mean[s]" (CPP 6).

In fact, female desire traps Eliot's poet in "verbal imprecisions"—"the slimy mud of words" mingles with other offensive discharges ("Choruses from the Rock," IX CPP 111). In "A Game of Chess," the neurotic wife tries to suck the very thoughts from her husband's head:

"My nerves are bad to-night. Yes, bad. Stay with me.
"Speak to me. Why do you never speak. Speak.
    "What are you thinking of? What thinking? What?
"I never know what you are thinking. Think."

    I think we are in rats' alley
Where the dead men lost their bones.

"What is that noise"
                    The wind under the door.
"What is that noise now? What is the wind doing?"
                    Nothing again nothing.

                            "Do
"You know nothing? Do you see nothing? Do you remember
"Nothing?"

    I remember
Those are pearls that were his eyes.
"Are you alive, or not? Is there nothing in your head?" (CPP 40–41)

It is the wife, rather than the silent husband, who poses as the aggressor in this encounter, and her goal seems to be to ruin him.[9] She not only empties his head but fills him up with the flotsam of other poets' dismembered creations, indiscriminately mixed with refrains from popular songs. Her automatic talking, like the sea, silences and transforms him, as it did King Alonso. "Those are pearls that were his eyes": blinded, he can no longer serve as a prophet. Instead, he is the jewel tucked in the oyster's slime.

    The sexual/spiritual alienation of Eliot's male appears in "Portrait of a Lady" as the "dull tom-tom" beat of the narrator's brain as he tries to ignore the woman's sexual "meaning": "Inside my brain a dull tom-tom begins / Absurdly hammering a prelude of its own / Capricious monotone" (CPP 9).[10] The Lady's conversation alludes to "velleities and carefully caught regrets" that, though ambiguous, are aggressive:

"You do not know how much they mean to me, my friends,
And how, how rare and strange it is, to find
In a life composed so much of odds and ends,
[For indeed I do not love it. . . you knew? you are not blind!
How keen you are!]
To find a friend who has these qualities,
Who has, and gives
Those qualities upon which friendship lives.
How much it means that I say this to you—
Without these friendships—life, what *cauchemar*!" (CPP 8)

The "tobacco trance" that Eliot's narrator slips into to escape the Lady's sexual impositions serves as an inept escape from her conversational advances.

"I keep my countenance," Eliot's narrator claims, "I remain self-possessed."

> Except when a street piano, mechanical and tired
> Reiterates some worn-out common song
> With the smell of hyacinths across the garden
> Recalling things that other people have desired.
> Are these ideas right or wrong? (CPP 10)

He lies, of course. Eliot's poet is *not* self-possessed—she makes him "recall things that other people have desired."

"'Perhaps you can write to me,'" she says, when he tells her he plans to escape abroad. "My self-possession flares up for a second," he claims; "*This* is as I had reckoned." No doubt he imagines he has asserted control over the situation. Instead, the Lady casts aspersions on the poet's motivations. A trip abroad becomes, she insinuates, a cowardly retreat from her advances:

> "I have been wondering frequently of late
> (But our beginnings never know our ends!)
> Why we have not developed into friends."
> I feel like one who smiles, and turning shall remark
> Suddenly, his expression in a glass.
> My self-possession gutters; we are really in the dark. (CPP 11)

The narrator claims that he's in the dark, but even Eliot's most pessimistic self-portraits force poet and reader inward, until concentrated self-examination becomes a transcendent perception. This dissolute Lady, for example, forces the poet to "remark" himself in the mirror, perhaps the mirror of poetry, to see just what he's doing, and so her sexual innuendo acts as the catalyst for a prelude to mysticism:

> And I must borrow every changing shape
> To find expression . . . dance, dance
> Like a dancing bear,
> Cry like a parrot, chatter like an ape.
> Let us take the air, in a tobacco trance— (CPP 11)

Of course, the "expression" the narrator finds for his thoughts is too animalistic to be divine, and the trance is not mystical but "tobacco," pedestrian. The "dull tom-tom" the poet hears sounds too much like his own name; it is thus a "false note" (CPP 9).

In letters to Aiken and Pound written during the composition of "Portrait of a Lady," Eliot encloses a draft entitled "Suppressed Complex," "one small verse," Eliot writes to Pound. "I know it is not good, but everything else I have done is worse. Besides, I am constipated and have a cold on the chest. Burn it" (L 87). The poet, dancing in the firelight like an avenging spirit, witnesses the woman's nocturnal distress before flying through the window at dawn. It is a strange aubade:

> She lay very still in bed with stubborn eyes
> Holding her breath lest she begin to think.
> I was a shadow upright in the corner
> Dancing joyously in the firelight.
>
> She stirred in her sleep and clutched the blanket with
>   her fingers.
> She was very pale and breathed hard.
> When morning shook the long nasturtium creeper in the
>   tawny bowl
> I passed joyously out through the window. (L 87)

In this draft, Eliot distances himself from the "hysterical" illnesses—migraines, for example—that his wife Vivien reputedly suffers. In some ways, the poet turned spirit poses as the very thought the woman screws her eyes shut against: her paleness and hard breathing denote, perhaps, a battle against arousal—especially when combined with the suggestive image of the shaking of the "long nasturtium creeper" in its "tawny bowl." Significantly, Eliot's spirit is able to escape, "joyously," the woman's solitary suffering.

Freud argues in *Dora: An Analysis of a Case of Hysteria*—and Eliot, following Charcot's and Janet's work with hysterics, was not unfamiliar with Freud's writings on the subject—that women with hysterical "complexes" often develop symptoms such as breathing or coughing troubles to express, or vent, suppressed desires for penetration. Thus, desire masquerades as revulsion or refusal, and hysteria is connected to female frigidity.[11] In *Dora*, Freud suggests that the "hysterical" woman's feelings of constriction and breathlessness are due to a "*displacement* of sensation" from the lower body to the throat and mouth (44). Freud imagines, that is, that Dora imagines (on some unrepresentable level) her mouth as another vagina and thus rejects anything she feels will be forced down it (food, kisses, etc.). Dora's "sensory hallucination" is quite like Eliot's woman's breathlessness in bed. Like Eliot, Freud inhabits Dora's suffering mind:

> I have formed in my own mind the following reconstruction of the scene. I believe that during the man's passionate embrace she felt not merely his kiss upon her lips but also the pressure of his erect member against her body. This perception was revolting to her; it was dismissed from her memory, repressed, and replaced by the innocent sensation of pressure upon her thorax, which in turn derived an excessive intensity from its repressed source. (45)

Freud's descriptions of displacement, repression and sexual disgust were no doubt available to Eliot as he composed "Suppressed Complex" ten years later (*Fragment of an Analysis of a Case of Hysteria* was published in 1905).

The poem's title is ambiguous, however. Though it purports to diagnose the distressed woman at its center, it could as easily refer to the poet, happily engrossed as he is with voyeuristic fantasies. Lyndall Gordon suggests that Eliot's sexual ambivalence springs from partially suppressed desires and competing sexual emotions: "there is always a genuine craving for experience and a fear that experience might so easily pass one by," she writes (39). This tension, Gordon implies, might serve as the impetus behind Eliot's mystical moments. In any case, Eliot's poetry reveals fears of the heterosexual experience that masochistic voyeurism and mystical flight help allay.

Once we suspect that the somewhat hysterical "complex" is unfixed—a contaminant that the writhing woman fails to contain—we can see Eliot's mystic poet as infected with the same symptoms. Certainly, Eliot complains, at length, of his own bodily infirmities as he composes these visions: constipation and a chest cold. Bottled up, Eliot presents himself in the same straits as his suppressed woman. Like her, he derives pleasure from his illness, and his demand that Pound "burn" his poem comes across as a masochistic wish.

In "Eliot and the Horrific Moment," Ronald Schuchard muses that much of Eliot's work was an attempt to avoid "the dispossessing horrors attendant upon 'personality'"—the "cream of the nightmare dream" and "the hoo-has coming to get you" (CPP 84)—and gain "artistic control" over them through poetry (193). "From the outset of his career," Schuchard says, "[Eliot] ransacked literature for evidence of controlled horror . . . and his poetry is a virtual repository of horrific epigraphs and allusions that are there to objectify and intensify the personal moments of spiritual terror." Schuchard argues that "Eliot took the horrific way to the beatific" and discovered "that the horror of life is often inexpressible, that it can be too intense for even the most objective correlative" (193). In his early work, Eliot's horrors often merge with whores who, drawing the "COFFIN the very last card" (CPP 85), inspire the hoo-has in his narrators.

Schuchard connects Eliot's "Whispers of Immortality" to his marriage. Vivien's psychosomatic illnesses, together with Eliot's own mental exhaustion, led them to share "what Eliot's most recent biographer, Peter Ackroyd, calls a *maladie à deux*," Schuchard writes, as Eliot performed a kind of "professed dispossession," his life become "a Jacobean nightmare of sexual mortality, compounded by his probable knowledge of the exploits of Bertrand Russell, who provided the cottage at Marlow" (196). Citing a confessional letter that Russell purportedly wrote to his mistress, Lady Constance Malleson, Schuchard argues that Eliot's suspicions of marital betrayal resulted in a "spiritual devastation" with far-reaching effects on his work.

Eliot's precipitous marriage to Vivien Haigh-Wood in June 1915 certainly presents his readers with an enduring mystery. What motivated him to abandon his stance against conjugal relations? Did he mean to explore a fearful heterosexual terrain in order to lay to rest, once and for all, his sexual attacks? Or did he assume that marriage would accomplish what European study and time had not—that it would prevent him from returning to a stultifying academic career in the United States and convert him into a mature, respected poet? Schuchard and others argue that Eliot conceived of his first marriage as a controlled horror, a continual confrontation that would serve as a rigorous martyrdom to fuel a flagging artistic spirit.

At a single stroke, Eliot's marriage certainly confounded his parents' plans, particularly his mother's desire that he return to Harvard to complete his doctorate and take a professorship in Philosophy. Though Eliot blamed the war for his change in plans, his letter to Professor Briggs expresses another motive. "I have decided to remain in London, or at least in England, and attempt to engage in literary work, hoping to be able to find a position in a school at the same time," he explains (L 110).

If, on the other hand, Eliot took the plunge in order to be "stimulated"—as Vivien so eloquently put it to Bertrand Russell—he was soon disappointed. "The only surprising thing," Eliot admits to his brother Henry, a week after the wedding, "is that I should have had the force to attempt it, and when you know Vivien, I am sure that you will not be surprised at that either. I know that you will agree that the responsibility and independent action has been and will be just what I needed" (L 104). Eliot's optimism foreshadows impending disaster. "Now my only concern is how I can make her perfectly happy," he concludes, "and I think I can do that by being myself infinitely more fully than I ever have been. I am much less suppressed, and more confident, than I have ever been."

Eliot's letter to his brother is littered with optimistic omissions. "Forgive the exclusively practical tone of this letter," he writes, after cataloguing his poetic assets (as if preparing a last will and testament). "I feel more alive than I ever have before," as if writing it will make it so. Closing, he says: "I want to send you her picture soon. Vivien is not very well at present, and this has knocked her out completely, so I do not want one taken yet" (L 105–6).

Throughout his letters, Eliot discusses Vivien's illnesses rather than their romantic activities. In fact, he forestalls "gossip" about their sexual life with confessions of health problems: "[I]t was a great anxiety all winter and spring," Eliot writes to Aiken, "as she kept having incidental troubles like teeth which set her back. I may say that this was not a case of maternity in any degree. Most people imagine so unless I explain. It has been nerves, complicated by physical ailments, and induced largely by the most acute neuralgia" (L 143).

Vivien soon figures as Eliot's worst nightmare as their symptoms become symbiotic. As Vivien's sick headaches, neuralgia, and vague menstrual infirmities impose a series of medical expenses on Eliot, his own hypochondria increases. On a brief hiatus from the marriage, Eliot writes Professor Woods from his family's summer home, hinting at future disappointments: "Unfortunately, I have just had word that my wife is very ill in London, so I must go at once, sailing Saturday. I do not anticipate that her illness will prevent my return before the opening of college; but if it is serious enough to detain me I will cable to you" (L 113). Five days later, Eliot returned to London, and wrote to his father to apologize for, again, precipitously going against the paternal edict. "I felt that my mistake was in hurrying home before I had got your letters, and so failing to get a balanced view of the situation; and secondly in blundering into a change of plan which was unjustified and unnecessary," he confesses (L 113–114). Despite this admission, Eliot made no concessions to his parents' academic plans for him. Instead, he confessed his financial pains: "We have planned a very economical mode of life, and Vivien's resourcefulness and forethought are inexhaustible. We are not planning how to make living easier: the question is how to live at all" (L 114).

Eliot discovered, of course, that married life would never be the visionary meeting of pure minds he described in fantasies of the Hyacinth girl.[12] After his marriage, Eliot's girls ("who stoop to folly" and then "resent" their mistakes) overrun his work, until "[a]ny man might do a girl in / Any man has to, needs to, wants to / Once in a lifetime, do a girl in" (CPP 83). The best woman, Sweeney suggests, is a dead quiet one; her virtue, at least, is certain. Her body radiates a comforting domestic space and stasis: "Nobody came / And nobody went / But he took in the milk and he paid the rent" (CPP 83). What the man actually *does* with his embalmed woman, there in the quiet, "dont apply." What's important, Sweeney argues, is that "there wasn't any joint" between them, since they are both in the same condition: "He didn't know if he was alive / and the girl was dead / He didn't know if the girl was alive / and he was dead / He didn't know if they both were alive / or both were dead" (CPP 84).

This process of contamination and corruption, female to male, Eliot begins to designate with the term "hysteria." Though a kind of sexual threat in Eliot's poetry emanates from aggressive males like Sweeney, a "primitive" violence can be traced back to the woman and her desire. In "Sweeney Erect," for instance, the whore's epileptic laughter (called "hysteria") makes Sweeney uglier and more elemental than he was at the poem's opening (no mean feat): he devolves before our eyes into a hairy beast with a sharp razor, menacing in his nudity. The poem opens with a scene—"a cavernous waste shore / Cast in the unstilled Cyclades," lined with "bold anfractuous rocks / Faced by the snarled and yelping seas"—that emphasizes the ancient and carnivorous nature of the woman's prostitution (which comes to evoke, for Eliot, all heterosexual contact). Sweeney is reduced to the "gesture of orang-outang" as he struggles, ineffectually, to separate himself from the woman's swamp:

> Gesture of orang-outang
> Rise from the sheets in steam.
>
> This withered root of knots of hair
> Slitted below and gashed with eyes,
> This oval O cropped out with teeth:
> The sickle motion from the thighs
>
> Jackknifes upward at the knees
> Then straightens out from heel to hip
> Pushing the framework of the bed
> And clawing at the pillow slip. (CP 25)

Sweeney's "rise" from the prostitute's primordial bed implies, in the narrator's esti-mation, a *backward* movement: "(The lengthened shadow of a man / Is history, said Emerson / Who had not seen the silhouette / Of Sweeney straddled in the sun.)" (CPP 26). The narrator's ironic look reduces Sweeney and his whore to their origins, and focuses on their vicious mouths.

The vivid and pointillist description—a "withered root . . . slitted below and gashed," "this oval O cropped out with teeth" —could evoke Sweeney's ape-like face, his naked body, as well as the epileptic woman's anatomy, exploded to fill the screen and transformed into a chewing orifice whose "sickle motion from the thighs" threatens all men. Her shrieking, either inchoate expression of a physical problem or an inexpressible reaction to Sweeney's anatomy, is noted as evidence of "the female temperament" (CP 25). Sweeney responds, of course, with violence: he "tests the razor on his leg / Waiting until the shriek subsides." The woman's laughter, howev-er, cannot be controlled. "The epileptic on the bed / Curves backwards, clutching at her sides." It is a disease that spreads and so "the ladies of the corridor / Find them-selves involved" and "disgraced,"

> Observing that hysteria
> Might easily be misunderstood;
> Mrs. Turner intimates
> It does the house no sort of good. (CP 26)

Thus, Eliot connects hysteria to prostitution, venereal disease, organic contagion, and animal sexuality. As the womb itself, hysteria serves to identify the "female tem-perament," which in Eliot's mind is also a corrosive lack of taste that "does the house no sort of good."

Finally, hysteria is a disturbance in the poet's attention that cannot be con-tained. It spreads, taking over the woman's body and then the yelping sea that her body becomes for the horrified man. (She is, literally, the wound that never heals.) The shriek of laughter echoes in the siren's cry and whores push their way into Eliot's rooms "padding on broad feet"—just as Doris does, bringing "sal volatile / And a glass of brandy neat" to check, if only for a moment, the flood of the woman's unconscious.

Eliot's early fantasies involve *leaving* the woman—before her sexual initiation—in prelude to a religious romance. The chaste woman "grieves" his loss, allowing the distanced poet to take satisfaction in her disappointment: "So I would have had him leave," he writes, in "La Figlia Che Piange." "So I would have had her stand and grieve, / So he would have left / As the soul leaves the body torn and bruised, / As the mind deserts the body it has used" (CPP 20). Eliot imagines the poetic conception to be immaculate. Poetry serves, eventually, as the messianic issue of this bloodless intercourse: a divine son for the Holy Father. In "Ash Wednesday" and *Four Quartets,* Eliot returns to this vision of poetry, linking the offended virgin and her "fugitive resentment" to the rising (male) spirit. Her eyes, her "rape," compel the poet's imagination, possess him and impregnate him with poetry: "Sometimes these cogitations still amaze / The troubled midnight and the noon's repose" (CPP 20).

As the Sweeney poems attest, however, what springs from the poet's head is not always divine. Sometimes, it is Mr. Apollinax, "the irresponsible foetus" who faces down Mrs. Phlaccus and Mrs. Cheetah—only to be *returned* to the womb/sea. Mr. Apollinax attempts revenge: he turns the tables on the insatiate American ladies, chewing them up with their own anarchic laughter. His struggle, like Prufrock's, however, is doomed as he is incorporated into the very "nature" he tries to escape.

"When Mr. Apollinax visited the United States," the poem begins, alluding to Bertrand Russell's visit, "His laughter tinkled among the teacups." Apollinax is Prufrock, reincarnated as a leering satyr—"I thought of Fragilion, that shy figure among the birch-trees / And of Priapus in the shrubbery / Gaping at the lady in the swing" (CPP 18), says the narrator. "In the palace of Mrs. Phlaccus," Apollinax's emits a deranging laughter to counter the women's conversation:

> His laughter was submarine and profound
> Like the old man of the sea's
> Hidden under coral islands
> Where worried bodies of drowned men drift down in the green silence,
> Dropping from fingers of surf. (CPP 18)

Apollinax's descent into the women's madness is as decapitating as Prufrock's exposure to their teatime conversation: "I looked for the head of Mr. Apollinax rolling under a chair," says the narrator. Both Apollinax and the ladies are combined in a promise of Dionysian excess: "I heard the beat of centaur's hoofs over the hard turf / As his dry and passionate talk devoured the afternoon." The narrator surveys the wreckage as an archaeologist:

> "He is a charming man"—"But after all what did he mean?"—
> "His pointed ears. . . . He must be unbalanced,"—
> "There was something he said that I might have challenged."
> Of dowager Mrs. Phlaccus, and Professor and Mrs. Cheetah
> I remember a slice of lemon, and a bitten macaroon. (CPP 18)

This "passionate talk"—perhaps the "modern" equivalent to a Bacchanalian revel—
is finally embalmed in the half-eaten remains of the tea party.

The bitten macaroons are not the end of Mrs. Phlaccus and her clan. Eliot's
underworld Eve returns again and again, rising from the ashes (or the waves) to ruin
the poet's reflections. Aphrodite gone mad, she climbs out of the desert's dust to the
din of falling towers, burning like a modern Medea. Aphrodite/Persephone becomes
the Great Mother of the Gods, as in the *Waste Land,* a destructive nature bent on
possessing her errant son/lover. She demands the poet's death in the "darkness on the
face of the deep" ("Choruses" CPP 107). He drowns in her body: "men who turned
towards the light . . . / Invented the Higher Religions. . ./ But their light was ever
surrounded and shot with darkness / As the air of temperate seas is pierced by the
still dead breath of the Arctic Current" (CPP 107).

Eliot implies that the woman has devoured the Father.[13] His absence creates a
cultural castration. Contact with the Great Mother's "decayed hole" creates empty-
headed poets, the Fisher King's wound, Tiresias "throbbing between two lives,"
"[d]ead mountain mouth of carious teeth that cannot spit" and "dry sterile thunder
without rain" (CPP 47). She, like Lil, aborts the miraculous birth. Eliot's "awful daring of a moment's surrender / Which an age of prudence can never retract" (CPP
49) results in "[d]ry bones [that] can harm no one," the empty chapel where "Ganga
[is] sunken" and "limp leaves" wait for rain. A feral, female jungle (reminiscent of
the pneumatic Grishkin) "crouch[es], humped in silence" over all (CPP 49).

This "great mother," prevented from reproducing—or "having" her son—murders *instead of* mothering. Lacan suggests that the woman's desire to have a son
equals her desire to *be* the phallus, the representative of power, because she can't *have*
it. The pregnant body, in this scenario, becomes a sign of her power. But in Eliot's
Waste Land, the woman is sterile. Her maternal lamentation is "perverse" and insa-
tiable—she will do whatever she can to fill herself. An enraged siren, a vampire, she
lures the poet into her black lair:

> A woman drew her long black hair out tight
> And fiddled whisper music on those strings
> And bats with baby faces in the violet light
> Whistled, and beat their wings
> And crawled head downward down a blackened wall
> And upside down in air were towers
> Tolling reminiscent bells, that kept the hours
> And voices singing out of empty cisterns and exhausted wells. (CPP 48)

Eliot buries the underside of his mind of Europe in his Lady: infantile desires, primitive ritual, superstition, human sacrifice, blood lust.

The *initiated* female body: pneumatic bliss, shaking breasts and the afternoon's fragments, slit and gashed below, *vagina dentata*, excessive "temperament," hysteria, nihilistic laugher and laughter, corrosive contact, chilled delirium, coffin, "lack of taste" and of God, epileptic seizure, loss of control, the unconscious blistering to the surface and engulfing all, yelping, anfractuous rocks ringing a barren shore, accidental stars, death by water: Eliot alludes to this conflation of emotions and events quite boldly in his prose poem, "Hysteria."

> As she laughed I was aware of becoming involved in her laughter and being part of it, until her teeth were only accidental stars with a talent for squad-drill. I was drawn in by short gasps, inhaled at each momentary recovery, lost finally in the dark caverns of her throat, bruised by the ripple of unseen muscles. An elderly waiter with trembling hands was hurriedly spreading a pink and white checked cloth over the rusty green iron table, saying: "If the lady and gentleman wish to take their tea in the garden, if the lady and gentleman wish to take their tea in the garden . . ." I decided that if the shaking of her breasts could be stopped, some of the fragments of the afternoon might be collected, and I concentrated my attention with careful subtlety to this end. (CPP 19)

"Hysteria" appears somewhat out of place in *Prufrock and Other Observations*, a volume devoted to witty monologues designed to finesse the decadence of urban life. The prose poem's flatness contrasts with the crafty lines of Eliot's brief portraits, and its frank treatment of sexuality proves "tasteless" against the decorous violence of the rest. "Hysteria" oozes physicality; its raucous laughter and shaking breasts make it a particularly vulgar *female* body. Though the narrator attempts to distance himself from the scene, he struggles from beginning to end to maintain his integrity . . . and fails. Ultimately, "Hysteria" lacks the irony that separates Eliot's narrators from the women they investigate. Even the narrator's "careful subtlety" and "concentrated attention" cannot recuperate this compelling vision and distance.[14]

The poem's title announces it as fundamentally distinct from the rest of the volume. The single word suggests several readings for what lies below, serving, first, as a diagnosis, and, second, as a condemnation. Because poem's shape mimics a dictionary definition, it could also be read as a figurative illustration, a gloss that illuminates more allusive moments in the rest of the volume.

Investigation and diagnosis are particularly male or "objective" activities designed to enforce boundaries, to contain indeterminacy or contamination in logical categories. Eliot's struggle for separation from and control of the woman soaks through every line of "Hysteria." The poem opens on the narrator's losing battle to describe and thus contain the ongoing fact of the woman's laughter. It is an active threat that cannot be captured, entirely, in language. The narrator's conflicting metaphors, circling out in time and space, reveal his impotence: "As she laughed I was aware of becoming involved in her laughter and being part of it, until her teeth were only accidental stars with a talent for squad-drill." Even the verbs the narrator chooses to illustrate the scene are imprecise—the woman "laughed," supposedly, as a discrete action in the past, yet the narrator is trapped in the glue of "becoming" and "being," an endless, awkward and passive structure that occludes him as the subject (or object) of such maniacal glee. In fact, the woman's "hysterical" laughter exceeds the poem and its frustrated language. She laughs at his inadequacies, his inability to shut her up, her ability to dis- or de-compose him. Her laughter is a volcano that expresses fury, disappointment, amusement, destruction, and her body shakes with this eruption.

The poem recalls other female bodies in Eliot's first slim volume, all of whom suffer from the "lack of taste" Eliot calls hysteria. As they break rules of social propriety, and affront the reader with uncontrollable excess, their transgressions bleed outward. In "Rhapsody on a Windy Night," a prostitute leaks into the streets, materializing as the cat "which flattens itself in the gutter, / Slips out its tongue / And devours a morsel of rancid butter" and as "female smells in shuttered rooms" (CPP 15). Finally she becomes the moon itself, beaming down on a dilapidated slum.

Eliot's narrator is "aware," at first, "of becoming involved in" and then "being part of" the woman's laughter. What's the difference? Remember that Mrs. Turner and the other ladies of the corridor find themselves "involved" in the whore's hysteria, implicated in the same potential lack of taste, disgrace, misunderstanding. Is this "becoming involved" a process of initiation, a prelude to "being part of" the female temperament?

According to the *Oxford English Dictionary*, to "involve" derives from the Latin *involv(ere)*, "(to) roll into or upon, to wrap up, envelop, surround, entangle, make obscure." Examples of the verb's use evoke Eliot's hellish visions of the woman's destructive body, spread out over the landscape: consumptive fires, visions of tombs and wombs, and polluted cities.

To "involve" is also "[t]o wind in a spiral form, or in a series of curves, coils or folds; to wreathe, coil, entwine," as might a sleeping snake. The image of the snake contains Eliot's fear of the Medusa as well as a terror of domesticity, since it gives rise to the image of the "threde which is involvde rounde about the Needle." Snakes, needles, marriage and sexuality are all "involved," dizzying the poet.

Involvement with the woman leads to language problems as well, as "to involve" is also to "envelop within the folds of some condition or circumstance . . . to beset with difficulty or obscurity . . . To entangle (a matter), to render intricate." Involved doctrines are plagued with "inexplicable contradictions," "great obscurity" and "numerous difficulties"; once again, beguiling women appear at the bottom of this verbal barbarity: "As wiliye as those shrewes that beguyle him haue holpe hym to inuolue and intryke the matter." No surprise, then, that involvement proves criminal. Eliot's narrator and the ladies in the corridor are all "entangled . . . in difficulties, perplexity," "embarrassed"[15] and "engaged . . . in circumstances from which it is difficult to withdraw," and thus "implicated in a charge or crime"—whether it be prostitution, hysteria or (as in Sweeney's case) murder. Ultimately, the woman's criminal laughter "roll[s] up within itself, . . . envelope[s] and take[s] in; . . . overwhelm[s] and swallow[s] up" the poor poet (OED). This process is not only destructive; it is reproductive of the woman—or her hysteria—since to involve is to "multiply (a quantity) into itself any desired number of times; to raise to a power." Soon the narrator is inside the woman and looking out—at the distant specter of her moving mouth: "her teeth were only accidental stars with a talent for squad-drill."

By "accidental stars," Eliot might mean to suggest that the woman's body, seen from the inside, forms an absurd cosmology with no particular plan. Ascribing such chaos to the woman's body, perhaps the poet intends to remark the senselessness of nature and female space. Haphazard bodies cannot be incorporated into the service of logical schemes, maps, ordered narratives, and constellations. Instead, accidental stars signify nature's power *over and against* man. Their "talent for squad-drill" is a ridiculous touch: their only order is a preparation for war.

Though this first sentence blurs the *vagina dentata* by blowing it up into cosmic proportions, the second sentence presents no visual trouble. It is, shockingly, graphic: "I was drawn in by short gasps, inhaled at each momentary recovery, lost finally in the dark caverns of her throat, bruised by the ripple of unseen muscles." The woman's laugh becomes an extension of her prehensile tongue; she uses it to reach out, capture, and swallow her paralyzed prey. Of course, "being part" of this monstrous digestive system is a terrifying transformation. What goes in as man exits as shit.

There is something inescapably sexual in this vision of annihilation, something *childish* and yet *experienced* in the poem's description. The narrator is effaced in "short gasps," and experiences "momentary recovery"; now, stuffed "the dark caverns of her throat," "the ripple of unseen muscles" squeezes him as he makes his way down. How is it that he can see "dark caverns" and "unseen muscles"? How does he know that he is "finally lost"? He could be recalling a first sexual experience: the trauma of erection, penetration, and impotence. He might be caught in an intense wish for an oral encounter. Mouths merge with vaginas, tongues with penises. The woman uses her laugh like a penis, penetrating the flaccid narrator, until she is pregnant by/with him. The woman is a giant snake, digesting her prey alive.

The poet witnesses his own rape and we, as readers, are invited as involved spectators. What's more, "an elderly waiter with trembling hands" witnesses the assault and he, too, appears disturbed by the spectacle and its implications. Wayne Koestenbaum, in "*The Waste Land:* T. S. Eliot's and Ezra Pound's Collaboration on Hysteria," and Tony Pinkney, in *Women in the Poetry of T. S. Eliot,* read the elderly waiter as the ineffectual "father" in a triangular family relationship (the narrator is the helpless son and the woman is the phallic mother). The waiter's stuttering serves as a "symptom" of male hysteria.

The waiter, "hurriedly spreading a pink and white checked cloth over the rusty green iron table, says: 'If the lady and gentleman wish to take their tea in the garden, if the lady and gentleman wish to take their tea in the garden . . ..'" The silenced poet identifies with the waiter's anxiety and his servile attempts to cover the embarrassing woman, to contain her in the garden, attempts that prove ineffectual. He can't even hide the iron table, and his stuttering exacerbates the woman's glee.

The waiter's comment is corroded into an ellipsis by the woman's persistent laughter—thus he is banished from the poem. Since the aging father cannot punish the hysterical mother, it is left up to the son/lover (as it has been from the beginning) to take care of her. He must "concentrate" his "attention" with "careful subtlety" against the "shaking of her breasts"[16]—which, in this landscape, fractures the afternoon and destroys its "order." Does the narrator really assume that his semi-sadistic, voyeuristic fantasy will eventually control the woman, reassert the expected order (father over son over mother), and thus convert the fragmented afternoon into a coherent narrative?

Actually, this strange poem with its uncanny fracturing into irreconcilable points of view highlights the impossibility of Eliot's ever completely "seeing" this woman—he is always "finally lost" as her body and laughter remain veiled. Distorted images, timelessness, and the displacement of affect magnify the poem's surrealistic landscape. Such condensed, illogical imagery suggests a dream. "Hysteria" forces the reader into the analyst's position: only "he" can bring the perpetrator to light, since the dreamer is helpless to wake from the nightmare.[17]

Eliot must have been aware of contemporaneous work done with psychoanalytic interpretations of dream work and hysteria because he was more than once involved in analysis himself, attended Janet's seminars in hysteria, and cared for a wife who suffered from "hysterical" symptoms such as hypersensitive nerves and an acute sense of hearing.[18] No surprise, then, that "Hysteria" reads like an interlude in the hysteric's talking cure. Eliot's laughing Lady compares to Anna O., the "seminal" protagonist of Freud's and Breuer's *Studies in Hysteria,* in that both demand and yet deny interpretation. Perhaps part of the Lady's pleasure lies (as does Anna O's) in stringing her reader along, engaging his attention with shocking images, mixing literal with figurative sense, occluding the sense—or source—of her ruminations. Like a dream, "Hysteria" teases the reader with mutilated reproductions of significant "scenes" from Eliot's "real" life, and our "pleasure" in watching this primal scene is more than a little sadistic.

Freud describes the relationship between analyst and hysteric as a battle to establish the primacy over the repressed reminiscence or "narrative." In *Studies in Hysteria,* for instance, Freud discusses his struggle to extract information from patients during early attempts at free association. (He would press his hand on the patient's forehead and tell her to remember what she had forgotten when he removed his hand—Eliot underwent this sort of manipulation at Margate). Despite Freud's forceful directions, patients balk. "They promised to say whatever occurred to them under the pressure of my hand, irrespectively of whether it seemed to them relevant or not, and of whether it was agreeable to them to say it or not—to say it, that is, without selecting and without being influenced by criticism or affect," Freud writes.

> But they do not keep this promise; it is evidently beyond their strength to do so. The work keeps on coming to a stop and they keep on maintaining that this time nothing has occurred to them. We must not believe what they say, we must always assume, and tell them, too, that they have kept something back because they thought it unimportant or found it distressing. (*Studies* 279)

Freud emphasizes the analyst's authority as the master of narrative and compares his method to the "crystal ball" of fortune-telling: "We must insist on this, we must repeat the pressure and represent ourselves as infallible, till at least we are really told something" (279). Freud attributes the confessing patient's reticence to the "mutilation" enacted by a mind resistance to disclosure, and describes the suspicious, even willful, nature of the patient's silence. "The longer the pause between my hand-pressure and the patient's beginning to speak," he says, "the more suspicious I become and the more it is to be feared that the patient is re-arranging what has occurred to him and is mutilating it in his reproduction of it" (279).

How can Eliot's narrator escape his involvement in the woman's laughter, her elemental and overwhelming body, her hysteria? He must, in a sense, lay hands upon her. He must wrest from her the "true" story, the master narrative, must counteract the "mutilation" of her mind. Writing serves a phallic power: as long as the narrator can record the woman's disease with careful subtlety, he can write her "end," even as he is paradoxically involved in and so mutilated by it.

But "Hysteria" is not, many readers admit, an appropriate or effective cure for the woman. Her disease rubs off on the narrator and, by implication, on Eliot himself. Perhaps this is why the poem is relegated to the close of the volume, and why many critics consider it a freak in Eliot's menagerie. As if to contain Eliot's embarrassment, critics disapprove—with Mrs. Turner—of this unseemly scene and omit it from their discussions of Eliot's genius.

The poem creates two central responses in critical readers. The few who tackle it do so as if dissecting a corpse in a murder investigation: they see it, that is, as containing "clues" to the perpetrator of a crime. James E. Miller's work is a case in point. In a chapter entitled "Faint Clews and Indirections: The Sub-Surface Life," Miller includes "Hysteria" in a brief parenthetical remark (18). In the same chapter, Miller mentions "Hysteria" as a source for psychobiographical readings of Eliot's marriage (26). Finally, in a chapter called "A Suppressed 'Ode': Confessional Poem," Miller cites "Hysteria" as the cover for this missing "Ode": "when the American edition of this volume was prepared, the title was changed to *Poems*, the contents rearranged, and 'Ode' was dropped in favor of the prose-poem 'Hysteria,' a probable portrait of Vivien. Eliot never again published 'Ode'" (42). Miller, whose project it is to exhume Eliot's homosexual proclivities, would like to classify "Hysteria" as, somehow, a trace of Eliot's sexual inversion, a psuedo-confession less damaging than those it has replaced.

Most critics drop "Hysteria" from their critical surveys (Lyndall Gordon's well-read biography, *Eliot's Early Years*, is a case in point). Eliot never mentions the poem in his published letters and a survey of his most salient biographers reveals an almost universal silence. These attempted suppressions are, themselves, a bit hysterical. If, as psychoanalysts such as LaPlanche and Pontalis claim, hysteria is a conversion disorder, then "Hysteria" is what it announces itself to be—Eliot's failure to create an emotion that lives only in the poem. Instead of containing and converting the woman's destructive laughter into "careful subtlety" and abstraction, the poet is possessed by it.

"Hysteria" can be condemned for the same reasons that Eliot faults *Hamlet*. The poem is "puzzling, and disquieting"; "the versification is variable"; "he has left in it superfluous and inconsistent [images] which even hasty revision should have noticed"; "[b]oth workmanship and thought are in an unstable relationship"; "probably more people have thought ["Hysteria"] a work of art because they found it interesting, than have found it interesting because it is a work of art"; and, finally, the poem "is full of some stuff that the writer could not drag to light, contemplate, or manipulate into art" (SP 47, 48).[19]

Needless to say, "Hysteria" is not an adequate objective correlative, "a set of objects, a situation, a chain of events which shall be the formula of that *particular* emotion; such that when the external facts, which must terminate in sensory experience, are given, the emotion is immediately evoked" (SP 48). "Hysteria" is *not* particular and never discrete. Its narrator, like Hamlet, is "dominated by an emotion which is inexpressible, because it is in *excess* of the facts as they appear" (48).

Eliot's projection of hysteria, of chaotic and preconscious nature into the "limitless" female body is in no way an original masculine insight. Unsurprisingly, Eliot fits into a monumental tradition. Adrienne Rich reminds us, in *Of Woman Born*, of the female body's connection to natural processes, and particularly of the womb's conflation with the ocean:

> The ocean, whose tides respond, like women's menses, to the pull of the moon, the ocean which corresponds to the amniotic fluid in which human life begins, the ocean on whose surface vessels (personified as female) can ride but in whose depth sailors meet their death and monsters conceal themselves . . . it is unstable and threatening as the earth is not; it spawns new life daily, yet swallows up

lives; it is changeable like the moon, unregulated, yet indestructible and eternal. (108)

Klaus Theweleit elaborates on this conflation in his history of fascism, *Male Fantasies*. Women have long served as the repository for sexual desires and godlessness, he says. "A river without end, enormous and wide, flows through the world's literatures," he writes, and it is woman.

> Over and over again: the women-in-the-water; woman as water, as a stormy, cavorting, cooling ocean, a raging stream, a waterfall; as a limitless body of water that ships pass through, with tributaries, pools, surfs, and deltas; woman as the enticing (or perilous) deep, as a cup of bubbling body fluids; the vagina as wave, as foam, as a dark place ringed with Pacific ridges; love as the foam from the collision of two waves, as a sea voyage, a slow ebbing, a fish-catch, a storm; love as a process that washes people up as flotsam, smoothing the sea again; where we swim in the divine song of the sea knowing no laws, one fish, two fish; where we are part of every ocean, which is part of every vagina. (283)

Theweleit puts it rather poetically himself as he describes the emotion that male writers pour into that sea: "He who has been inside the right woman, the ultimate *cunt*—knows every place in the world that is worth knowing."

> And every one of those flowing places goes by the name of Woman . . . the ocean that covers two-thirds of the earth's surface and all its shorelines, the irreproachable, inexhaustible, anonymous superwhore, across whom we ourselves become anonymous and limitless, drifting along without egos, like 'masses of rubble,' like God himself, immersed in the principle of masculine pleasure. (284)

The difference between Eliot's and Theweleit's emotion is the tenor, or terror, in the sublime feeling they describe. While Theweleit claims that man feels the limitless anonymity as the experience of God (the swimmer is "like God himself"), Eliot's poet experiences it as God's absence. Theweleit describes Eliot's masculine erasure as masculine pleasure. (Perhaps, as Eliot's body of work suggests, these are one and the same.)

While his poems describe paralyzed and occluded men, Eliot poses as the satyr in letters to male friends, adopting a jocular disdain for society, family and heterosexual relations. Along with "Portrait of a Lady" and "Prufrock," Eliot shares with his friends misogynist doggerel about "King Bolo's big black queen / That famous old breech l(oader)" (L 42). A crude satirist, Eliot draws an exaggerated portrait of his African lady, suggesting that she represents a savage desire to eat penis and to penetrate her male subjects—King Bolo included among them. Though cartoonish, Eliot's African Queen serves as another incarnation of his devouring Aphrodite, and his portraits of "civilized" women differ only slightly. In Eliot's estimation, contemporary women are guilty of the same perversities and excesses as the African Queen, though they sublimate them in social intercourse.

In peevish diatribes against the boredom of life at Oxford, for instance, Eliot accuses faculty wives of excessive fecundity, claiming that they produce packs of unruly children to ruin their academic husbands. In one letter, Eliot draws two bell-pulls for himself, side by side, labeling the first for "visitors" and the second for "professors and their wives" — "the second should have no bell," Eliot proclaims, gleeful (L 74).[20] Perhaps because he is not, himself, a professor, a young Eliot sees men of letters as feminized shadows who waste their time creating "easy-chair aesthetics," which is simply "vaporing in the void."

So Eliot sets up a series of transitive links: female sexuality → male impotence → intellectual sterility → physical reproduction → male vapors. It seems a variation on the old theme of "books or babies." Eliot's persistent ribaldry occludes his investment in these matters (such as a philosophically informed poetic) and seems to be a pose designed to distance himself from the woman's or wife's contamination, as well as from Prufrock's male vapors and sexual inadequacies.

Eliot goes to great pains, in fact, to erect barriers between his personal life and his poetic personae, perhaps to prove himself "one of the boys" and thus to make vital connections—as with Pound—in the publishing world. At the time, it appeared that the man-of-action stance was more likely to sell copy than the sensitive approach, so Eliot played cards and smoked big cigars instead of making visits to influential maiden aunts. In letters to Aiken, Eliot is irreverent, gaudy, and hyperbolically gauche; for Pound, Eliot poses as the Davy Crockett of the poetic frontier. For both, Eliot condemns other men's prissiness regarding such characters as King Bolo and his Big Black Kween. He writes to Pound: "I have corresponded with Lewis, but his puritanical principles seem to bar my way to Publicity. I fear the King Bolo and his Big Black Kween will never burst into print. I understand that Priapism[21], Narcissism etc. are not approved of, and even so innocent a rhyme as '. . . pulled her stockings off / With a frightful cry of "Hauptbahnhof!!'[22] is considered decadent" (L 86). Thus, Eliot casually projects his own gynephobia and sexual inadequacies onto those who have rejected him.

In a letter to Aiken, dated 19 July 1914, Eliot encloses a sample of his Bolovian verse. The homoerotic content of this exchange between college friends is NOT subtle, adding fuel to several critical camps wherein Eliot's "suppressed" homosexuality is still debated. "I will send you this to go to sleep on," Eliot writes to his friend.

> Now while Columbo and his men
> Were drinking ice cream soda
> In burst King Bolo's big black queen
> That famous old breech l(oader).
> Just then they rang the bell for lunch

And served up—Fried Hyenas;
And Columbo said "Will you take tail?
Or just a bit of p(enis)?" (L 42)

King Bolo's "big queen" "breech loader" titillates her readers with ambiguity: is "she" a man in drag?

Eliot extends the joke by poking fun at academics, who, he implies, are so caught up in analysis and documentation that they become the butt of their own jokes. The "fine flavor" of the salvaged "double entendre" in the last lines of the poem, he writes, is owed to the detective work of "two inseparable friends," "Hans Frigger"(a celebrated poet) and "Herr Schitzel."

In a subsequent letter to Aiken, Eliot sends another bit of Columbo, making his references to homosexual intercourse clear:

Now while our heroes were at sea
They pass'd a German warship.
The captain pac'd the quarterdeck
Parading in his corset.
What ho! they cry'd, we'll sink your ship!
And so they up and sink'd her.
But the cabin boy was sav'd alive
And bugger'd, in the sphincter. (L 59).

Despite his bravado with male friends, Eliot's anxiety about his own masculinity is apparent because he ends the letter with this assertion: "I should find it very stimulating to have several women fall in love with me—several, because that makes the practical side less evident. And I should be very sorry for them, too."

Bandying about Priapism, penetration, and all sorts of sadistic colonization, Eliot diverts his readers from the passive nature of his own poetic. He uses ribald, all-American misogyny to draw a line in the sand between himself and Prufrock. As he explains to Pound: "There can be no contemplative or easychair aesthetics . . . only the aesthetics of a person who is about to do something."(L 86–87) [23] Such sweeping dismissals are no doubt intended to throw Pound off his scent.[24] As Eliot writes this, he ponders his own surrender to the monumental history of European ideas.

In a letter to Aiken, Eliot says he's suffering from a "nervous sexual attack" and hints at its source: "I hate university towns and university people, who are the same everywhere, with pregnant wives, sprawling children, many books, and hideous pictures on the walls" (L 75). Again, the pregnant wife seems to be to blame for all the chaos and hysteria. "Come let us desert our wives and fly to a land where there are no Medici prints, nothing but concubinage and conversation," Eliot says, conveniently ignoring his lack of a Mrs. (L 74). In another letter to Aiken, Eliot expands his disgust with women, marriage and middle class reproduction to include an "exe-

crable" English taste. The whole milieu makes him sick: "Oxford I do not enjoy," he
writes: "the food and the climate are execrable, I suffer indigestion, constipation,
and colds constantly; and the university atmosphere." He will never come to like
England, Eliot tells his American friend. But what is the alternative? Should he submit to his parents' life and "compromise and conceal my opinions and forfeit my
independence" the way they have, all for the sake of the children? Or should he take
Henry James' asexual life as a model, and spend his money after fifty on a Parisian
boulevard? "I dread returning to Cambridge," he confesses to his friend,

> and the nausea of factory whistles at seven and twelve o'clock (one doesn't mind
> it so much at night—one doesn't *see*, then) and the college bell, and the people
> in Cambridge whom one fights against and who absorb one all the same. The
> great need is to know one's own mind, and I don't know that: whether I want
> to get married, and have a family, and live in America all my life, and compro-
> mise and conceal my opinions and forfeit my independence for the sake of my
> children's future; or save my money and retire at fifty to a table on the boule-
> vard, regarding the world placidly through the fumes of an aperitif at 5 p. m.—
> How thin either life seems! (L 88)

All of Eliot's fears can be traced back to the woman, who propagates either this horrible English taste that makes him suffer "dyspepsia" or the expectation of marriage
that will make the States a prison of ringing bells.

Eliot's attempts to assert himself as the cock of the walk are feeble at best, and
he seems to know this because he undercuts himself at every turn. Eliot's alter-egos
are not Don Juans but blustering drag queens, ineffectual scholars, funny nephews.
Eliot's morbid representations of Christ's passion, littered throughout the *Waste
Land*, "Gerontion" and his religious poetry, echo this misbegotten masculinity. In
Eliot's "modern" world, the Mother always wins, breeding an elemental impotence,
cruel culture, dead art.

Does Eliot's misogynist discourse express, eventually, its inverse? Is he really
confessing a masochistic wish? Does Eliot, as some critical readers suggest, identify
himself with the wronged woman? Perhaps Eliot creates antagonistic heterosexual
positions for himself, as he does for his saints, in order to simultaneously experience
and condemn terrifying and intriguing sexual matters. His poet's violent capitula-
tion is bound with pleasurable sensations, after all. Though Prufrock is destroyed by
the sirens, he describes his dissolution in sensual terms: "We have lingered in the
chambers of the sea," he moans, recalling vaginal metaphors, "By sea-girls wreathed
with seaweed red and brown / Till human voices wake us, and we drown" (CPP 7).
What does this fantasy of obliteration afford Eliot's mystic in training?

"Virtues / Are forced upon us by our impudent crimes," claims Gerontion
(CPP 22)—"unnatural vices" (such as oral copulation?) "are fathered by our hero-

ism." Eliot's eroticizes his "castration" into a mystic communication; the poet must submit to pain in order to enjoy the Absolute. Assuming that "Hysteria" serves as another of his poet's sexual fantasies, we can identify a few of Eliot's erotic wishes: voyeuristic masochism, passive oral sexuality, and an equally passive sadism. We can read "Hysteria," in fact, as expressing the desire to replace the mother through a process of reverse birth.

This climax is opposed to the standard Oedipal desire that Freud finds at the root of every male narrative of desire or power: "It is the fate of all of us, perhaps, to direct our first sexual impulse towards our mother and our first hatred and our first murderous wish against our father. Our dreams convince us that that is so" (*Interpretation* 296). In contrast, Eliot's "Hysteria" might convince us that he sees the lover (could-be-mother) as a rival whose sadistic power must be turned against her. Does the fumbling waiter, a shadow of the missing father, represent Eliot's wish for a rapport with the Father?

James E. Miller, Jr. insists, in *T. S. Eliot's Personal Waste Land*, that much of Eliot's definitive poetry reveals and revels in homoerotic desire—particularly the drafts for "Prufrock" and *The Waste Land*. Miller argues that "The Love Song of J. Alfred Prufrock" is addressed to Jean Verdenal, Eliot's closest friend at the boardinghouse in Oxford (Eliot dedicated *Prufrock and Other Observations* to Verdenal's memory after he was killed in WWI). Eliot uses Verdenal in much the way that Dante uses Beatrice, Miller says, and Eliot's explorations of mysticism are motivated by his desire to take on the female role in a love affair with the Father.

Tony Pinkney reads "Hysteria" as Eliot's shocking inversion of Freud's "traditional" subject-object and gender positions, and grounds his reading in a Kleinian notion of the child's "pre-Oedipal" horror and fascination with particular female body parts (such as the breasts) which "he" wants to incorporate and possess wholly. Freud argues that jokes are an essential part of the patriarchal power structure, and so ensure that the woman retains a subordinate (or absent) position during their telling; "it is therefore all the more scandalous," Pinkney says, "that in Eliot's text this structure is turned on its head."

> Not only does this female laughter deconstruct the binary oppositions of self and other, subject and object; it equally turns inside out the triangular structures of patriarchal authority in its own miniature version of Bakhtinian carnival. The generic indeterminacy of 'Hysteria' is another facet of this wholesale deconstruction; neither prose nor poetry, it too bears witness to the power of the woman's laughter to interrogate the dualisms into which the social world is structured. (21)

In this scenario, Eliot wants to restore patriarchal legitimacy to the mother-father-son triangle, to silence the mother and return father and son to positions of superiority. Eliot's anxiety of influence can be traced not to his literary father but to his "real-life" mother, according to Pinkney (23–24). Eliot uses poetry to over-write her, as "Hysteria" employs a form of automatic writing to buttress the narrator's ego "against the psychotic disintegration the woman menaces" (Pinkney 20).

As a ritual designed to bind the narrator's traumatic wound and restore phallo-centric order, "Hysteria" fails. The narrator's attempts to replace the woman in her subordinate position only expose his impotence and psychic disintegration: "He is left with a collection of brilliant *apercus*, or of descriptive details whose very excess gives them a quality of phantasmagoric intensity that has more in common with the Kleinian paranoid-schizoid than it does with the coherent social world the ego is try-ing to restore" (Pinkney 22–23).

Both Pinkney's and Miller's readings ignore Eliot's pleasure in this "possession." Of the four sentences in "Hysteria" allocated to describing the woman's disease, three are devoted to the narrator's rapture. His final sally seems a token effort, at best. The last sentence allows the narrator to "have it" both ways: he enjoys a con-trolling position in this masochistic fantasy. Though he sees himself as the beaten, he can manipulate the fantasy by revealing his script-writing abilities at its conclu-sion, asserting himself as the author of this fantastic "hysteria."[25]

In "A Child is Being Beaten," Freud makes the connection between male masochism, repressed homosexuality and voyeurism,[26] arguing that masochistic men "invariably transfer themselves into the part of a woman" (126). Certainly, Eliot's poet complains of "becoming involved" in the woman's laughter and body, and then of "being a part" of it. In the male masochist's fantasy, Freud suggests, "the persons who administer chastisement are always women, both in the phantasies and in the contrivances" (126). The man may express homoerotic desire and yet fantasize about a "heterosexual" encounter, says Freud, by taking a "feminine" attitude during the beating fantasy. "In [the case of] the boy," Freud argues, the beating fantasy "starts from the inverted attitude, in which the father is taken as the object of love."

> The boy . . . changes the figure and sex of the person beating [from male to female], by putting his mother in the place of the father; but he retains his own figure, with the result that the person beating and the person being beaten are of opposite sexes. . . . The boy evades his homosexuality by repressing and remodeling his unconscious phantasy; and the remarkable thing about his later conscious phantasy is that it has for its content a feminine attitude without a homosexual object-choice. By the same process, on the other hand, the girl escapes from the demands of the erotic side of her life altogether. She turns her-self in phantasy into a man, without herself becoming active in a masculine way, and is no longer anything but a spectator of the event which takes the place of the sexual act. (127–128)

Eliot's narrator inhabits both the male and female masochists' positions as outlined by Freud. That is, he views the scene from the position of the "girl" who looks on, as well from the position of the boy who loves to be beaten by his mother (a mere stand in for his father). So we could say that Eliot's narrator thus "escapes from the demands of the erotic side of his life altogether by converting himself in phantasy into a man, without becoming active in a masculine way—and so he is no longer anything but a spectator of the event which takes the place of the sexual act." And the event that takes the place of the sexual act is not a beating, but an *eating*.

Eliot's poet appears in more than a few classical and biblical disguises in his early poetry—wounded males such as St. John of the Cross, Prufrock, John the Baptist, Lazarus, Tiresias, and even Christ. An amalgamation of emasculated and masochistic religious prophets, Eliot's poetic voice culminates, as he suggests in his Notes for the *Waste Land*, in the androgynous Tiresias.

It is Christ who ultimately lurks behind this classical facade, "the third who walks always beside you . . . / Gliding wrapt in a brown mantle, hooded" (CPP 48), Christ the Tiger, who "devours" the citizens of the *Waste Land*. "In depraved May," says Gerontion, the months of "dogwood and chestnut, flowering judas," the prophet will be

> . . . eaten, . . . divided, . . . drunk
> Among whispers; by Mr. Silvero
> With caressing hands, at Limoges
> Who walked all night in the next room;
> By Hakagawa, bowing among the Titans;
> By Madame de Tornquist, in the dark room
> Shifting the candles; Fräulein von Kulp
> Who turned in the hall, one hand on the door. (CPP 21–22)

"After such knowledge," laments Gerontion, "what forgiveness?" Christ will return as the Prufrock's snickering Footman, the tiger, the pale rider—an annihilator rather than a savior.

Eliot attempts to differentiate between Madame de Tornquist's and Madame Sosostris' mumbo-jumbo (voodoo—as in *Sweeney Agonistes*), candle-shifting, and the poet's mystical visions. Women in the Unreal City have carnal desires and crave hearts, minds, bodies. Poets long for spiritual food[27] and are eventually "ruined" by this desire. Just as Salomé and her mother demand John the Baptist's head for his sexual refusal, Eliot's Lady cuts the poet off:

> Would it have been worth while,
> To have bitten off the matter with a smile,
> To have squeezed the universe into a ball
> To roll it toward some overwhelming question,
> To say: "I am Lazarus, come from the dead,
> Come back to tell you all, I shall tell you all"—
> If one, settling a pillow by her head,

> Should say: "That is not what I meant at all.
> That is not it, at all." (CPP 6)

Eliot's turns the poet's failure into the poem's refrain: "That is not it, at all." The poet strives for mystical utterance and merely reproduces the Lady's senseless repetition.

Eliot's misanthropic prophet/poet is unable to force the moment to its crisis. Instead, his benediction—like Tiresias' "Shantih shantih shantih" (CPP 50)—shatters into female tongues. Mystical communication ends "not with a bang but a whimper" (CPP 59) and there is, finally, no perfect order or incantation for Eliot's poet, only absorption into the woman's verbal and physical madness. Transfigured, the poet serves as a male Cassandra, and his metaphorical death, like Philomel's and Ophelia's, goes, it would seem, unheeded.

Eliot cites Jane Harrison in his seminar work, and in her *Themis* Harrison connects dying god rituals to initiation and ordination ceremonies. Harrison argues that myths "which embody the hiding, slaying and bringing to life again of a child or young man" can "reflect almost any form of initiation rite" and that the ancient Greek Kouretes ceremonies she investigates actually "had to do with a rite of the initiation of a sort of medicine-man, a rite nearer akin to our Ordination than to either Baptism or Confirmation" (20). Though Harrison claims that *Koures* is "a word impossible to translate," she tentatively defines it as "Initiated Young Men." The Koures participate in mysterious tribal rituals and so achieve the status of medicine men, passing on the secrets. Their job is to "initiate others, [to] instruct them in tribal duties and tribal dances, [to] steal them away from their mothers, conceal them, make away with them by some pretended death and finally [to] bring them back as new-born, grown youths, full members of their tribe" (Harrison 19–20).

Harrison also discusses ritual communion in pre-Classical Greek society, "the eating of raw flesh." Totemic religions, Harrison argues, which stress non-differentiation between worshippers and god, use "red and bleeding feasts" to initiate mystics into adult and mysterious societies.[28] "As a rule a savage abstains from eating his totem," Harrison writes. "The man is spiritually, mystically, akin to his totem, and as a rule you do not eat your relations" (123). But "at certain times and under certain restrictions a man not only may, but must, eat of his totem, though only sparingly, as of a thing sacro-sanct," Harrison says. "This eating of the totem is closely connected with its ceremonial multiplication. You abstain from your totem as a rule because of its sanctity, i.e. because it is a great focus of *mana*; you eat a little with infinite precautions because you want that *mana* and seek its multiplication" (123–124).

What Harrison calls non-differentiation, Georges Bataille, in *Death and Sensuality*, calls continuity. Like Eliot, Bataille believes that "the domain of eroticism," particularly the heterosexual model, "is the domain of violence, of violation" (16). "What does physical eroticism signify if not a violation of the very being of its practitioners?—a violation bordering on death, bordering on murder?" (17). Bataille's term for this fusion and death, "dissolution," recalls Eliot's death by water. "In the process of dissolution, the male partner has generally an active role, while the female partner is passive. The passive, female side is essentially the one that is dissolved as a separate entity. But for the male partner the dissolution of the passive partner means one thing only," Bataille concludes: "it is paving the way for a fusion where both are mingled, attaining at length the same degree of dissolution" (17). The discontinuous self, Bataille argues, finds itself thus "violated" by death: "The most violent thing of all for us is death which jerks us out of a tenacious obsession with the lastingness of our discontinuous," or individual, "being" (16).

Bataille links sacrifice to religious eroticism, as does Eliot. "In sacrifice," Bataille writes, "the victim is divested not only of clothes but of life (or is destroyed in some way if it is an inanimate object)." Thus, in a kind of strip tease,

> [t]he victim dies and the spectators share in what his death reveals. This is what religious historians call the element of sacredness. This sacredness is the revelation of continuity through the death of a discontinuous being to those who watch it as a solemn rite. A violent death disrupts the creature's discontinuity; what remains, what the tense onlookers experience in the succeeding silence, is the continuity of existence with which the victim is now one. (22)

In other words, a violent sacrifice—like Prufrock's dissolution in the sirens' sea—shows the spectator, or in this case the reader, a sacred revelation: the poet's "continuity" or immortality in the silence that succeeds him, the silence that is "continuity of existence" or God. Like Eliot, Bataille insists on the spectacular and erotic nature of the religious ritual: "Only a spectacular killing, carried out as the solemn and collective nature of religion dictates, has the power to reveal what normally escapes notice" (22).

Harrison's and Bataille's discussions of religious sacrifice speak to Eliot's desire to multiply his own cultural *mana* through poetic self-immolation. His poet is violated and consumed by a ravenous readership—women who come and go trading bon mots on reproduction Renaissance art like bon bons. So the poet serves as the culture's totem animal and his consumption ensures a ceremonial multiplication. Sacrifice leads to sanctification: "Sacrifice is simply either 'holy doing' or 'holy making,' . . . *sanctification*, or, to put it in primitive language, it is handling, manipulating *man*," explains Harrison.

> When you sacrifice you build as it were a bridge between your *mana*, your will, your desire, which is weak and impotent, and that unseen outside *mana* which you believe to be strong and efficacious. In the fruits of the earth which grown by some unseen power there is much *mana*; you want that *mana*. In the loud-roaring bull and the thunder is much *mana*; you want that *mana*. It would be well to get some, to eat a piece of that bull raw, but it is dangerous, not a thing

to do unawares alone; so you consecrate the first-fruits, you sacrifice the bull, and then in safety you—communicate. (137)

One of Eliot's ancillary aims seems to be to create a mystical or intellectual position of superiority for himself, to establish himself as a voice of the tribe. His sacrificial poetic rituals work to "initiate" a male poet into a realm of spiritual power. Sacrificial rituals, according to Harrison, can be conflated with primitive rites of passage, as such rites often represent a "Second Birth" in the son's metaphorical transformation into a totem animal (130). Harrison illustrates this process with a Hindu purification ceremony for "rebirthing" a child born under a bad horoscope: "[H]e has to be born again of a cow," says Harrison, " . . . dressed in scarlet, tied on a new sieve and passed between the hind legs of a cow forward through the forelegs to the mouth and again in the reverse direction to simulate birth." And so "[t]he child is new born as a holy calf. This is certain, for the father sniffs at his son as a cow smells her calf" (131). According to this logic, rituals that involve the eating of totemic animals allude to the process of "eating" sons so that they can be reborn through the Father.

Freud's fantastic reading of the totemic meal elaborates on the Father's crucial role in these proceedings. Freud attributes the ceremony's generative power to its ability to tap into ambivalent or contradictory Oedipal emotions:

> One day the brothers who had been driven out came together, killed and devoured their father and so made an end of the patriarchal horde. United, they had the courage to do and succeeded in doing what would have been impossible for them individually. . . . Cannibal savages as they were, it goes without saying that they devoured their victim as well as killing him. The violent primal father had doubtless been the feared and envied model of each one of the company of brothers: and in the act of devouring him they accomplished their identification with him, and each one of them acquired a portion of his strength. The totem meal, which is perhaps mankind's earliest festival, would thus be a repetition and a commemoration of this memorable and criminal deed, which was the beginning of so many things—of social organization, of moral restrictions and of religion. (*Totem and Taboo* 176)

Freud likens his "tumultuous mob" of savages to children, seeing them "filled with the same contradictory feelings which we can see at work in the ambivalent father-complexes" of children and neurotics (177). These primitives hate their father because he takes all the women for himself, presenting "a formidable obstacle to their craving for power and their sexual desires"; at the same time, the sons admire the father for enjoying the power he denies them. As Freud sees it, the act of eating the father, or his totemic representation, allows these "children" to satisfy their violent hatred for the father while identifying with him (177). This communion ritual expresses a suppressed affection as remorse, according to Freud, and so "[t]he dead father [becomes] stronger than the living one had been" (178). He becomes a god.

Freud continues his fantasy narrative by suggesting that the totem meal, by regulating divisive sexual desires through an incest taboo, allows the primal brothers to "rescue" the homosocial organization that made them strong before the murder of the living father:

> The new organization would have collapsed in a struggle of all against all, for none of them was of such overmastering strength as to be able to take on his father's part with success. Thus the brothers had no alternative, if they were to live together, but—not, perhaps, until they had passed through many dangerous crises—to institute the law against incest, by which they all alike renounced the women whom they desired and who had been their chief motive for dispatching their father. In this way they rescued the organization which had made them strong—and which may have been based on homosexual feelings and acts, originating perhaps during the period of their expulsion from the horde. Here, too, may perhaps have been the germ of the institution of matriarchy . . . which was in turn replaced by the patriarchal organization of the family. (178–79)

The totemic meal, Freud concludes, also enacts a promise *not* to kill the Father again, thus ensuring reconciliation with him, his protection in the future, and his forgiveness. That way, the "brothers" can enjoy the father's power without fear of annihilation.

Freud's tale of the father's ritual devouring, the killers' remorse, and the new homosocial (eventually patriarchal) organization that springs from the re-enactment of this "communion" over the Father's dead body sounds a bit like Eliot's fantasies of paternal reconciliation in the *Waste Land*, "Gerontion" and *Ash Wednesday.* Eliot's poet and poetry attempts to force its audience to "accept the rule of the dead father," as Jane Gallop puts it in *Reading Lacan* (107). Lacan's re-interpretation of Freud's social Genesis divides the picture into before and after—the "unlivable rivalry of ego versus ego" that invests Freud's primal horde with Lacan's "imaginary order" converted, through the totem ritual, into "the truly social structure" of Lacan's symbolic order, "the rule of the dead father" (Gallop 107). In a sense, Eliot connects his desiring Lady with the primal horde and imbues her with pre-conscious or pre-social thought (though, ironically, Eliot's dowagers are always the enforcers of a stifling social structure). Against the matriarch, Eliot's poet yearns after the truly social structure of the totemized society, the symbolic order or the rule of the dead father.

Eliot's *Waste Land* suggests that the male landscape is "polluted," indeed, with something like maternal "lamentation" that sterilizes both land and people. Eliot's readings of Frazer stress the connection between a healthy king, god or totem and a healthy tribe. Unlike Eliot's modern man, Frazer's "savage cannot fail to perceive how intimately his own life is bound up with the life of nature, and how the same processes which freeze the stream and strip the earth of vegetation menace him with extinction" (V, 3). Frazer's "primitive" knows the experience of dissolution and can re-experience that sublimity through ritual. The "evolution" of consciousness, or social structures, according to Frazer, relegates this experience to the recesses of the mind.

Eliot's poems suggest that the classical model described by Frazer and imitated by so many of his fellow poets lacks a certain liberating violence, a violence necessary to remind readers of this vivid dissolution. Perhaps this is one reason why Christ's passion serves as Eliot's poetic touchstone. In "Journey of the Magi," Eliot's pagan narrator ponders the immaculate birth: "this Birth was / Hard and bitter agony for us, like Death, our death," he says. "We returned to our places, these Kingdoms, / But no longer at ease here, in the old dispensation. . . / I should be glad of another death," he concludes (CPP 69). Finally, Eliot's bloody (or bloodless) feasts serve that this "other" religious and erotic communion/death—baptisms of fire designed to rebuild totemic relationships.

In poems such as "The Love Song of J. Alfred Prufrock," "Portrait of a Lady" and then the *Waste Land*, Eliot conceives a divinely inspired—though imperfect— poet who acts as a medium for the unspeakable Word.[29] Certainly, Eliot walks a thin line as he compares his ineffectual poet to a savior, so he's careful to undercut his representative, to call into question his ability to follow in such grandiose footsteps. "I am no prophet," Prufrock avers, dismissing his likeness to John the Baptist. Instead, he's another Lazarus, an animated corpse "come from the dead . . . to tell you all" (CPP 6).

In these terms, poetic language approaches an emotional and intellectual experience outside of individual "reality." Eliot's work proposes poetry as the language of a missing or forgotten religious ritual, recalling Lucien Lévy-Bruhl's notion of "collective representations": expressions whose emotional and spiritual life transcend individual generations to convey an experience of "respect, fear, adoration" for the other (*How Natives Think* 13). Eliot draws from such reverential descriptions of the symbolic community possible in language, and even his most cynical pieces suggest that poetry is a sanctified medium. Prufrock becomes, in death, the collective consciousness of a lost generation, converting the first person to a plural: "We have lingered in the chambers of the sea," he intones, "By sea-girls wreathed with seaweed red and brown / Till human voices wake us, and we drown" (CPP 7). Prufrock's plight, though peculiar, is not particular. Indeed, it proves oracular, and so unreadable, as Eliot's poet "sees" past, present and future—individual and collective history, love and sexuality, consciousness, religion, the afterlife.

Ultimately, these are inextricably linked in Eliot's lexicon, and poetry provides the essential glue: "Every phrase and every sentence is an end and a beginning, / Every poem an epitaph" (CPP 144). By the time Eliot composes the *Waste Land*, he regards poetry as a receptacle for God's voice, the thunder that promises (but perhaps denies) rain. Here, and elsewhere, Eliot's poet speaks as if possessed and, though necessarily imperfect, as God's translator for a population afflicted with spiritual blindness. "These fragments I have shored against my ruins," Eliot's Fisher King/Tiresias says, speaking for a disintegrating City.

In "Choruses from the Rock," Eliot writes that "the soul of Man" must, properly, "quicken to creation" (CPP 111); the poet serves, then, as a womb for the Word. Set against this artistic and spiritual quickening is female abjection: meaningless shapes such as the sea, "slimy mud," sleet and hail, emotions. All of these present and oppose themselves to the artist's eye as he labors to give birth to "the perfect order of speech, and the beauty of incantation":

> Out of the formless stone, when the artist united himself with stone,
> Spring always new forms of life, from the soul of man that is joined to the soul
> of stone;
> Out of the meaningless practical shapes of all that is living or lifeless
> Joined with the artist's eye, new life, new form, new colour.
> Out of the sea of sound the life of music,
> Out of the slimy mud of words, out of the sleet and hail of verbal imprecisions,
> Approximate thoughts and feelings, words that have taken the place of thoughts
> and feelings,
> There spring the perfect order of speech, and the beauty of incantation.
> ("Choruses from 'The Rock'" CPP 111)

Eliot's poetry seeks to re-order this messy body into the expression of a pure emotion that, he insists, exists nowhere *but in* the poem. Poetry cannot serve, says Eliot, as a representation of individual experience or suffering; instead, it must transform bodies into words, emotions into minds. The poem ultimately prevents earthly incorporation as it *converts* sordid bodily affairs into poetic apperception. Eliot strives for what Wallace Stevens, in "Of Modern Poetry," calls "[t]he poem of the mind in the act of finding / What will suffice."

Eliot's last poem conceives of the perfect poem as an epitaph, "the complete consort" of male and female "dancing together" under the end and beginning that is "God":

> . . . every phrase
> And sentence that is right (where every word is at home,
> Taking its place to support the others,
> The word neither diffident or ostentatious,
> And easy commerce of the old and the new,
> The common word exact without vulgarity,
> The formal word precise but not pedantic,
> The complete consort dancing together)
> Every phrase and every sentence is an end and a beginning,
> Every poem an epitaph. ("Little Gidding," CP 144)

The ultimate dis-embodier, the epitaph transforms matter into phrases and sentences, vulgarity into precision, commonness into formality. The epitaph/poem, erected over the woman's body, provides "easy commerce" between this world and the next. Eliot's dream poem works the magic of transubstantiation—matter or mother into God.

3.
Transformations

THROUGH HIS WORK, ELIOT ATTEMPTS TO CHART A PLACE FOR HIMSELF ON the maps of gender, sexuality, religion, politics and poetics that will afford him metaphysical vision. In "The Death of St. Narcissus," Eliot satirizes the burgeoning cult of the personality; motivated by egotism verging on onanism, Narcissus's "sacrifice" goes unremarked by God or His people, and so the culture Narcissus dances for remains unregenerate. Eliot uses such persona poems to try on off-center sexual and gender roles, as well as to denigrate what he designates as predatory female sexuality and to celebrate the emasculate—celibate—male.

In "The Love Song of J. Alfred Prufrock" and the *Waste Land*, Eliot returns to the dying god narrative, casting his male protagonists as dying sons and lovers, and the voracious women who surround them as the earth goddesses who demand their return. Eliot's allegorical approach suggests that twentieth century culture is on the brink of apocalypse not only because of the doomed relationship between dying son and demanding lover/mother but, more importantly, because of the culture's complicity in the son's unregenerate sacrifice. The *Waste Land* inhabitants look the other way, rejecting the Father who demands his son's death and rebirth. A godless people have no poetry, and a people without poetry, Eliot implies, have no God. Up to and including *The Hollow Men*, Eliot seems concerned with pointing out this cultural lack. It's not until he undergoes his own religious conversion and begins to write "religious" poetry like *Ash Wednesday* that Eliot's goal appears to be to supply an answer for this lack.

With *Ash Wednesday* Eliot's allegorical poetry undergoes a subtle change. The sacrificial relationship that in "Prufrock," "Gerontion" and the *Waste Land* is either interrupted, thwarted or impossible in *Ash Wednesday* comes to signify a spiritual rebirth. Though visions of a cultural desert still provide the backdrop for *Ash*

Wednesday, Coriolan, "Choruses from 'The Rock,'" and *Four Quartets,* cultural Armageddon now signifies not God's absence, but proof of His presence and promise for the penitent poet. Camped in exclusively Christian and certainly Catholic[1] terrain, Eliot's poet doubles as ecstatic visionary, performing a *solitary,* spiritually erotic role. Not surprisingly, Eliot's evil Eves are recuperated as well, transformed from demanding lovers to sexless (and silent) mothers like the Virgin Mary.

In *Ash Wednesday,* in fact, Eliot declares a new "muse" for himself—a divine female figure, "torn and most whole," who operates as his audience and icon, the "rose of memory" that is "now the Garden / where all loves end" (CPP 62). As ideal mother, Eliot's silent Lady is *never* a lover and *always* a martyr. This new and improved Lady provides a fitting Anglo-Catholic substitute for the pagan earth mother who instigates the dying god's sacrifice in poems such as "Prufrock." She conforms perfectly to the sacrificial role demanded of her by the Father's rule—giving up body, voice and desire for His divine purpose. Free from original sin, she serves as the poet's divine intercessor.[2] The Virgin's womb provides the best objective correlative for the poet's mind, in Eliot's estimation: a sanctified, still place where he can hear and repeat the Word. Because of this purity, "dry bones in the desert" (that could be read as images of the ailing tradition, the poet's ancestors, a missing God, or all three) sing in her/his presence.[3]

All this is a long time coming, though Eliot's readers and critics are quick to place him on the side of the Word and God the Father. Eliot spends the early stages of his poetic career cultivating himself as the enlightened "savage," a "scientist" of poetry with interests in the evolution of religious ritual and social practices. His own commitment to a particular religious tradition and idea of God remains, perhaps deliberately, obscure.

There are hints of his growing allegiance to Anglo-Catholicism, however. Essays such as "Tradition and the Individual Talent" preview Eliot's impending reliance on Christian narrative and iconography, and suggest that he lays his poetics over the Trinity in order to cast himself as a priest, if not as a latter-day prophet. It is my contention that Eliot's Catholic identifications are more complex than most readings allow. Though Eliot calls for a social structure, embodied in a culture's art, that is religious by necessity and firmly entrenched in patriarchal practices, it is not clear that Eliot intends to be one of the founding fathers of such a new age.

While Eliot's gynephobia and misogyny are painfully evident in both his poetry and prose—his essay on *Hamlet* is particularly revealing—his own identification with a virgin "femininity" or sexless maternity is not as obvious. Even as Eliot investigates the possibilities of the dying god narrative in the modern setting, that is, he identifies with the "veiled sister," the innocent female virgin/victim, rather than with the rejuvenated Father or his celestial original. Just as his Narcissus remembers being a young girl who is raped by the old man in the woods, Eliot's poet, modeled on Tiresias, suffers all as a woman, and remembers that pain as the sweetest. In the classical paradigm, Eliot is more likely to see himself in Psyche, then, than in Amor, and in Eliot's Christian paradigm, he adopts Mary as a touchstone. Thus he aligns himself with a position outside of the three-part god. His poet is the pure vessel, the "holy" womb (that Eliot calls, for the sake of science, a "catalyst"). Thus Eliot's "conversion" process begins, as he transforms the "feminine" from a voracious hysteria into a sacred stillness, the word within the Word, and thus the proper purview of the poet. At the same time, Eliot makes his move in the direction of the Church of England.

Inklings of Eliot's shift toward orthodox Christianity can be found, as I remarked above, in "Tradition and the Individual Talent" (1919), his "seminal" or germinal essay on poetic conception. First collected in *The Sacred Wood*, this essay describes the poet as a mystical vessel in which the materials of poetry—emotions and "feelings" —fuse to create the "new emotion of art," and this new emotion alters, irrevocably, the "existing order." In other words, the poet is possessed by something very much like the godhead as he gives birth to a "new" poetry, an active vision that revises past, present and future.

This extended metaphor for poetic conception offers a twist on the Adamic myth, a process of father-son conception—or a mode of motherless reproduction—that Nina Baym exposes and rejects in "Melodramas of Beset Manhood." Baym cites a novelistic and critical "tradition" in American literature that she calls a "myth of artistic creation" predicated on Adam: the "unconventional" novelist (or poet) recreates literature in the absence of social or domestic ("female") pressure. Thus, the writer transfers "the American myth from the Adamic hero *in* the story to the Adamic creator *of* the story" as "unconventionality is interpreted as a direct representation of the open-ended experience of exploring and taming the wilderness, as well as a rejection of 'society' as it is incorporated in conventional literary forms" (77). Crowing over the *Waste Land* as a father-son production, Ezra Pound subscribes to this mythic pregnancy as he celebrates Eliot's impregnation by the "Uranian muse," congratulating himself as the C-sectioning physician of a new poetry and, at the same time, suggesting his role as the poem's progenitor when he jokes about his contribution—his "upjut of sperm."

Eliot seems to see the creative process in more passive terms. Ever intrigued by images of rape and violation, Eliot identifies, in a sense, with the absent woman in the Adamic myth. Yet "[t]here is no place for the woman author in this scheme," says Baym. "Her roles in the drama of creation are those allotted to her in a male melodrama: either she is to be silent, like nature," as in *Ash Wednesday*, "or she is the creator of conventional works, the spokesperson of society," as in "Portrait of a Lady," "Prufrock" and the *Waste Land* (Baym 77). Eventually, as his religious poetry reveals, Eliot's genuine lady must indeed keep silent, conflated with an idealized nature.

But as Eliot struggles to articulate the process of poetic reproduction, his woman splits in two; Eve is differentiated from Mary. Eve serves, in Eliot's mythology, as the betrayer, the body that tempts Adam from his union with the divine. Mary is afforded another role in this drama—she plays the ravaged virgin, the metaphysical rape victim, and, finally, the sexless mother of God's son.

Eliot's "pure" girl is penetrated by the divine in much the same way that the poet in "Tradition and the Individual Talent" is seized, possessed, *ravished,* by monumental emotions and feelings. In this essay, Eliot demands the poet's "submission" to a higher Authority—a vague reference to the God that wanders through Eliot's poetry after the *Waste Land.* "Submission" rings with erotic and religious significance in Eliot's work. Indeed, one could assert that religion *is* eroticism, a masochistic pleasure, in Eliot's world, as his vision of that authority, or Absolute, takes on increasingly sacrificial overtones. The body that suffers, of course, yields to the mind that creates (or the body that suffers creates the mind—at one point, Eliot alludes to the poet's submission as an "amputation," though he quickly denies the resonance). Poetry becomes the issue of the poet's ecstatic "violation," as traces of the Absolute form new combinations in his wounded mind. Perversely, Eliot's poet is Mary, the mother of a new God (who is both Father and Son), or, simply, a portal to the divine.

"Throughout patriarchal mythology," says Adrienne Rich in *Of Woman Born,*

> dream-symbolism, theology, language, two ideas flow side by side: one, that the female body is impure, corrupt, the site of discharges, bleedings, dangerous to masculinity, a source of moral and physical contamination, 'the devil's gateway.' On the other hand, as mother the woman is beneficent, sacred, pure, asexual, nourishing; and the physical potential for motherhood—that same body with its bleedings and mysteries—is her single destiny and justification in life. (34)

This separation of mind and body, eroticism and sexual intercourse, good woman (virgin) from whore, mother from lover, informs Eliot's mythic re-creation of poetry and sexual relations. Particularly key to Eliot's conception of the "good" woman is her suffering. Eliot identifies himself with that suffering as the essence of "goodness." "It is as if the suffering of the mother," Rich writes, "the primary identification of woman *as* the mother—were so necessary to the emotional grounding of human society," and by implication to the grounding of Eliot's "new" poetry, "that the mitigation, or removal, of that suffering, that identification, must be fought at every level, including the level of refusing to question it at all" (30).

Fathering and mothering; suffering; submission; self-obliteration: these issues, though silent or silenced in Eliot's poetry, orchestrate it from behind the scenes. In "Tradition and the Individual Talent," Eliot goes to great pains to create a new genealogy for poetry that leaves out the woman *as the male poet takes her place.* Indeed, Eliot is engaged in recuperating the sexual or experienced female by exiling her. Eliot's method of banishment, however, is identification. He redeems his woman, that is, becoming her. Rich comments that "poetry was where I lived as no-one's mother, where I existed as myself" (31). For Eliot, poetry serves as the place where he has no mother and needs none to reproduce—cellular division will do quite well. Though he shrouds his early fantasies of maternal appropriation in scientific rhetoric, Eliot's eroticism is religious in nature. His "Tradition and the Individual Talent" describes an Immaculate Conception—if anything, he exists in poetry as his own divine mother. This is how he colonizes the wilderness (so to speak).

As Julia Kristeva points out in "Stabat Mater," Christianity brings the "resorption of femininity within the Maternal . . . to its peak" (163). In fact, Kristeva's motivating questions can be applied to Eliot's poetic conception. Does this "reduction," she wonders, represent simply a "masculine appropriation of the Maternal" that is itself merely "a fantasy masking primary narcissism"? Or is it (also) a form of "enigmatic . . . masculine sublimation," a "taming" of the economy of primary narcissism that, in the tradition of da Vinci and then Freud, "is a requirement for artistic, literary or painterly accomplishment"? (163) Eliot's "Tradition and the Individual Talent" certainly sets itself up as an exercise in taming the "female" or feminine in the interests of a "strong" national literature or art. For poetry to be immortal, Eliot's poet must adhere to the same "compelling imaginary construct" as the Mary narrative. Eliot must invent for his poet a deathless and sexless "biography . . . similar to that of Jesus"; he must assign him "letters patent of nobility"; and he must reveal our relationship to and from such a poet as "the prototype of love relationships," incorporating in that love courtly and child love, "thus fitting the entire range that goes from sublimation to asceticism and masochism" ("Stabat" 164–65).

Eliot's poetry is predicated on a masculine sublimation of epic proportions, as his poet gives birth to poetry through a procedure akin to in-vitro fertilization. Eliot compares poetic "implantation" to the combination of elements in a sterilized environment. He exalts this "horrifying" space by converting it into virgin territory and calling it "the poet's mind," a purely masculine environment. This conversion depends, in part, on the mystifying nature of Eliot's prose. His discussion is steeped in eccentric imagery and metaphor, as well as in pseudo-scientific, philosophic and aesthetic explications, and so his argument is alternately concrete and abstract. The result is an elusive and frustrating treatise that skirts concrete understanding and thus suggests a mystical transaction between poet and spirit in which the spirit (what Eliot calls Tradition) holds sway.[4]

Whenever it seems that Eliot might compare the poet's mind directly to a womb, his discussion veers into abstract territory, obscuring the metaphor. Eliot further circumvents this identification by larding his essay with didactic passages designed to denigrate vaguely "female" habits of reproduction and reading, implying that scribbling women pollute the poetic or artistic process. One of the salient issues of this elliptical essay, for instance, is Eliot's insistence on the poet's escape from "personality." As he vaguely defines it, "personality" is connected with what Eliot sees as female narcissism:

> Poetry is not a turning loose of emotion, but an escape from emotion; it is not the expression of personality, but an escape from personality. But, of course, only those who have personality and emotions know what it means to want to escape from these things. (SP 43)

The cult of personality serves as the smuggest of female "sins" in "Prufrock," for example. Eliot uses indirection to avoid identification with the women who come and go. Though he supposedly includes himself and the reader (presumably male) in his condemnation—"We dwell with satisfaction upon the poet's difference from his predecessors" (SP 38)—the implication is that Eliot and his ideal reader have personality and emotions enough to know what it means to escape them. For Prufrock, there is no escape from the woman's "personality" except death.

In a rather sarcastic move, Eliot alludes to superficial social Madams who tout their interest in Michelangelo over crumpets and "plum[e] [themselves] a little with the fact" that the French are more critical and thus less "spontaneous" in their reading habits. Eliot's terse rejoinder smacks of the schoolmaster's superiority. ". . . [W]e might remind ourselves that we should be none the worse," he says, "for articulating what passes in our minds when we read a book and feel an emotion about it, for criticizing our own minds in their work of criticism" (SP 37).

It is no surprise that Eliot's rhetoric is most caustic when the boundaries between this feminine other and himself are uncertain. In his "Preface to the 1928 Edition" of *The Sacred Wood*, Eliot admits to rigid prose. "There are, it is true, faults of style which I regret," he confesses, "and especially I detect frequently a stiffness and an assumption of pontifical solemnity which may be tiresome to many readers" (vii). This stiffness could be a by-product of Eliot's attempt to differentiate his own voice from that of prating fools such as Prufrock, who, in the company of tea-time tarts, cannot say what they mean. Prufrock and other scapegoats are, to Eliot's chagrin, often confused with his "real-life" personality as readers assume that Eliot's popular poems are exercises in confession. (Eliot later suggests—in a perversely offhand gesture—that his *Waste Land* is a personal grouse against life rather than the voice of a dissatisfied generation.)

Another scathing essay in *The Sacred Wood* reveals Eliot's loathing for these dowagers and their eunuchs. In "Hamlet," written in the same year as "Tradition and the Individual Talent," Eliot deplores what he sees as the unwarranted excess of emotion in Shakespeare's famous play and the equally flamboyant criticism that it draws upon itself. "Hamlet the character has had an especial temptation for that most dangerous type of critic," Eliot writes: "the critic with a mind which is naturally of the creative order, but which through some weakness in creative power exercises itself in criticism instead" (SP 45). These minds been mutated by ambition and so "find in Hamlet a vicarious existence for their own artistic realization," Eliot sneers (SP 45). And so they give birth to freaks.[5]

Eliot connects various "weakness[es] in creative power"—Shakespeare's and his readers'—to the "guilty" woman's contamination. "Shakespeare's *Hamlet,* as far as it is Shakespeare's, is a play dealing with the effect of a mother's guilt upon her son, and . . . Shakespeare was unable to impose this motive successfully upon the 'intractable' material of the old play," Eliot says (SP 46–47). Questioning the legitimacy of the play, Eliot implies that the evil mother proves the "intractable material" that infects the whole with "artistic failure" (47) and thus turns it into a bastard. "In several ways the play is puzzling, and disquieting as is none of the others," Eliot says.

> Of all the plays it is the longest and is possibly the one on which Shakespeare spent most pains; and yet he has left in it superfluous and inconsistent scenes which even hasty revision should have noticed. . . . Both workmanship and thought are in an unstable position. We are surely justified in attributing the play . . . to a period of crisis. . . . It is the 'Mona Lisa' of literature. (SP 47)

As Jacqueline Rose points out in *Sexuality in the Field of Vision,* Eliot's obsession with the bad mother turned lover, or Madonna turned whore, lurks behind his knee-jerk condemnation of *Hamlet* and its critics. Rose diagnoses Eliot's rejection of the play as misogynist revulsion: he fears the woman's abjection and the patriarchy's inability to control her, she says. Eliot is no anomaly; he experiences the fears of a male generation worried about the World War's inroads against white male superiority, as droves of young men sacrifice themselves for King and country while their mothers, lovers and wives pick up the economic slack on the home front.

Eliot's comment about *Hamlet* being the Mona Lisa of literature seems like an afterthought. It speaks volumes, however. No doubt Eliot was aware of Walter Pater's essay on Leonardo da Vinci, and particularly familiar with Pater's rhapsodic passage regarding the famous face in *La Gioconda.* Unlike Eliot, Pater suggests that this portrait is da Vinci's masterpiece precisely because it is an objective correlative for his "love of the impossible," somehow represented by a fascination with two ideas, "the smiling of women and the motion of great waters" (34). Pater claims that the "germinal principle" for the well-known portrait is again "the unfathomable smile, always with a touch of something sinister in it, which plays over all Leonardo's work" (46).

Where Pater waxes enthusiastically about da Vinci's admiration for the woman he paints as well as his identification with her, given his sensual "secret" (a physical love for men), Eliot is horrified by excess. Pater's passage of description is "overblown" in Eliot's terms, but since it illustrates perfectly the "problem" *Hamlet* presents for Eliot, it is worth quoting at length:

The presence that thus rose so strangely beside the waters, is expressive of what in the ways of a thousand years men had come to desire. Hers is the head upon which all "the ends of the world are come," and the eyelids are a little weary. It is a beauty wrought out from within upon the flesh, the deposit, little cell by cell, of strange thoughts and fantastic reveries and exquisite passions. Set it for a moment beside one of those white Greek goddesses or beautiful women of antiquity, and how would they be troubled by this beauty, into which the soul with all its maladies has passed! All the thoughts and experience of the world have etched and moulded there, in that which they have of power to refine and make expressive the outward form, the animalism of Greece, the Lust of Rome, the reverie of the middle age with its spiritual ambition and imaginative loves, the return of the Pagan world, the sins of the Borgias. *She is older than the rocks among which she sits; like the vampire, she has been dead many times, and learned the secrets of the grave; and has been a diver in deep seas, and keeps their fallen day about her; and trafficked for strange webs with Eastern merchants: and, as Leda, was the mother of Helen of Troy, and, as Saint Anne, the mother of Mary . . .* The fancy of a perpetual life, sweeping together ten thousand experiences, is an old one; and modern thought has conceived the idea of humanity as wrought upon by, and summing up in itself, all modes of thought and life. *Certainly Lady Lisa might stand as the embodiment of the old fancy, the symbol of the modern idea.* (46–47 italics mine)

This image of the woman as a beautiful vampire who contains "all modes of thought and life" in the modern world is the "horror" Eliot tries to avoid in his discussions of "Hamlet" . . . and yet this horror fascinates and compels him in his own work. There is nothing this immortal woman won't do. Indeed, Pater's reverie verges on blasphemy—he is certainly guilty of recreating the Mona Lisa as a narcissus, a sensual, pagan god. Da Vinci's sensitivity to femininity and maternity, as Pater sees it, becomes Eliot's despised excess. How can she (the quintessential mother/lover) be the "monument" Eliot tries to reconstruct through his own suffering body and creative mind? An objective correlative must remain just that. Correlate. An object. Abject. This excessive woman refuses these roles.

Does Eliot struggle to construct his own monument over the mother's historical body, her limitless "desire"? Certainly, he continually fights against this woman, and her sucking soul: ". . . how would they be troubled by this beauty, into which the soul with all its maladies has passed!" Pater proclaims. How indeed?

Perhaps to compensate for the woman's tendency to involve the world in her body, Eliot works assiduously to rob her of this experience—to ground her, entirely. No deathless mother/lover characterizes the *Waste Land*. Instead, Eliot's depictions of modern contamination suggest that the woman's sexual relations, domesticated, depressing and mundane, are to blame for physical and spiritual infertility. Eliot pays particular attention to the woman's sexual "folly": "Her brain allows one half-formed thought to pass: / 'Well now that's done: and I'm glad it's over,'" Tiresias says of the promiscuous typist (CPP 44). Women like the typist use sex, Eliot implies, to "get" a man and thus to advance themselves. There is no desire involved in their offering, no sacrifice involved in their coupling. The aborting Lil is no better:

> It's them pills I took, to bring it off, she said.
> (She's had five already, and nearly died of young George.)
> The chemist said it would be all right, but I've never been the same.
> You are a proper fool, I said.
> Well, if Albert won't leave you alone, there it is, I said.
> What you get married for if you don't want children? (CPP 42)

Eliot's woman refuses to be a good mother. Instead, the sterile wife demands attention, performance, from the hapless poet turned husband: " . . . Stay with me. / 'Speak to me. Why do you never speak. Speak'" (CPP 40).

Margarete J. Sandelowski traces a historical interest in infertility that began in the mid-1800s and which, by the end of the century, focused itself on the woman's role in marital sterility. Sandelowski connects an increasing worry about infertility rates—a fear unsubstantiated by statistics—with suspicions about women's increasing sexual choices and independence:

> [T]he origins of infertility have consistently been linked to individual choices or actions, suggesting that if infertile individuals cannot be blamed for the obstructions and genital infections directly responsible for their not having children, they can be blamed for the past actions that predisposed them to developing these conditions or that initiated the causal chain of infertility. (39)

Thus, in the last decades of the nineteenth century, when Eliot was born, the public spotlight turned towards women's "new educational and occupational aspirations, their assertions of independence and claim to political rights, and a declining birth rate among what many viewed as the most desirable segments of the population" (Sandelowski 42). Eliot traces the problem of cultural sterility to the ambitious woman's door as well. Her acquisitive sexuality underlies his falling cities. The siren sings to the hero, luring him to the rocks. The errant typist's ennui pervades a sterile coupling. Lil is to blame for her health because she elected to have an abortion. Sweeney's prostitutes are "epileptic" and "hysterical" and infect Sweeney with their syphilis.

On all counts, the wrong "sort" propagates itself in Eliot's *Waste Land*. The nymphs have departed and so Mrs. Turner and her daughters comb the river for treasures. Changing demographics at the turn of the century proved "traumatic" for those interested in infertility as a sign of racial and economic precariousness in the United States, says Sandelowski:

> Between 1800 and 1900, the total white fertility rate decreased 50 percent, at
> least half of the decline attributable to a reduction of childbearing within mar-
> riage. The years between 1870 and 1915 were especially significant because they
> were characterized partly by increasingly visible differences in the fertility rates
> of native white upper-income women and their poorer, black, and immigrant
> counterparts, native white births lagging far behind those of the other groups.
> (43)

Elective abortions appeared to exacerbate to this trend, and so physicians actively
attempted to restrict the option. In addition, an imperative sprang up that women
conform to the "divine" role of wife and mother and a "socially conscious gynecol-
ogy" developed to address it: "Physicians believed that childbearing preserved the
true woman, protected her from the physical and emotional ravages of her own biological cycles, and protected society from decline and extinction" (Sandelowski
43–44).

This sort of medical and psychological theory no doubt troubled the Eliots as
they contended with Vivien's menstrual ailments. The increasing availability of birth
control and women's expanding social roles altered the perception of infertility, especially in marriage. "The failure to reproduce at all," as in Eliot's and Vivien's case,
"or in sufficient numbers was increasingly viewed as a consequence of the failure to
want to reproduce" (Sandelowski 44), and this is certainly how many of Eliot's
friends and biographers saw his marriage. Eliot's "barren" marriage was indeed the
prototype of the modern waste land, and his nervous wife proved an easy villain: "In
medical literature, marital sterility was increasingly constructed as a social disease, a
disorder of civilization and modern living, involving culpable, largely female acts of
omission and commission" (Sandelowski 45). Horace R. Bigelow, a nineteenth century gynecologist, for example, demanded that women receive a "system of education" emphasizing maternality, since "conjugal onanism" was the result of "the rest-
less condition of modern women who aspired to absolute equality with men"
(Sandelowski 45).

Doctors such as Bigelow, worried about sterility in the upper classes, argued for
suppressing women's "intellectual" rather than physical labors; though sterility rates
were the same for all classes, doctors promulgated the idea that poverty and labor
were conducive to increased birth rates, while indolence and wealth were not
(Sandelowski 46). A popular treatise by T. G. Thomas, published in 1891, cata-
logues the "depreciating habits of civilized life" that predispose white, upper class
women to sterility. "These habits, almost wholly in the domain of female agency,
included neglect of proper nutrition and outdoor exercise, brain fatigue, impropri-
eties of dress, imprudence during menstruation, and the prevention or termination
of pregnancy" (Sandelowski 46). At the turn of the century, then, nativist fears of
racial suicide and the "unchecked fertility" of the lower classes and immigrant pop-
ulations, as well as a burgeoning eugenics movement, brought childless white

women under attack. An early twentieth century campaign against venereal disease and its consequences, spearheaded by Prince Albert Morrow, failed to take the onus off women. Though Morrow argued that men's sexual activities outside of marriage were responsible transplanting the "diseases of vice" into innocent wives' "beds of virtue" (Sandelowski 49), women were still cast as conspirators in aristocratic sterility, while men were dismissed as "passive accomplices" (Sandelowski 50).

Eliot uses the *Waste Land* to lament this conspiracy. Aristocratic sterility has led to spiritual bankruptcy, and now the not-so-meek inherit the earth: "He who was living is now dead" and "We who were living are now dying," while "There is not even solitude in the mountains / But red sullen faces sneer and snarl / From doors of mudcracked houses" (CPP 47). Finally, "hooded hordes" swarm over the endless plains to the sound of maternal lamentation (CPP 48). In a section cut from "The Fire Sermon," Eliot links the London workplace to American economic and racial fears:

> London, the swarming life you kill and breed,
> Huddled between the concrete and the sky;
> Responsive to the momentary need,
> Vibrates unconscious to its formal destiny,
> Knowing neither how to think, nor how to feel,
> But lives (only) in the awareness/transformations of the observant eye.
> London, your people is bound upon the wheel!
> Phantasmal gnomes, burrowing in brick and stone and steel! (WL 31)

Eliot links this soulless reproduction of semihuman workers, if only by proximity, to the typist's bored copulation. The clerk carbuncular is, after all, "One of the low on whom assurance sits / As a silk hat on a Bradford millionaire." The typist's sexual liberties contribute to his feelings of social aggression, as he "munches with the same persistent stare, / He knows his way with women and that's that!" (WL 33).

In another section of the *Waste Land* wisely omitted from the final draft, Eliot condemns the scribbling upper class woman for her indolent intellectuality. In short, Fresca is guilty of a degenerate reproduction of the word as she lolls in bed eating bon-bons and dribbling bad poetry. She is another portrait of Eliot's Lady, a social prostitute who indulges every one of her perverse desires at the expense of culture:

> Fresca! in another time or place had been
> A meek and weeping Magdalene;
> More sinned against than sinning, bruised and marred,
> The lazy laughing Jenny of the bard.
> (The same eternal and consuming itch
> Can make a martyr, or plain simple bitch);
> Or prudent sly domestic puss puss cat,
> Now autumn's favorite in a furnished flat,

> Or strolling slattern in a tawdry gown,
> A doorstep dunged by every dog in town. (WL 27)

The issue of Fresca's self-indulgence is bad writing: "Women intellectual grow dull," Eliot claims, "And lose the mother wit of natural trull" (WL 27). Eliot equates female "intellectuality" with "dull" sexuality, severing both from "mother wit" and thus "natural" behavior.

Eliot is an easy study in male paranoia and gynephobia. Pronouncements such as this—"*Hamlet*, like the sonnets, is full of some stuff that the writer could not drag to light, contemplate, or manipulate into art"—provide strong evidence for Eliot's vendetta against the Dark Lady (SP 48). Citing Gertrude as *Hamlet's* excess and comparing the play to da Vinci's dark lady, Eliot as much as tells us that he sees the sexual woman/queen as the source of artistic crisis and failure. (Of *his own* artistic crisis and failure, we might add, reading the essay as condemnation and confession, just as we tackle his poetry of the same period. Vivien plays a fine Gertrude while Eliot's "Prufrock" and *Waste Land* are certainly "full of some stuff" that Eliot can never completely "drag to light" or manipulate properly.) Eliot's extended descriptions of Hamlet's disgust and Shakespeare's artistic "problem" cement our suspicions that he uses both as convenient scapegoats for his own sexual and social neuroses. Drawing on images of mental disease and infection, Eliot hints that Gertrude is the virus that starts a chain reaction of symptoms ending in the cataclysm of public attention or "interest." "Hamlet is up against the difficulty that his disgust is occasioned by his mother, and that his mother is not an adequate equivalent for it; his disgust envelops and exceeds her. It is thus a feeling," Eliot concludes, "which he cannot understand; he cannot objectify it, and it therefore remains to poison life and obstruct action" (SP 48). In short, the mother is a mental plague.

Gertrude's character is infectious, Eliot insinuates, because, though inferior and insignificant, it cannot be dominated by the artist who creates it. In fact, it is "*because* her character is so negative and insignificant" that "she arouses in Hamlet the feeling which she is incapable of representing" (SP 48–49). The same could be said, of course, for all of Eliot's Ladies. His description of Shakespeare's impotence reads like a confession, as when he describes Hamlet's feigned yet very real madness as "a form of emotional relief." Here, Eliot hits rather close to home:

> The intense feeling, ecstatic or terrible, without an object or exceeding its object, is something which every person of sensibility has known; it is doubtless a subject of study for pathologists. It often occurs in adolescence: the ordinary person puts these feelings to sleep, or trims down his feelings to fit the business world; the artist keeps them alive by his ability to intensify the world to his emotions. . . . We must simply admit that here Shakespeare tackled a problem which proved too much for him. Why he attempted it at all is an insoluble puzzle; under compulsion of what experience he attempted to express the inexpressibly horrible, we cannot ever know. We need a great many facts in his

biography . . . We should have to understand things which Shakespeare did not understand himself. (SP 49)

In "Tradition and the Individual Talent," Eliot insists that an author's biography should remain irrelevant if not inaccessible, but in "Hamlet" he undercuts the idea. Indeed, we think, Gertrude must be a ghost imported from a "reality" that, as Eliot suggests, we can never know.

Likewise, Eliot's elaborate escapes from the "feminine" merely call attention to its influence on his work. What we at first take to be rejection or revulsion can serve as a masked reproduction, an identification or obsession with the sexual, and sinful, woman. Eliot's failure to control and dismiss Gertrude's excess in "Hamlet" is no fluke. In fact, his imagery often "exceeds the facts" of his philosophical and aesthetic discussions, as his abstract pronouncements about objective correlatives take the backseat to his evocations of sleeping citizens, avid adolescents, horrified artists drugged up with emotion, and the pathologist's study. The harder Eliot works to sanitize his study, the more "individual" his struggle becomes. As Eliot campaigns vigorously to amputate "personality" from the poet and poetry, his peculiar imagery compels us to use that very poetry to expose his "private" desires, mortification and obsessions.

Maud Ellmann argues that Eliot actually "smuggle[s] personality back into [his] poetics in the very terms [he] use[s] to cast it out." "Eliot . . . insists that poetry originates in personal emotion, implying that the author's subjectivity pervades the text," she writes, "yet at the same time he deplores this intervention" (3). Eliot's poetic suffers from "slippage" and "blur," Ellmann claims, and involves as much expression of self as repression of it (4). Ultimately, his "play of metaphor deranges the machinery of logic," embarking the reader on "a metaphoric odyssey" (39).

Despite condemnation, protestation and calculated indirection (what we might call philosophical sleight of hand), Eliot reveals his reliance upon conception and procreation as the model for poetic reproduction in "Tradition and the Individual Talent." His task, it appears, is to redeem this process for a patriarchal poetry through a Christian/Catholic twist. Perhaps, as Eliot accuses his foes of doing, he too is engaged in setting before us the "implication . . . of some pleasing archaeological reconstruction" (SP 37). The work Eliot struggles to approve—in this essay as in much of his poetry—here through the pleasantly distancing lens of a microscope, is the heterosexual act. In this "seminal" essay, Eliot transforms the womb into the site of divine intervention, designating the now holy space as masculine. As such, it is bodiless—the poet's "mind," perhaps a vague vision of the Holy Ghost.

Eliot begins by finding fault with what he sees as an alarming trend in literary studies: the attempt to discover "the peculiar essence of the man" (SP 37). ". . .[W]e endeavour to find something that can be isolated in order to be enjoyed," Eliot says. "Whereas if we approach a poet without this prejudice we shall often find that not only the best, but the most individual parts of his work may be those in which the dead poets, his ancestors, assert their immortality most vigorously" (SP 38). As I suggested earlier, Eliot infers that this improperly "satisfying" and prejudicial activity is female. In essence, Eliot implies that women isolate sons from their fathers, as in "Prufrock," no doubt in order to enjoy them free from the patriarchal contract.

In order to break the mother's hold, Eliot insists upon the poet's lineage, emphasizing his possession by his forefathers.[6] "No poet, no artist of any sort," Eliot reiterates, "has *his* complete meaning alone. *His* significance, *his* appreciation is the appreciation of *his* relation to the dead poets and artists" (SP 38, emphasis mine). As Stephen H. Clark notes, " . . . the 'simultaneous order' that is here invoked is an exclusively masculine enclave. To participate in the 'mind of Europe' involves the perpetuation of a patriarchal authority stemming back beyond Homer to 'Magdalenian draughtsmen'" (168). Just as Eliot's poet and audience must be male, we can assume that the dead ancestors he speaks of are fathers, just as we might acknowledge that the "prejudice" Eliot mentions here originates in mothers bent on confining knowledge to "whatever can be put into a useful shape for examinations, drawing-rooms, or the still more pretentious modes of publicity" (SP 40).

In an attempt to further masculinize poetic conception, Eliot "define[s] this process of depersonalization and its relation to the sense of tradition" as objectively or scientifically as possible. Still, it is impossible to eliminate the sense that human relations underlie Eliot's "conception of poetry as a living whole of all the poetry that has ever been written" (SP 40).[7] It is difficult for Eliot to maintain that poetic impregnation is like the introduction of an inert metal into a chamber full of gas without alluding to copulative imagery. "I . . . invite you to consider," Eliot says, "as a suggestive analogy, the action which takes place when a bit of finely filiated platinum is introduced into a chamber containing oxygen and sulphur dioxide" (40).

And so Eliot opens his essay with a homily to familial reproduction, citing the power of dead ancestors to assert their immortality "most vigorously" through their poet son by demanding the sacrifice of his "most individual parts" and his "peculiar essence as a man." At the same time, Eliot rejects traditional notions of manhood, such as the celebration of difference or "following the ways of the immediate generation before us in blind or timid adherence to its successes"—a mimesis which Eliot obliquely connects to "the impressionable period of adolescence" (SP 38).[8] Though Eliot indicts these processes of initiation and reproduction (of the father's law), he deliberately mystifies the act(s) necessary to comply with and simultaneously alter the ideal "order."

All we can glean from the essay is that Eliot's conformity requires a special consciousness of Tradition, which has become "a matter of much wider significance" than we'd reckoned. "It cannot be inherited," Eliot advises, "and if you want it you must obtain it by great labour" (38). Yet there are no operational instructions for this labor. Rather, it is something visited upon the would-be poet akin to possession by the divine. What Eliot describes is an immediate "involvement" in something larger than the self, a feeling in the bones, and an acute consciousness that comes from outside the poet:

> [Tradition] involves, in the first place, the historical sense, which we may call nearly indispensable to anyone who would continue to be a poet beyond his twenty-fifth year; and the historical sense involves a perception, not only of the pastness of the past, but of its presence; the historical sense compels a man to write not merely with his own generation in his bones, but with a feeling that the whole of the literature of Europe from Homer and within it the whole of the literature of his own country has a simultaneous existence and composes a simultaneous order. This historical sense, which is a sense of the timeless as well as of the temporal and of the timeless and of the temporal together, is what makes a writer traditional. And it is at the same time what makes a writer most acutely conscious of his place in time, of his own contemporaneity. (SP 38)

Eliot emphasizes the metaphysical nature of this conceptual act by reiterating its "connectedness" with the past, present and future generations, as well as its transcendence of human mortality and time: a man writes with *all* generations of writers in his bones.

Eliot equally mystifies the "birth" of the new piece of art. His poet, who submits to this labor and is thus possessed by a concatenation of dead voices, somehow transforms past, present and future as he produces the new work of art:

> The necessity that [the poet] shall conform, that he shall cohere, is not onesided; what happens when a new work of art is created is something that happens simultaneously to all the works of art which preceded it. The existing monuments form an ideal order among themselves, which is modified by the introduction of the new (the really new) work of art among them. The existing order is complete before the new work arrives; for order to persist after the supervention of novelty, the *whole* existing order must be, if ever so slightly, altered; and so the relations, proportions, values of each work of art toward the whole are readjusted; and this is conformity between the old and the new. (SP 38–39)

This is indeed a miraculous birth. Eliot's rhetoric reinforces the idea that this transaction is superhuman and that only the faithful are called to participate in it, those "aware of great difficulties and responsibilities" (SP 39) involved in transmitting the Word.

In Eliot's estimation, this sanctified process of creation and self-sacrifice entails a severe, inescapable, judgment: "In a peculiar sense [the poet] will be aware also that he must inevitably be judged by the standards of the past. I say judged, not amputated, by them . . ." (SP 39). Eliot acknowledges the consequences of this particular rebirth—particularly for a poet raised to recognize the hortatory goals of nineteenth century idealized masculinity: steady material or economic gain, the sublimation of sexual and other wasteful energy into gainful industrial pursuits, individuality apart from the masses and, thus, the pursuit of a particular kind of cultural progress—technological rather than intellectual.[9] Eliot's description of the poet at work contradicts this image of the man at work. "What happens," Eliot explains, "is a continual surrender of himself as he is at the moment to something which is more valuable. The progress of an artist is a continual self-sacrifice, a continual extinction of personality" (SP 40). If anything is amputated from the poet, it is "himself as he is at the moment," his will or phallic identification.[10]

A casual reader of Eliot's essay might assume that Eliot calls for a drastic amputation; he may read Eliot's manifesto as an attack on manhood itself. That reader may be correct; after all, Eliot's "conception of poetry" (SP 40) involves not only conformity but self-sacrifice, surrender to "something . . . more valuable" than individual success, judgment on all levels (past, present and future), great difficulties and responsibilities and, finally, the extinction of personality. These are demands placed on the turn of the century wife as she is exhorted to fulfill her role as the divine or ideal mother. If she does not show herself to be ready to subjugate her desires to this end, as Ben Barker-Benfield suggests, the social structure—supported by the medical and scientific community—will only be too glad to "fix" her, usually with a literal amputation: clitoridectomy and castration. Barker-Benfield argues that the successful suppression of women's sexuality came to represent, by the turn of the century, the proper working order of civilization; unbounded, desiring women "represented man's loss of control over himself" (349). "[I]t may well be that disorderly women were handed over to the gynecologist," Barker-Benfield suggests, "for castration by husbands unable to enforce their minimum identity guarantee" (356). That is, they were handed over for what we now call female genital mutilation, and abhor as a third-world practice. Thus, the castration of the middle- or upper-class woman in the family was either metaphorical or literal.

Ironically, this amputation was not seen as a violent imposition but rather as a willing, even joyful, self-sacrifice to "something greater." Barker-Benfield notes that women often offered themselves up for castration, thinking that their emotional "problems" would be solved through the operation.

The birth of Eliot's poetry entails, certainly, the same "hard and bitter agony" for the poet, the same death of the "self" and rebirth in the divine other. As with the cult of ideal motherhood, Eliot redeems or exalts this sacrifice by envisioning it as a divine call. He suggests this, for example, in "Journey of the Magi," as one of the wise men remembers his journey to see the infant god:

> . . . I had seen birth and death,
> But had thought they were different; this Birth was
> Hard and bitter agony for us, like Death, our death.
> We returned to our places, these Kingdoms,
> But no longer at ease here, in the old dispensation,

With an alien people clutching their gods.
I should be glad of another death. (CPP 69)

In the two poems following "The Journey of the Magi," Eliot reiterates the connection between a death of the self and a miraculous rebirth. "A Song for Simeon" refers to "this birth season of decrease" (CPP 70) and "Animula" ends with an altered prayer, "Pray for us now and at the hour of our birth" (CPP 71). These deaths promise spiritual, if not social, salvation—the body is amputated but the spirit is increased.

As Eliot seeks to separate the poet from his suffering, laboring body, he paradoxically calls attention to the physical nature of his task. Describing the act of creation as a scientific experiment with minerals and gases, careful to emphasize the process as a chemical transaction rather than an emotional effect, Eliot attempts to focus on the spiritual or metaphysical nature of the quickening rather than its physical analogy. Interestingly enough, the same emphases, theological questions and paradoxes invest discussions of Mary's virginity before and after the miraculous birth. Some of these discussions, particularly those which argue that Mary maintained an intact hymen even after childbirth, the labor for which was painless and comparable to passing gas, are as inventively scientific as Eliot's.[11]

A mixture of metal and gas takes place, he says. The mind digests and transmutes "passions" into poetry (an acid) but remains frigid— "inert, neutral, and unchanged," Eliot insists. "When the two gases...are mixed in the presence of a filament of platinum," Eliot claims, "they form sulphurous acid."

> This combination takes place only if the platinum is present; nevertheless the newly formed acid contains no trace of platinum, and the platinum itself is apparently unaffected: has remained inert, neutral, and unchanged. The mind of the poet is the shred of platinum. It may partly or exclusively operate upon the experience of the man himself; but, the more perfect the artist, the more completely separate in him will be the man who suffers and the mind which creates; the more perfectly will the mind digest and transmute the passions which are its material. (SP 41)

Eliot's descriptions of this conception call up the physical nature of this supposedly sanitized space. The poet's mind mimics the womb: "a receptacle for seizing and storing up numberless feelings, phrases, images, which remain there until all the particles which can unite to form a new compound are present together" (SP 41). The process of "fusion" which Eliot describes as the definitive moment of conception suggests a physical union: "it is not the 'greatness,' the intensity, of the emotions, the components, but the intensity of the artistic process, the pressure, so to speak, under which the fusion takes place, that counts" (SP 40).

If Eliot's poet serves as a divinely selected womb for poetry, then his gaseous visitor, Tradition, is something like the Holy Ghost. This abstraction serves, in both cases, to exalt and mystify the paternal element in Eliot's passive act of poetic conception. Maud Ellmann points out that Eliot's essay shrouds an authoritarian past's "iron hand ... by sentimentalising its paternalism" (37). Ellmann argues that Eliot masks this patriarchal coercion in "the rhetoric of organicism": "He speaks as if tradition had emerged according to the laws of nature," she says, "rather than through the social, economic and political exclusions which institute the canon by expelling any works that challenge its hegemony. Spongeous and capacious," Ellmann concludes, Eliot's naturalized sense of the holy Father or tradition "absorbs all friction into the serenity of its organic form" (37–38).

Just what does Eliot gain from this exalted view of a tradition that demands self-sacrifice and extinction from its sons? Ellmann claims that Eliot gains "his place with the immortals" because his willing submission to this divine order "universalises his identity at the very moment that he seems to be negated" (38). Thus Ellmann subscribes to Eliot's identification with Christ's passion and crucifixion. At moments, it's true, Eliot clearly posits himself as the savior of culture and history; much of his characteristic criticism smacks of the pulpit. As Elisa Kay Sparks puts it: "Eliot's . . . descriptions of the creative process can be seen as typical examples of the strategies of logocentrism, or more specifically phallogocentrism. [He] creates an opposition between a valued Origin associated with masculinity and devalued supplement associated with femininity," she continues. That devalued supplement, Sparks argues, is the emotion or "nature" that Eliot connects with the guilty woman. "[Eliot] thus participate[s] in the fairly common attempt to create a totally male myth of the engenderment of the word/world," Sparks concludes (73).

But this identification with the Father is shaky, at best, as Eliot often denies his own authority with the same breath he uses to assert it. Looked at askance, Eliot's mystification and naturalization of the poetic conception reveals his attempt to idealize a subservient feminine—the maternal as defined by the patriarchy—and then to inhabit that space. In "The Function of Criticism" (1923), Eliot reiterates his sense of the poet's masochistic and subordinate role in the reproduction of tradition and the "unconscious community" which underwrites it:

> I thought of literature then, as I think of it now, of the literature of the world, of the literature of Europe, of the literature of a single country, not as a collection of writings of individuals but as 'organic wholes,' as systems in relation to which, and only in relation to which, individual works of literary art, and the works of individual artists, have their significance. There is accordingly something outside of the artist to which he owes allegiance, a devotion to which he must surrender and sacrifice himself in order to earn and to obtain his unique position. A common inheritance and a common cause unite artists consciously or unconsciously: it must be admitted that the union is mostly unconscious. Between the true artists of any time there is, I believe, an unconscious community. And, as our instincts of tidiness imperatively command us not to leave to the haphazard of unconsciousness what we can attempt to do consciously, we

are forced to conclude that what happens unconsciously we could bring about, and form into a purpose, if we made a conscious attempt. The second-rate artist, of course, cannot afford to surrender himself to any common action; for his chief task is the assertion of all the trifling differences which are his distinction: only the man who has so much to give that he can forget himself in his work can afford to collaborate, to exchange, to contribute. (SP 68–69)

Eliot leaves us with the suspicion that this essay, like "Tradition and the Individual Talent," involves a masochistic self-condemnation (along with a defense of "friends" like Ezra Pound). Is Eliot perhaps one of the "second-rate artists" he dismisses as incapable of a purely motivated sacrifice? After all, collaborations, exchanges and contributions are not activities we necessarily identify with Eliot's artistic process, nor are they a hallmark of the modernist era.

In "Tradition and the Individual Talent," as in his *Waste Land*, Eliot's "fragments" concede quite a bit about his personal obsessions, objects of desire and identifications. In this case, they reveal Eliot's fascination with family structure and intrigue, as the balance of power shifts away from the aristocracy (the patriarchy, in other words) and into the hands of the middle-class. Here, Eliot quotes from and discusses, briefly, Tourneur's *The Revenger's Tragedy*, where the danger to the honorable and god-fearing middle-class in this social cataclysm is represented as the aristocracy's unbounded sexual desire. The Duke and his sons, that is, would like to take the virtue of the upper-middle-class daughter, caught minding her own business on the fringes of the court. Because these crimes are perpetrated, in part, by the economic and political machinations of the Duke's bastard and step-sons (and their mother's complicity in them), Tourneur's play deals with some of the same collapsing social, sexual and family mores as Eliot's *Waste Land*. (In his essay devoted to a discussion of the Jacobean playwright, "Cyril Tourneur" (1930), Eliot claims that *The Revenger's Tragedy* can only be compared to *Hamlet* [SE 166], so clearly he feels that the play suffers from some of the same "problems" as Shakespeare's.) Thus, Eliot's allusive and elusive discussion provides a fittingly mysterious conclusion to his exploration of poetic conception.

Eliot provides a short passage from one of Vindice's monologues as an example of what he calls the "combination of positive and negative emotions" that form "a new art emotion":

> And now methinks I could e'en chide myself
> For doating on her beauty, though her death
> Shall be revenged after no common action.
> Does the silkworm expend her yellow labours
> For thee? For thee does she undo herself?
> Are lordships sold to maintain ladyships
> For the poor benefit of a bewildering minute?
> Why does yon fellow falsify highways,

And put his life between the judge's lips,
To refine such a thing—keeps horse and men
to beat their valours for her? ... (SP 42)

Eliot congratulates himself on taking the passage out of a somewhat obscure context: "I will quote a passage which is unfamiliar enough to be regarded with fresh
attention in the light—or darkness—of these observations," he says. Eliot is obviously interested, again, in original sin—particularly the "poor benefit of a bewildering minute" that such seductive machinations yield, and the mortality and/or
damnation that result from such a fall from grace. In this context, sexual desire is
deadly, and the woman's "beauty" is the agent of divine retribution. Eliot is also
interested in the virginal woman as the victim—here Vindice's dead lover—of a
voracious male desire. (This male desire seems conflated, in the *Waste Land*, with the
acquisitive female domesticity or social ambition that substitutes for sexual intrigue
or power.)

More often than not, Eliot's poetry expresses a fascination with martyred
women like Vindice's dead lover and his threatened but still virtuous sister.
Ambitious mothers are pitted against these tragic women in *The Revenger's Tragedy*
and Eliot's *Waste Land*. In Tourneur's play, Vindice's mother is willing to sacrifice her
daughter's virtue to win favor in the court, while the Duke's second wife plots with
her sons to overthrow him, overlooking their sexual crimes (one of them rapes a
chaste nobleman's wife, causing her to commit suicide). The *Waste Land*, particularly, contains a bevy of undone women for whom Eliot expresses fondness and/or
sympathy: Philomel, Ophelia, Magdalene, the Hyacinth girl. All of them have been
"rudely forced."

In "The Fire Sermon," these voices blend with a penitent Eliot's; in a sense, all
invite God's "burning" presence to avenge or redeem the transforming "event."
These women are "undone," that is, but their voices blend into prophecy as they
utter apocalyptic cant:

> "Trams and dusty trees.
> Highbury bore me. Richmond and Kew
> Undid me. By Richmond I raised my knees
> Supine on the floor of a narrow canoe.

> "My feet are at Moorgate, and my heart
> Under my feet. After the event
> He wept. He promised 'a new start.'
> I made no comment. What should I resent?"

> "On Margate Sands.
> I can connect
> Nothing with nothing.

> The broken fingernails of dirty hands.
> My people humble people who expect
> Nothing." (CPP 46)

As readers have suggested, this collapsing reverie could be an attempt at expiation for the enduring guilt Eliot suffers for "wronging" his wife, Vivien. More likely, it is a "prayerful" attempt to expiate what he sees as his own sexual guilt, and an escape— through divine intervention—from the heterosexual demands of marriage. As another reader of this passage has commented, the "burning" imagery evokes the pain of venereal disease as well as the cheerful fires of God's love. The crumbling passage also provides Eliot with a neat segue-way to a masochistic rhapsody celebrating God's power to fuse sinner and sexuality into a divine utterance: "Burning burning burning burning," the poem continues. "O Lord Thou pluckest me out / O Lord Thou pluckest // burning" (CPP 46). These forced women eventually merge in *Ash Wednesday's* silent Lady. Significantly, Eliot (as the bodiless poet) merges with her as well.

In a short draft excised from the final version of the *Waste Land*, Eliot further explores the connection he's forging between poet, "injured bride," and avenging God. Here, the virginal bride reappears from the dead as the "wrong'd Aspatia," the "very inconvenient dead," and her unfaithful lover records his punishment at her— and God's—hands (WL 117). Her grief and trauma transforms her into a hellish vision of the Eumenides[12] or Medusa:

> That hand, prophetical and slow
> (Once warm, once lovely, often kissed)
> Tore the disordered cerements,
> Around that head the scorpions hissed!

Eliot's narrator confesses, passionately, his inability to "expiate the fault," even with "remorse unbounded" and "grief intense." Though (or perhaps *because*) his punishment is in excess of the supposed crime, the narrator ends in a note of ecstasy:

> God, in a rolling ball of fire
> Pursues by day my errant feet.
> His flames of ~~pity/horror~~/anger/~~passion~~ and ~~of ire~~/desire
> Approach me with consuming heat. (WL 117)

Eliot's ambivalence about God's anger/desire is clear in the number of nouns he's considered and crossed out, and the mystery of his final choice is never resolved. Thus, Eliot knits together God's passion with anger, pity, horror and desire, using the wronged woman as a "catalyst" for this visitation.

Though his poetry is straightforward on these matters, Eliot occludes his poetry's investment in a peculiar, virginal sexuality by deliberately interrupting the passage he cites from Tourneur's play. It's a passage which, he claims, depends upon what surrounds it for its emotional charge; he has deliberately tamed—dis-charged it, that is. "In this passage," Eliot says,

> (as is evident if it is taken in its context) there is a combination of positive and negative emotions: an intensely strong attraction toward beauty and an equally intense fascination by the ugliness which is contrasted with it and which destroys it. This balance of contrasted emotion is in the dramatic situation to which the speech is pertinent, but that situation alone is inadequate to it. This is, so to speak, the structural emotion, provided by the drama. But the whole effect, the dominant tone, is due to the fact that a number of floating feelings, having an affinity to this emotion by no means superficially evident, having combined with it to give us a new art emotion. (SP 42–43)

So much for halting at the frontier of mysticism. In his "Cyril Tourneur," Eliot describes the predominant emotion in the play as "some horror beyond words," which springs from the poet's "inner world of nightmare" (SE 166). This "cynicism, . . . loathing and disgust of humanity" are "immature" responses or emotions, Eliot claims in 1930, because "they exceed the object. Their objective equivalents are characters practising the grossest vices..." (SE 166). Yet Eliot is willing to concede that, though "the play is a document on humanity chiefly because it is a document on one human being, Tourneur," the piece captures the "death-motive" well enough to be a "triumph"—"for the hatred of life is an important phase—even, if you like, a mystical experience—in life itself," Eliot concludes (SE 166).

Eliot's discussion of the "new emotion" in art hinges on the vague apprehension of some "enemy" waiting in the wings. The triumphant "death-motive" or the "loathing and horror of life itself" which Eliot identifies in "Cyril Tourneur" seems to be this "new emotion" of art which he wants readers of "Traditional and the Individual Talent" to see in the quoted passage, the artistic triumph that Eliot ascribes to "a highly sensitive adolescent with a gift for words" (SE 166). This horror, Eliot later claims, provides a wholeness of vision often lacking in first attempts: "[O]ccasionally the intensity of the vision of its own ecstasies or horrors, combined with a mastery of word and rhythm, may give to a juvenile work a universality which is beyond the author's knowledge of life to give, and to which mature men and women can respond" (SE 166). It's clear that Eliot identifies himself with the "young" Tourneur and his loathing of others, and particularly of the "hatred of life" that Eliot claims soaks through Tourneur's lines.[13] Who, again, is the enemy of their Absolute?

In Tourneur's play, lewd schemers surround the doomed hero. The Duke, a "royal lecher," has poisoned Vindice's fiancée because her "purer part would not consent / Unto his palsy lust" (I.i.33–34). In the meantime, the Duke's ill-favor and spendthrift behavior has bankrupted and killed Vindice's father; the Duke's son,

Lussurioso, plans to ruin the virtue of Vindice's sister, Castiza. Other crimes of similar motives afflict the court. The Duchess's youngest son has raped a nobleman's chaste wife—she kills herself because of the shame. (He assumes he'll get off through the political power of his stepfather). The Duchess and the Duke's illegitimate son are having a revenge affair. The Duchesses's other two older sons plot a coup d'état. The old Duke continues to arrange illicit tête-à-têtes in the bushes, while Vindice's mother is easily persuaded to sell her only daughter's virtue to the Duke's son. Significantly, mothers are most untrustworthy in this tragedy: adulterous, incestuous and murderous, like the Duchess, they are easily swayed into prostitution. The only pure women in the play are dead (like Vindice's fiancée and the raped wife of the nobleman) or in jeopardy, like Vindice's virginal sister, Castiza.

Clearly, "grace" is in short supply in this world—almost all of these intrigues end in blood. Even Vindice, after slaying the entire court and turning it over to Antonio, the wronged nobleman widower, is sent to the gallows. Yet his death, like Hamlet's, provides an escape from a violent, material world and assures him a kind of immortality. Furthermore, his sacrifice is ennobled by his purpose: to thwart a corrupt and corrupting state of affairs, to reinstall an "ideal" order. The dead hero becomes the consciousness of the play, a historical record of wrongs avenged. Perhaps this is what Eliot sees as the play's triumph over the adolescent "horrors" which it records and a way in which the poetic hero can align himself with the self-sacrificing virgin.

The passage that Eliot excerpts in "Tradition and the Individual Talent" actually continues with a scathing indictment of masquerade (particularly women's vanity) and its consequences. The desire that such masquerade produces, warns Vindice, ends in madness: "'Tis we are mad in sense, they but in clothes," he pronounces (III.v.81). He addresses the skull of his beloved, which he has dressed up in fine clothing and painted with poison for a fatal rendezvous with the hapless old Duke (who has killed the poor virgin for resisting his lechery):

> Does every proud and self-affecting dame
> Camphor her face for this, and grieve her Maker
> In sinful baths of milk,—when many an infant starves
> For her superfluous outside,—all for this?
> Who now bids twenty pound a night, prepares
> Music, perfumes, and sweetmeats? All are hushed,
> Thou may'st lie chaste now! It were fine, methinks
> To have thee seen at revels, forgetful feasts
> And unclean brothels; sure 'twould fright the sinner
> And make him a good coward, put a reveller
> Out of his antic amble,
> And cloy an epicure with empty dishes.
> Here might a scornful and ambitious woman
> Look through and through herself; see, ladies with false forms

You deceive men, but cannot deceive worms.—
Now to my tragic business. Look you, brother,
I have not fashioned this only for show
And useless property; no, it shall bear a part
E'en in its own revenge. This very skull,
Whose mistress the Duke poisoned with this drug,
The mortal curse of the earth, shall be revenged
In the like strain, and kiss his lips to death. (III.v. 83–104)

The horror of the skull beneath the skin, of the woman's sexuality and ambition, is no unfamiliar emotion in Eliot's poetry. The violent death or destiny implied as the consequence of such masquerade and seduction is a predominant theme in Eliot's work. As he discusses the playwright, a decade after writing "Tradition and the Individual Talent," Eliot remarks that a phrase like "[t]he poor benefit of a bewildering minute" "seem[s] to contract the images in [an] effort to say everything in the least space, the shortest time" (SE 168). In a sense, Eliot has already borrowed this phrase for his *Waste Land,* as he writes about "The awful daring of a moment's surrender / Which an age of prudence can never retract" (CPP 49).

Stephen Clark argues that the speech which Eliot quotes and discusses "marks a casting off of obligation: Vindice will henceforth participate freely and independently in the intricate choreography of the play's intrigue" (170). He is free from the woman's sexual wiles, Clark suggests, "[a]nd so a kind of aesthetic repletion becomes possible in contemplating the victim: she no longer has the deceiving beauty of the living, but an alternative and more potent allure in death." Clark sees this "repletion" as Eliot's way of recuperating the feminine through sacrifice of her body: "fear of mortality can be tamed, utilized almost, through the violation and sacrifice of the female body: the propitiatory offering to a new spiritual or symbolic order" (170). Thus Clark argues that Eliot, by employing a passage which savagely refers to the patriarchy's potential redemption in the virgin's bloody sacrifice, identifies himself with the priest of the new order, rather than the sacrificial victim. Another reader might see Eliot's identification with a masquerading hero whose own death is assured through the process of revenge and/or redemption.

Likewise, Eliot chooses to obliterate himself in the "expression of a *significant* emotion"—the infamous third party that has "its life in the poem and not in the history of the poet." It seems that Eliot connects the "emotion of art" with an impersonal superhuman; the poet must sacrifice himself to this significant order or other, like Vindice's fiancée and then himself, in order to transform his desire/personality into something sacred: poetry. "And the poet cannot reach this impersonality," Eliot repeats in conclusion, "without surrendering himself wholly to the work to be done" (SP 44).

There is something sacred about this surrender to authority. First of all, it identifies the poet with the hero, whose job it is to "revenge" himself on the enemies of the ideal order. This identification includes an idealization of the "good," virginal woman and a condemnation of ambitious sexuality, nearly always feminized. Second, it assures the self-sacrificing poet of some immortality, as the record of his deeds serves to reinforce the new order and his place in it.

Thus, Eliot oscillates between an idealization of the suffering victims of human desire (all, in some way, injured brides) and an identification with their repentant spoilers, whose transgressions must be punished with God's passion. Idealization and identification collide in "Tradition and the Individual Talent." We recall the implied violence in Eliot's poetic transformation: it is the "intensity of the artistic process, the pressure, so to speak, under which the fusion takes place, that counts" (SP 41). This fusion is at once a "rude forcing" and a rebirth or redemption. Here, Eliot describes it as the consuming heat of the virgin's and God's wrath.

It could also be compared to a strange, self-constructed initiation rite: a kind of symbolic or spiritual circumcision/castration. Drawing from Frazer's studies of "primitive" societies, Bruno Bettelheim ascribes such *Symbolic Wounds* to "the adolescent's attempts to master his envy of the other sex, or to adjust to the social role prescribed for his sex . . ." (21). Eliot's self-mutilated poet mimics the wounded woman; the tradition "forces" him to give birth to a new poetry. Bettelheim, like Eliot, sees this potential or actual violence as a positive force that might be desired by, appropriated by, the male: "[I]n our discussion of initiation and circumcision we have been far too engrossed in what looks like destruction (damage to the genitals) and have overlooked the more hidden fascination with pregnancy and birth," Bettelheim writes. "It may be that what has been linked narrowly and pessimistically with castration, truly a destruction of life, will come to be seen as resulting rather from the most constructive desires, those concerned with progeny, with new life" (22). Eliot is certainly concerned with creating a new life—for poetry and for himself—and he seems to suggest that self-wounding (metaphorical or actual) sparks such reproduction.

Finally, the poet's surrender to a higher authority allows him to transcend the same natural borders as the dying god and thus aligns him with this figure. The slain god, or his human representative, journeys into the afterlife without fear and then returns to bear witness. Eliot clearly alludes to this journey as he concludes "Tradition and the Individual Talent," suggesting that the poet "is not likely to know what is to be done unless he lives in what is not merely the present, but the present moment of the past, unless he is conscious, not of what is dead, but of what is already living" (SP 44). But he travels as Persephone rather than Odysseus, as Mary rather than Christ.

4.
Madness or Mysticism
Eliot's Dream-Crossed Twilight

It seems to be widely believed that any contact with the occult is rather like contact with an infectious and incurable disease.

—Leon Surette, *The Birth of Modernism*

Eliot began writing a kind of spiritual autobiography in an age that was not cordial to the genre.

—Lyndall Gordon, *Eliot's Early Years*

INVESTIGATIONS OF ELIOT'S POETICS CITE HIS 1927 RELIGIOUS CONVERSION AS A definitive shift in his epistemological speculations, and thus in his art. This move is the culmination of a long process of private speculation, image-making, indirection and ambivalence. As Eliot abandons his reliance on science and philosophy in favor of the metaphysics of orthodox Christianity and Catholicism, he envisions his poet as a masochistic mystic. At the same time, Eliot's impulse to regard the poet as an androgynous priest or prophet—a "witness" of cultural disintegration and an advocate for spiritual rebirth on a grand level—yields to a more private purpose. After *The Hollow Men*, Eliot's apocalyptic imagery and his arch pronouncements slip from the public sphere; his poet's torment seems private, personal, and his relationship to God speaks of individual rather than cultural atonement. And so his crazy-quilt arrangements of broken images, and his scathing comments on urban blight, give way to a sobering "confessional" mode in *Ash Wednesday* and his final *Four Quartets*.

Eliot's confirmation to the Church of England signals a disavowal of several crucial factors in his early poetic persona. It serves to negate, once and for all, his humanistic, Unitarian upbringing—Eliot strikes against his family's, particularly his grandfather's and mother's, emphasis on Protestant social reform as the single purpose of any "good" citizen. Eliot's conversion further separates him, physically and spiritually, from his "hysterical" wife and the Bloomsbury set that described their married social life. It also severs him from other fashionable modernists. Last, and certainly not least, Eliot rescripts the artist's relationship to "his" audience, casting the cultural purpose of art in religious terms. In the process, Eliot changes the medium of his public communication, as this series of turns ends—at long last—in the ritualistic, even "classical," drama that Eliot proposes as the most effective mode of "ceremony" for the arts. Thus, Eliot's conversion marks his cruelest and most satisfying failure. In quest for a "deeper union," that is, Eliot sacrifices poetry *en route*.

In anticipation of his first truly confessional poem, Eliot's *Hollow Men* ends a "witty" indictment of secular humanism with the poet's yearning after an orthodox relationship with a familiar Christian God. As his imagined "civilized" world ends with a whimper, Eliot's poet prepares for the work of penitence, the limbo of purgatory, that he will experience in *Ash Wednesday*. And as his relationship to the "material" of poetry changes, so does his relationship to the monumental tradition he once touted as the end to all artistic endeavors. Though Eliot continues to describe the poet's job in grandiose social terms in essays such as "The Social Function of Poetry," where he suggests that the poet's job is to refresh the culture's language, to set aesthetic standards, and to "translate" art for the masses, his poetry reveals a more private purpose. Eliot reconceives his poetry as prayer, and thus implies that the acts of writing and reading poetry are individual endeavors—the penitent speaking with God.

At the same time, Eliot's primary identification shifts. His poet is no longer prophet or priest, or even sacrificial virgin. Instead, he becomes "dry bones" that sing God's praise in the desert. Again the passive receptacle for the "new" emotions of poetry, Eliot shifts his gaze to the quintessential Christian icon for pure femininity or maternality: the Virgin Mary. And so Eliot's evil lady, his siren Eve, disappears from the scene, transformed into the silent Lady.

By adopting Mary as his muse, Eliot swaps Christian for classical imagery without abandoning his reliance on the dying god theme. Frazer shows how Christian lore appropriates Eastern and then classical myths and rituals, and contemporary studies of the transformation of pagan rituals into "canonized" Christianity emphasize the appropriation of such rituals to cement a popular power base and to assure that lingering matriarchal social and political practices are transformed to serve an ironclad patriarchy.

These goals are analogous to Eliot's, at least as he alludes to them in his criticism. In "The Function of Criticism," he condemns those who listen for what he calls the "inner voice" in order to find a universal sensibility or self. As far as Eliot is concerned, this act is the true measure of the "lower" classes, and its popularity transforms modern life into a purgatory: "The possessors of the inner voice ride ten in a compartment to a football match in Swansea, listening to the inner voice, which breathes the eternal message of vanity, fear, and lust" (SP 71). Though this activity, at its best, aspires to a mystical examination of subjectivity, Eliot rejects it as "an exercise far beyond the strength of our football enthusiasts." Communion, in Eliot's opinion, must not be taken lightly:

> It is an exercise, however, which I believe was of enough interest to Catholicism for several handbooks to be written on its practice. But the Catholic practitioners were, I believe, with the possible exception of certain heretics, not palpitating Narcissi; the Catholic did not believe that God and himself were identical. (SP 71)

Mr. Murry is most guilty palpitating narcissi in this scenario, and must be held responsible for rekindling this misguided and dangerous interest in the "inner voice." "'The man who truly interrogates himself will ultimately hear the voice of God,' Mr. Murry says. In theory," Eliot concludes, "this leads to a form of pantheism which I maintain is not European . . . "—and so must be torn down and replaced, since to be European is to be next to godliness (SP 71).

Eliot mocks the inner voice as an organizing deity by portraying its negative consequences for an orderly and *right* thinking society. A social contract predicated on self-assertion rather than surrender, on the individual rather than the collective, will eventually blow apart. "Why have principles," Eliot asks, "when one has the inner voice?"

> If I like a thing, that's all I want; and if enough of us, shouting all together, like it, that should be all that you (who don't like it) ought to want. . . . And we can not only like whatever we like to like but we can like it for any reason we choose. We are not, in face, concerned with literary perfection at all—the search for perfection is a sign of pettiness, for it shows that the writer has admitted the existence of an unquestioned spiritual authority outside of himself, to which he has attempted to conform. We are not in fact interested in art. We will not worship Baal. 'The principle of classical leadership is that obeisance is made to the office or to the tradition, never to the man.' And we want, not principles, but men. (SP 72–73)

By "classical," Eliot seems to mean "traditional," patriarchal, Christian. Somehow, he has rehabilitated the term, put it in the service of monotheism.

Eliot works a similar alchemy on the pagan women—Demeter, Philomel—that he has identified himself with as suffering for something "outside" of themselves. He repeats one of the best Christian public relations jobs when he combines vague allusions to pagan earth goddesses and overwrites them with the Virgin Mary. So there is nothing original about Eliot's Christian "recuperation" of the feminine through the "purified" image of the Virgin (herself begotten, finally, by Immaculate Conception). Nor is it surprising that Eliot eventually identifies himself with this image and subject position. Eliot follows a long line of masochistic Christian foot-steps as he appropriates Mary's role to "conceive" his monumental poetry, a move that he anticipated (vaguely) in "Tradition and the Individual Talent." As Julia Kristeva reminds us in "Stabat Mater," the sanctified maternal is the "proper" potion for giving birth to mystical matters: "the most intense revelation of God, which occurs in mysticism, is given only to a person who assumes himself as 'maternal,'" she says (162). St. Augustine and others, for example, "played the part of the Father's virgin spouses, or even . . . received drops of virginal milk directly on their lips." So "[f]reedom with respect to the maternal territory then becomes the pedestal upon which love of God is erected," Kristeva explains (162).

According to Kristeva, even Eliot's hysterical impotence in the face of the fem-inine, as confessed in "Hysteria" and other poems, is to be expected, since Mary-identified mystics "throw a bizarre light on the psychotic sore of modernity." That wound is "the incapability of contemporary codes to tame the maternal" (162). Only "the orthodox constituent of Christianity," like the Eliot of *Ash Wednesday*, can redeem the woman as he "sanction[s] the transitional function of the Maternal by calling the Virgin a 'bond,' a 'middle' or an 'interval,' thus opening the door to more or less heretical identifications with the Holy Ghost" ("Stabat Mater" 162–63). By 1930, Eliot certainly risks charges of heresy—and offending his staid Boston Brahmin relatives—as he identifies with this Holy Ghost. But perhaps this is his goal, as Eric Sigg suggests: "[T]o escape the kind, if not the degree, of culture that surrounded his youth was just what Eliot . . . set out to do" (2).

In fact, Eliot's move alienates not only family and friends but also the contem-porary critical establishment. While fellow critics and publishers embraced the new Eliot, warts and all, as a cultural cash cow (his "Prufrock" and *Waste Land* sparked at least two generations of undergraduate imitators and spawned the New Critics), contemporary readers regard his radical religiosity as a corrosive conservatism—the ravings of a middle-aged man in crisis. We are apt to diagnose Eliot's faith as evi-dence of a God complex and as a failure of his original (and thus definitive) mod-ernist poetic *or* as an acknowledgment of personal failures. Eliot's implication that these personal failures are in fact cultural, that his experience of sin and redemption is universal, is an intellectual heresy. It smacks of an unacceptable alibi for private neuroses and perversions.

Lyndall Gordon appears to apologize for Eliot's Anglo-Catholic approach as she asserts that he had always intended to make the "divine 'touch'" a priority in his poetry, especially the *Waste Land*, but that secular fashion, intellectual vanity and Pound's editorial patronage prevented him from making those claims overtly. Her apology is rather defensive, and seems aimed at a secular—and so intellectually vain—critical establishment. The *Waste Land* "originated in the purely personal record of a man who saw himself as a potential candidate for the religious life," says Gordon, "but was constrained by his own nature and distracted by domestic claims"

(EEY 118). In Gordon's biography, Eliot is the thwarted preacher, prevented from reaching the pulpit by social and familial expectations. He eventually used his poetry, she implies, as a way of sneaking the sermon into a more fashionable package. Eliot's religious poems, in this scenario, express spiritual lofty ambitions and an accounting for his "sins," rather than an escape from them. In other words, Gordon touts Eliot's conversion as a positive step.

Conversely, the bulk of current critical and popular readings of Eliot attribute his conversion to his gynephobia and his hatred of domesticity. Specifically, critics and biographers such as Peter Ackroyd and Tom Matthews read Eliot's *Ash Wednesday* as an abandonment of Vivien and his atonement for that "sin." Secondarily, they view his alliance with the Church of England as an official repudiation of the embarrassingly mercantile flavors of his St. Louis roots, the humanist influence of his grandfather, Andrew Greenleaf Eliot, and his mother's overbearing intellectual and social ambitions. Finally, James E. Miller, Jr., and those sympathetic with Michael Hastings' portrayal of the Eliot marriage in *Tom and Viv*, see Eliot's conversion as a means not only of cutting Vivien out of his life but of expressing a latent homosexuality.

If, as Leslie Fiedler suggests in *Love and Death in the American Novel*, the American male's romance involves lighting out for the territories to escape social constraints (nearly always embodied by women, as Nina Baym points out), it would appear that Eliot uses intellectual mysticism as a passport to the final frontier. After all, Eliot hails from what used to be the frontier, and the forces—mother, home—that threaten to engulf and consume him have already colonized these territories.

The male American writer, Baym explains, pits himself against a literary tradition epitomized by scribbled nuisances, "flagrantly bad best-sellers written by women" (70). "Personally beset in a way that epitomizes the tensions of our culture," Baym says, "the male author produces his melodramatic testimony to our culture's essence" (70). This could easily summarize Eliot's purpose in the *Waste Land*, *The Hollow Men*, and his *Four Quartets*. Baym attributes this male "melodrama of beset manhood" to a need to rewrite the masculine "self" as motherless, appropriating Adamic mythology. Re-reading Eliot's poetry and poetics through a late-twentieth century lens, or the harsher lights of feminist and psychoanalytic theories of subjectivity, Eliot's bid for religious salvation becomes a masochistic melodrama of epic proportions, a *Moby Dick*. We can assume that Eliot hopes to trade his earthly mother for a celestial Father, or to supplement the lack of his father's approval with a divine call.

In 1930, the year that Eliot released *Ash Wednesday*, Freud published *The Future of an Illusion*. In it, he elaborates on themes introduced in *Civilization and its Discontents*, arguing that the "oceanic" feeling that some equate with a sense of the divine can be read as the return of "an early phase of ego-feeling" (20). He elaborates:

The derivation of religious needs from the infant's helplessness and the longing for the father aroused by it seems to me incontrovertible, especially since the feeling is not simply prolonged from childhood days, but is permanently sustained by fear of the superior power of Fate. I cannot think of any need in childhood as strong as the need for a father's protection. Thus the part played by the oceanic feeling, which might seek something like the restoration of limitless narcissism, is ousted from a place in the foreground. The origin of the religious attitude can be traced back in clear outlines as far as the feeling of infantile helplessness. (20)

Eliot's conversion evokes Freud's condescension in many contemporary readers. His final "turn" to God suggests that he seeks the restoration of a limitless narcissism. Certainly, *Ash Wednesday* can be read as an extended expression of infantile helplessness, and this plea for unmitigated union with the Father smacks of homoeroticism, a celebratory impotence in the face of the maternal, and an eroticized view of the death and afterlife Eliot once claimed to fear. In this revisionary light, Eliot's leanings toward ascetic life, his announcement of celibacy, his abandonment of Vivien and his religious poetry appear as neurotic attempts to avoid abjection. His faith becomes his fetish. With his eyes firmly fixed on God, that is, Eliot avoids the horror of heterosexuality and the female body.

Thus we tend to view Eliot's conversion as a cowardly attempt to suppress the catalysts of his obsessive-compulsive disorders, his "sexual attacks," which we can interpret as anxiety about his sexuality and subjectivity. This means that we diagnose Eliot's impulse to religious witness or Christian mysticism as a symptom of pathology, and remember that hysteria is defined as a "conversion disorder." Religious feeling, confronted with the skepticism of the twentieth-century, becomes egotistical delusion.

While Eliot's religious poetry reveals a personal record of failure and partial atonement, our readings of that poetry say quite a bit about our own obsessions with cultural witness. Eliot's faith must be an alibi, we think, for some unspoken or unspeakable crime. In her discussion of moral or Christian masochism, Kaja Silverman describes the "strikingly self-contained" economy of moral masochism (*Male Subjectivity* 196), where the subject is given over to self-mortification and fantasies designed to mimic Christ's passion. Silverman cites the standard elements of the Christian masochist's tableau: the necessary external audience, the body on display, and the organizing fantasy or image of Christ's crucifixion. "What is being beaten here," Silverman explains, "is not so much the body as the 'flesh,' and beyond that sin itself, and the whole fallen world" (197). Eliot's later poetry and his plays (particularly Celia's death on the anthill in *The Cocktail Party*) reveal his fascination with these bloody images of Christ's martyrdom. Silverman points out that erotic fantasies centered on Christ's mortification pit the subject "against the society in which he or she lives, makes of that figure a rebel, or even a revolutionary of sorts"

(197–98). This fantastic battle would appear to be Eliot's, particularly the "desire to remake the world in another image altogether, to forge a different cultural order" (Silverman 198).

Here, in a nutshell, is Eliot's "sin" in contemporary critical eyes. His conversion confesses an overweening egotism and a threatening divestiture of phallic power, a renunciation of masculinity (and, we might add, of a particular ideal for American democracy), since "the exemplary Christian masochist also seeks to remake him or herself according to the model of the suffering Christ, the very picture of divestiture and loss," an offensive heresy even in secular circles. And "[i]nsofar as such an identification implies the complete and utter negation of all phallic values, Christian masochism has radically emasculating implications, and is in its purest form intrinsically incompatible with the pretensions of masculinity" (Silverman 198).

It is a strange family romance that Eliot takes as the model for his own, as Silverman recounts it. "[I]t is after all through the assumption of his place within the divine family that Christ comes to be installed in a suffering and castrated position" (198), usually the place reserved for the good daughter, wife and mother rather than the father. Fascinated with moral masochism, Eliot's religious poetry allows him to experience and re-experience Christ's psychic disintegration, a pain that becomes exquisite pleasure:

> The Christian, of course, lives his or her life in perpetual anticipation of the second coming. The figural meaning which this anticipation implants in present sufferings makes it possible for them to be savored as future pleasures, with time folding over itself in such a way as to permit that retroactivity to be already experienced now, in a moment prior to its effectivity. Such is the fundamentally perverse nature of Christian suspense and the pain it sanctifies and irradiates, a suspense which works against anything approximating psychic coherence. (Silverman 200)

This masochistic suspense characterizes Eliot's *Four Quartets*, where "the impossible union" (CPP 136), or "the still point of the turning world" (CPP 119) that Eliot searches for in *Ash Wednesday*, is revealed as Incarnation, a space where past and future are mingled in the present moment, and where what Eliot describes as the "flame of incandescent terror" and "torment" is "Love," a desire for God (CPP 143–44). Eliot clearly identifies with Christ as he describes his desire for divine union in "Burnt Norton":

> The inner freedom from the practical desire,
> The release from action and suffering, release from the inner
> And the outer compulsion, yet surrounded
> By a grace of sense, a white light still and moving,
> *Erhebung* without motion, concentration
> Without elimination, both a new world

And the old made explicit, understood
In the completion of its partial ecstasy,
The resolution of its partial horror.
Yet the enchainment of past and future
Woven in the weakness of the changing body,
Protects mankind from heaven and damnation
Which flesh cannot endure. (CPP 119)

That which flesh cannot endure seems to be Eliot's fantasy—even damnation, in these terms, seems better than enchainment in the changing body (body, in Eliot's world, ever identified as a "female").

Eliot's conversion, then, marks a series of turns, both for himself and for his critical readers. As Eliot turns to God, we turn away from Eliot and his God. In an ironic twist, Eliot's transformed from prophet to pariah, from world-weary Tiresias to headpiece filled with straw.

Our struggles and Eliot's seem to surround the issue of subjectivity or "self" determination. While Eliot looks to God as the beginning and end of consciousness, his disillusioned peers turn inward, to the unconscious, hoping to tap into cultural memory or timeless existence there. As if to goad them and to secure their rejection (another masochistic impulse), Eliot declares his intention to forget the "inner voice."

Eliot's move toward the Church of England began much earlier than 1927 and the first rumblings of *Ash Wednesday*, of course. That poem seems to be the culmination of a long process of turns and returns to the same subjects. Eliot's earliest works are equally filled with images of incarnation, redemption, and prophecy, though many of these images are negative. The young Eliot dwells on the bloodiness of Christ's sacrifice and the impotence of his disciples. Eliot's " martyrs"—Saint Narcissus, Prufrock and Tiresias—are all wounded in flamboyant ways. In "Gerontion," once intended as a prelude for the *Waste Land*, a dour old cripple portrays "Christ the Tiger" as a childish impotence: "The word within a word, unable to speak a word, / Swaddled with darkness" (CPP 21).

It's entirely possible that Eliot first distrusted his fascination with religious consciousness and what he thought of as potentially mystical experiences. Judging from the ambivalent representation of these moments in his early poetry, Eliot may have ascribed these experiences and interests to a "perversion" in his personality that produced self-deluding hallucinations. Eliot certainly turned the same critical eye on himself that he leveled on those seduced by the inner voice, like the palpitating narcissi he condemns in "The Death of Saint Narcissus" and "Gerontion." No doubt Eliot includes himself in his scathing criticism of those confused between personal "feelings" and the genuine material of poetry. As we learned in the previous chapter, Eliot's scientific terminology in "Tradition and the Individual Talent" covers an investment in Christian narratives and consciousness, re-defining a process of Immaculate Conception and incarnation as a chemical reaction. This investment in Christianity, however, is never far from the surface, despite Eliot's attempts to mask it with "objective correlatives." In fact, Eliot's insistence on the poet's "surrender" is always charged, in his own lexicon, with religious eroticism.

Readers such as Donald Childs, Jewel Spears Brooker, William Skaff, Lyndall Gordon and David Spurr explore how Eliot grappled with inexplicable visionary experiences early in his writing career. They argue that Eliot's early interests in comparative religious studies stemmed from attempts to explain, validate or dismiss the "mystical" moments he experienced as a young man. Eliot was always careful to differentiate between hallucinatory experience and what he thought of as divine union. Keenly aware of the continuity between auto-eroticism (masturbation, masochism), egotism and mysticism, Eliot's early work explores the psycho-sexual dangers inherent in any attempt to achieve a "deeper communion" with God. In Eliot's terms, self-worship and sexual perversions are the by-products of such attempts. "The Death of Saint Narcissus," we recall, describes the self-destructive attempts of an onanist to see himself as infused with God's presence. The Sweeney poems emphasize the animalistic and devolutionary nature of sexual intercourse—which some of Eliot's fellow modernists (Lawrence comes to mind) viewed as the modern equivalent of transcendence. Sweeney and his ilk portray the act as a mercenary and diseased "union" that ensures, rather than thwarts, mortality. "Prufrock" and "Portrait of a Lady" further develop the genteel danger attendant upon any urbane communion.

These early and definitive poems portray what Eliot sees as a fundamental confusion between "impossible union" and disease, between the mystic's experience and hysteria. Perhaps Eliot's readings in William James and Evelyn Underhill underscored for him the difficulties inherent in any study of religious consciousness. James, for example, devotes a large portion of his discussion of mysticism in *The Varieties of Religious Experience*—which Eliot read as part of his studies in alternate modes of consciousness—to a discussion of the pathological consequences of asceticism. Likewise, Underhill explores the highly subjective nature of "mystical" experience. James suggests that "saintliness" and mysticism are often misread as evidence of mental illness and that, on the other hand, hysteria is easily mistaken for mysticism. The dividing line, in James's description, is between self and other—the hysteric suffers from self-pleasuring hallucinations while the mystic delivers him or her "self" over to the divine completely. James stresses the tendency for asceticism to develop into a narcissistic preoccupation, as the penitent receives sexual pleasure from pain and self-denial. James never makes clear, however, even in his most pragmatic diagrams of the four qualities particular to saintliness, where communion ends and narcissism begins. Eliot's poetry explores these pathologies, pairing false prophets such as Prufrock with hyperbolic poetic pronouncements designed to expose the production of such metaphysical meaning as, at best, ridiculous and destructive.

Despite Eliot's savage rejections of narcissi seduced by inner voices, his approaches to mystical experience prove personally significant. Before 1927, Eliot presents a modern savior only to undercut the effort by suggesting its potential pathology. Though he deliberately distances himself from questionable subjectivity in "Prufrock" and "Portrait," even Eliot's most pessimistic portrayals yearn for penetration by the divine. Thus, each of his early poems proves a study in indulgence, pleasure, punishment and denial. Perhaps this ambiguity and ambivalence derives from the difficulty that Eliot and other religious philosophers found in differentiating between mind and body, communion and hallucination, mysticism and madness, male and female, and—most interestingly—self and other. It could be that the idea of God served quite well as an impossible amalgamation between self and other for such tortured thinkers and artists.

Thus, though Eliot's poetic personae pose as the objects of his intellectual derision, they also serve as his alter egos, despite his compelling arguments for an impersonal poetry. Readers are quick to point out that Eliot serves more often than not as the butt of his own practical jokes: that he poses as Prufrock, Gerontion, Tiresias, and Saint Narcissus. Even casual readers of Eliot's work don't miss the idea that he entertains a peculiar fondness for Prufrock's perversities and Gerontion's self-indulgent world-weariness.[1] Furthermore, readers remain divided in their readings of Eliot's art and criticism as prophetic or pathological, visionary or symptomatic. Was Eliot indeed the voice of a generation? Or was he, rather, giving tongue to a cultural hysteria, serving as a repulsive return of the repressed, the gaping wound?

As many signs point to the latter as to the former. Even Eliot's most famous poetic process is interrupted by a series of "nervous breakdowns" and hospitalizations. Wayne Koestenbaum suggests that the *Waste Land* is a hysterical text, marked by symptoms such as displacement and glossolalia, and produced by a process of "analysis" and transference instigated by Ezra Pound.[2] The hysterics that Eliot portrays as laughing Medusas, "suppressed complexes" and deferential tools bleed into backgrounds for cruel self-portraits. Though Eliot may have wanted to operate on such figures from afar, he ends by participating, again and again, in their excesses— returning compulsively to the scene of the crime.

It requires no stretch of the imagination to describe Eliot's poetic career as a spiritual journey. At the risk of seeming as glib as contemporary readers would have us see Eliot, the current academic backlash against Eliot and the New Critical methods of literary investigation (the latter perhaps falsely founded in his name) may stem in part from a vicious suspicion of religious consciousness and hierarchical experience, of neo-conservative rhetoric which imputes to a select few the possibility of transcending the tyranny of subjectivity. Certainly, contemporary descriptions of Eliot's "new life" as an Anglican worshipper emphasize Eliot's will to power in the privileging of a classical, or intellectual, mysticism and the spiritual elite it erects to "translate" for the masses. Donald Childs, in his "*Metamorphoses,* Metaphysics, and Mysticism from 'The Death of Saint Narcissus' to *Burnt Norton,*" argues that by the time Eliot composes *Ash Wednesday* he has rejected the "romantic" mysticism that St. Teresa and St. John of the Cross supposedly practiced—both sources for the figure of Saint Narcissus—to promote, instead, the classical mysticism of Aristotle, Aquinas and Dante (19). As Childs explains it, Eliot develops his choice in the Clarke Lectures, pointing out that such classical mystics "properly" locate the divine outside of the self, rather than confusing the passion for God with sexual love. "Like Ovid's Narcissus," Childs reminds us, "romantic mystics are not aware of the extent to which the thing they see is themselves" (19). Childs cites Eliot's attendant "epistemological and metaphysical dilemma" as our own: "as human beings we can never be sure that we are ontologically rapt, and not merely trapped in the psychologism of Narcissus, vainly lusting after our own image" (20).

William Skaff develops another strand of Eliot's scholarly researches to the same end, detailing how Eliot's work with Frazer developed into his own brand of mysticism as the modern metamorphosis of primitive religious consciousness. Eliot saw classical mysticism as a means of capturing Bradley's Immediate Experience (43), in other words, and developed from it an art that depends upon a kind of "mystical participation" between poet and audience. Skaff and others argue that, in Eliot's mystical scheme, intellectual communion is maintained by a select group of (male) priests. These shamans become, through prophetic words and performances of the untranslatable mysteries, responsible for the conscious life and rebirth of their culture.

Though, as Childs suggests, Eliot eventually proposed classical mysticism—the concentrated pursuit of intellection out of the self and into the Other, a motherless or bodiless communion—as the proper means of achieving a divine union, his mystical poetry remains caught up in the sensual aspects of the experience. Obviously, Eliot couldn't blithely categorize and escape the "mad and strange" aspects of personality. Instead, as he concludes in his dissertation, at each turn "calamity menaces our theory." This emotional chaos resurfaces in Eliot's religious poetry, especially in *Four Quartets,* as "undisciplined squads of emotion," the forces that rob Eliot's language of its ability to represent "another intensity," the "home" that has been "lost" and which he can only fight to recover: ". . . a further union, a deeper communion / Through the dark cold and the empty desolation, / The wave cry, the wind cry, the vast waters . . ." (CPP 129). Personality—Eliot portrays it as madness (female trouble) expressed through language—threatens to obliterate the secret mysteries. On another level, Eliot seems to be in love with this failure, or at the very least obsessed with it, returning to it again and again.

Religious eroticism and transcendence—celebrated as impotence, interrupted communion—propels Eliot through the latter part of his poetic production: *The*

Hollow Men, Ash Wednesday, and his final, enigmatic, disturbed and disturbing poetic sequence, *Four Quartets.* These familiar poetic landmarks reflect several "turns"—conversions in Eliot's metaphysics, poetic form, subject matter and purpose. Each turn springs from Eliot's conception of God as "an adequate synthesis for the dialectic of private and public, personal and impersonal, individual and societal, which serve[s] him not only in his philosophical, but also in his religious, esthetic, and socio-political thought, and in his poetic theory and practice" (Skaff 14).

> No one bothered his head about the theological disputes of a little sect of a small, despised people.
>   —Theodor Reik, *Dogma and Compulsion*

Eliot's expanding investigation of his own religious consciousness, his moments of mystical insight, coincides with his most stringent social and cultural commentary. As he criticizes the modern "citizen" for his reliance on emptied forms of discourse and communion (or his lack of either), Eliot suggests that his construction of a deliberately emasculated poet can provide the model for all cultural redemption. The masochistic poet—who, as an echo of the "old guy," Guy Fawkes, enjoys an annihilating reunion with a vicious God and a yearly resurrection—turns repeated religious punishment into poetic ecstasy. In a sense, he maps out, through his fractured or amputated body, through the "sense" of his stigmata, the journey into the twilight kingdom. Thus, Eliot transforms his own fear of death and the afterlife, as well as his fear of heterosexual intercourse, into a positive lack: if nothing else, *The Hollow Men* begins to transform these fears, through their repeated expression, into their opposite. Eliot's poet claims to desire, to embrace, sex and death. At last, Eliot's hollow man submits to a sexualized death, a union with God.

After the bleak close of the *Waste Land* in a somewhat painful approximation of a Christian benediction ("The Peace which passeth all understanding")[3], Eliot's scathing criticism of modern worship in *The Hollow Men* comes as no surprise. Eliot begins the 1925 poem with two epigraphs. The first comes from Joseph Conrad's *Heart of Darkness:* "Mistah Kurtz—he dead." The next hails from English lore: "A penny for the Old Guy." Eliot concludes the poem by sifting together nursery rhyme and liturgy (The Lord's Prayer), truncating and fracturing both to emphasize the violent, meaningless struggle of modern men to transcend their mortal circumstances. So "the hollow men" are Eliot's vision of modern worshippers, filled with the "shadow" endemic to all men (something between indifference and a lack of conscience, and certainly the presentiment of mortality). They also serve as the antithesis for Eliot's "savior," the culture's representative killed—ritually—in order to secure the cultural and spiritual life of the tribe. After all, Fawkes was put to death for his attempt to assassinate the Protestant king and Parliament; his execution and the reenactment of it each year provide a foundation for the Church of England's monopoly. Perhaps Eliot also intends this apocalyptic and ironic poem to betray the unconsciously savage methods modern societies employ to combat or perpetuate the "shadow." Eliot's poem suggests, in fact, that the cure for cultural death and social alienation is worse than the disease. As Fawkes himself proclaims, "A desperate disease requires a dangerous remedy."

In "The Hollow Men," Eliot creates a multiple personality reminiscent of Gerontion: "stuffed men / Leaning together / Headpiece filled with straw." This quasi-schizophrenic narrative voice forms as the stuffed men lean together to become one headpiece, whose "dried voices. . . whisper together" in "quiet and meaningless" phrases. Eliot wants to show the modern community as sterile, ineffectual, incapable of meaning. As potential leaders of the modern culture they represent, the hollow men have lived past their time; they are not good role-models; they have not submitted to the tradition, their ancestors or God. Instead of giving voice to the decline of civilization and cultural soul, and by their sacrificial testimony reanimating it, they have become the neurotic "victims" of a damaged and damaging nature. As they compare their utterances, for example, to "wind in dry grass" and "rats' feet over broken glass / In our dry cellar," they recall the opening of "A Game of Chess," as the husband derides, silently, his wife's querulous demands for answers. To her question, "What are you thinking of?," he answers, "I think we are in rats' alley / Where the dead men lost their bones."

Eliot is no doubt referring to the emasculated condition of the "prophets" in his canon. They have been unmanned, Eliot suggests, by the devouring public, represented by hungry, hysterical women: "Rachel *née* Rabinovitch," for instance, who "tears at the grapes with murderous paws" (CPP 35), or the rank feline smell of "Grishkin in a drawing-room" (CPP 33).

Though there are no women present in "The Hollow Men," their enervating presence lurks in the hollow men's impotence, their failure to "mean" in this wrecked landscape. Devouring women pose as "Mother" Nature, the bleak body created by Darwin's evolutionary science: scouring wind and scavenging rats supplant humanity, survive where human culture cannot. All humans, in fact, will return to Nature's harsh womb, as in *Ash Wednesday*, as meaningless bones.

The Hollow Men recalls the murderous sterility of scenes from Eliot's *Waste Land*, where dogs dig up corpses from gardens, the cruel month of April breeds lilacs from the dead land, and the gurgle of the polluted river evokes distraught visions of mortality in the Fisher King's abandoned son: "[w]hite bodies naked on the low damp ground / And bones cast in a little low dry garret, / Rattled by the rat's foot only, year to year" (CPP 43). Here, as in *The Hollow Men*, Eliot connects meaningless human intercourse with nature's indifference—abandoned graves and empty churches give home to rats, bones, and dry grass. The promise of rain is a tortuous reminder of disconnection and death, the destruction of civilization's record in apocalyptic catastrophe. In the *Waste Land*, the wind's song laments the "decayed hole," the empty chapel surrounded by tumbled graves:

> In this decayed hole among the mountains
> In the faint moonlight, the grass is singing
> Over the tumbled graves, about the chapel
> There is the empty chapel, only the wind's home.
> It has no windows, and the door swings,
> Dry bones can harm no one. (CPP 49)

The horror that a fearful Eliot reports in *The Hollow Men* is indeed this pervasive lack of transcendence: an inability to "mean" anything. Like Dante's *Inferno*, Eliot's poetic vision records a surreal dream landscape hashed together from Biblical and medieval storehouses. The inhabitants of Eliot's hell on earth are consigned to "Shape without form, shade without colour, / Paralyzed force, gesture without motion" (CPP 56). Eliot's poem argues that life has become a kind of purgatory, where "[t]hose who have crossed / With direct eyes, to death's other Kingdom / Remember us—if at all—not as lost / Violent souls, but only / As the hollow men / The stuffed men" (CPP 56). To be remembered as violent, lost or even soulless (as Kurtz) would be a better than to be forgotten. Memory is survival. Here Eliot suggests that the loss of voice and sight contribute to the disintegration of culture.

Seeing and believing go hand in hand, and society's eyes have been blinded to God. Vision, insight, and thus language are impaired. Those who cross over to "death's other Kingdom" pass with "direct eyes": they have seen what the Hollow Men refuse to, or dare not, see—"Eyes I dare not meet in dreams" (57). Eliot makes a distinction in the poem between "death's other Kingdom," "the twilight kingdom," and "death's dream kingdom"; this comparison implies that the hollow men are the living dead, zombies, and that their only escape is into death's dreams, where the eyes they wish to avoid are transformed into images of classical decay, lost childhood, nature's triumph over civilization: "Sunlight on a broken column" or "a tree swinging." Perhaps Eliot critiques the impulse, born on the psychoanalyst's comfortable couch, to ascribe every neuroticism and unhappiness to an inner fault, to material in the unconscious (death's dream kingdom), rather than to a fault in society, the ideology underlying that society, or the "god" that gives it shape. Eliot suggests that believing in the unconscious comforts the modern citizen because it allows him to hide behind the "deliberate disguise" of the scavenger, Death himself: "Rat's coat, crowskin, crossed staves / In a field / Behaving as the wind behaves / No nearer. . ." The unconscious is more comforting than God because it allows the hollow man to distance himself from that Other kingdom: "And voices are / In the wind's singing / More distant and more solemn / Than a fading star" (57). The hollow man wants to "be no nearer / In death's dream kingdom" to the eyes he dares not meet— no nearer," that is, to "that final meeting / In the twilight kingdom."

Clearly, Eliot identifies his poet with Guy Fawkes, who possessed the conviction of his beliefs—for which he would kill and then was killed. Eliot's poem is equal parts hostility and homage. After all, Mr. Fawkes rules over a "the dead land" where "stone images are raised" to him and "receive / The supplication of a dead man's hand" (57). Despite the bleak prospect, there is something uncannily, even surrealistically, sensual about this "supplication," the caress of this "dead man's hand" on the poet's supposedly dead libido. The poet wonders whether it will be the same in "death's other kingdom," whether he will again find himself "[w]aking alone / At the hour when we are / Trembling with tenderness," only to use "[l]ips that would kiss" to "[f]orm prayers to broken stone" (57–58). This strange dream of failed transcendence, hard as it may try to condemn the empty motions that constitute it, eroticizes its failure. Impotence becomes coitus interruptus, spiritual miscarriage. Eliot might refer, here, to his own inability to consummate or continue his marriage, his "saintliness" as he decided (after returning from a visit to his family) to live a celibate life. So he celebrates two failures at once, wallowing—as any good moral masochist might—in their ineffectual bids at spiritual supremacy.

Eliot's intentions for the poem are as mysterious as his portrayal of the "perpetual star / Multifoliate rose / Of death's twilight kingdom" (which seems to be a spiritualized, or fetishized, vision of the vagina). Does Eliot mean to suggest that incarnation and salvation are impossible dreams—"[t]he hope only / Of empty men" (58) and male masochists who flagellate themselves with the impossibility of spiritual union? Certainly, "[t]he eyes are not here," as the poet proclaims. "There are no eyes here." Eyes can represent, in this dream landscape borrowed from such surrealists as Dalí, insight, intellect, observation, the watchful face of the state (the missing police from the *Waste Land*). These missing eyes are ever present in their absence; the poet's blindness, his impotence, signals the very opposite, then. His impressive lack serves as his power, his sensual satisfaction. In fact, "In this last of meeting places / We grope together / And avoid speech / Gathered on this beach of the tumid river // Sightless" (58).

Eliot ends the poem with condemnation of all human intercourse, particularly sexual, and again his repeated protestations, his sermonizing, reveal his interest in the subject:

> Between the idea
> And the reality
> Between the motion
> And the act
> Falls the Shadow
> > *For Thine is the Kingdom*
>
> Between the conception
> And the creation
> Between the emotion

And the response
Falls the Shadow

Life is very long

Between the desire
And the spasm
Between the potency
And the existence
Between the essence
And the descent
Falls the Shadow
For Thine Is the Kingdom (CPP 59)

Eliot romances death, eroticizes the sacrificial moment, as his "shadow" visits the sexual scene. Death is the third who penetrates every desiring moment, is the regenerative spasm, is the cruel orgasm, is God's unspeakable face. Thus pain and obliteration fuse with pleasure for Eliot's poet—this moment of human intercourse is awful, a vision of the Eternal Footman snickering at man's impotence. There is no salvation, no transcendence. In effect, the Shadow decapitates the nursery rhyme and interrupts the Lord's prayer, cutting off the big "bang" with a whimper, suffocating the hollow man's stuttering voice mid-prayer. In an uncanny fashion, Eliot implies that we can know God's presence by his total absence, by the poet's inability, by the culture's lack . . .

For Thine is
Life is
For Thine is the

This is the way the world ends
This is the way the world ends
This is the way the world ends
Not with a bang but a whimper. (CPP 59)

The poet trails off into silence, a whimper of masochistic amputation.

Eliot sums up the impression left by *The Hollow Men* best in his essay on Dante, as he describes the mental "state" that Dante creates in his Divine Comedy. Dante, Eliot tells us, "reminds us that Hell is not a place but a *state*; that man is damned or blessed in the creatures of his imagination as well as in men who have actually lived; and that Hell, though a state, is a state which can only be thought of, and perhaps only experienced, by the projection of sensory images; and that the resurrection of the body has perhaps a deeper meaning than we understand" (SE 211–12).

Dante's is a *visual* imagination. It is a visual imagination in a different sense
from that of a modern painter of still life: it is visual in the sense that he lived

in an age in which men still saw visions. It was a psychological habit, the trick of which we have forgotten, but as good as any of our own. We have nothing but dreams, and we have forgotten that seeing visions—a practice now relegated to the aberrant and uneducated—was once a more significant, interesting, and disciplined kind of dreaming. We take it for granted that our dreams spring from below: possibly the quality of our dreams suffers in consequence.

—T. S. Eliot, "Dante" (SE 204)

Ash Wednesday troubles Eliot's critics. While they agree that the mythical or occult method, borrowed from Joyce and enhanced with Frazer's myths, characterizes much of Eliot's work until *Ash Wednesday*, they claim, as does Linda Leavell, that this poem "seems to elude explication, especially an explication based on allusions" (147). Drawing on his impressions of Dante's accessible "universality," Eliot claims that an allegorical, or visual, method—detached from immediate "meaning"—is the most vivid and "disciplined kind of dreaming" available to poets and readers. In short, Eliot's enigmatic poem describes a mystic set of visions, dreams that he claims come from above rather than below.

Leavell characterizes the method she finds in *Ash Wednesday* as the "ritual method"—"a projection from immediate meaninglessness toward the infinite unknowable, the ineffable Name," or "the future"—which she claims is an amalgamation of mythic and "nonsense" methods (148). Leavell describes the end of *The Hollow Men* as an attempt to show the failure of such ritual to transcend individuality and mortality: "Like vain prayer and like nonsense verse, [the poem] cannot reach beyond itself. Like whistling in the dark, it can only provide at best a small solace or charm against impending horror" (149). In contrast, Leavell asserts, *Ash Wednesday* celebrates the impending horror and our inability to understand or fill it. "The poem requires explication no more than the finest nonsense verse," Leavell says, "and yet it holds just beyond our grasp a meaning more profound than perhaps any in modern poetry." (I argue, of course, that this celebration goes on in *The Hollow Men* as well. Eliot's instrument of self-torture is just not as finely calibrated in that earlier poem. That is, he has not yet created his most sensual hell. His work on that score is more obvious in *Ash Wednesday*, as Leavell points out in her essay.) In her concluding sentence, Leavell takes her claim a step further: "While the rhythm of *Ash Wednesday* suggests a liturgy," she says, "truly a common prayer, its ritual runs deeper than Anglicanism, deeper even than Christianity, as deep as man's primal cry to his Maker" (152).

Encomia for Eliot's religious insight aside, Leavell's reading grapples with the critical difficulties occasioned by Eliot's metamorphosis from witty and ironic allusiveness to a deadly investigation of the "mysteries." Leavell reminds us that Hugh Kenner, in his *Invisible Poet*, marks *Ash Wednesday* as a dividing line for Eliot. While his language in poems before *Ash Wednesday* tended toward "a certain succinct impenetrability," Kenner argues, his work after this landmark poem seems to aim for "ritual translucency" (Leavell 152). Indeed, the poem practices an allegory that seems phantasmagoric and associational; Eliot would suggest that this a metaphysical manifestation: an epiphany in the truest sense of the word.

Ash Wednesday opens with a continuation of the self-flagellating stutters that close out *The Hollow Men*:

> Because I do not hope to turn again
> Because I do not hope
> Because I do not hope to turn
> Desiring this man's gift and that man's scope
> I no longer strive to strive towards such things
> (Why should the agèd eagle stretch its wings?)
> Why should I mourn
> The vanished power of the usual reign? (CPP 60)

There is certainly something off-putting to Eliot's change in pace, poetic material and tone. His humble protestations seem like the hand-wringing self-promotions of a latter-day Uriah Heep. The impulse to dismiss such sermonizing as the usual agèd nonsense—a 51–year-old man passing himself off as a dying sage—is overpowering. A man putting his house in order so forcefully and vocally reminds us of the peevish efforts of other "old" men to run the lives around themselves. (Emma Woodhouse's constantly ailing father, whose weak stomach determines the meals and bedtimes of all his hapless companions, comes immediately to mind.) To describe this "later" Eliot as a religious freak, repulsive in his obsequious enthusiasms for an indifferent or punishing God, is to regain the ironic distance (or, at the very least, the distance) his religious poems deny us. Richard Aldington does just this in his 1931 comic novel, *Stepping Heavenward*, describing a Midwestern saint's purgatorial journey through England with his neurotic wife. The novel is a barely veiled attack on Eliot for his conversion, his holier-than-thou attitude, and his fascination with the moral and physical masochism of the saints.

Ash Wednesday is perhaps Eliot's first overtly—and, for some, regrettably—confessional poem. Its patently Catholic material suggests, to the uninitiated, a traitorous alliance. (Is this why Leavell categorizes allusions to the confessional, original sin and the Catholic liturgy as "nonsense"?) The converted Eliot becomes the Guy Fawkes of modern literature, described as a pathetic neurotic rather than the sacrificial lamb he wanted to be. *Ash Wednesday* explodes, in a sense, the established themes and sentiments of the mythic method that Eliot claims to admire in Joyce. In 1902, Joyce writes to Lady Gregory to complain that "[t]here is no heresy or no philosophy which is so abhorrent to my church as a human being," and to share with her his resultant manifesto: "I shall try myself against the powers of the world. All things are inconstant except the faith of the soul, which changes all things and fills their inconstancy with light. And though I seem to have been driven out of my country here as a misbeliever I have found no man yet with a faith like mine," he says, gearing up for Stephen Dedalus. In a 1907 lecture he called "Ireland, Island of Saints and Sages," Joyce proclaimed again against the Catholic Church, linking it with political tyranny and the brain drain:

> The soul of the country is weakened by centuries of useless struggle and broken treaties, and individual initiative is paralysed by the influence and admonitions of the church, while the body is manacled by police, the tax office, and the garrison. No one who has any self-respect stays in Ireland, but flees afar as though from a country that has undergone the visitation of an angered Jove. (171)

Joyce concludes his diatribe by pointing out the state of affairs left in Ireland by this "flight of the wild geese" from its rigid borders, usually to democratic havens like the United States:

> From 1850 to the present day, more than 5,000,000 emigrants have left for America, and every post brings to Ireland their inviting letters to friends and relatives at home. The old men, the corrupt, the children, and the poor stay at home, where the double yoke wears another groove in the tamed neck; and around the death bed where the poor, anaemic, almost lifeless body lies in agony, the rulers give orders and the priests administer last rites. (172)

In *Ash Wednesday*, Eliot appears to embrace the church and its police, tax men, and jailers as he turns his back, once and for all, on any alliance with his home country. He gleefully accepts the double yoke of spiritual—and bodily—slavery that Joyce rejects, posing as the poor, anemic, almost lifeless body of the subjugated old man. He pledges his allegiance to anti-humanistic tyranny at the expense of his, and by implication our, very "being."

Joyce's reliance upon Dionysian structures of myth and meaning serve as a deliberate rejection of the orthodox structure in Ireland, a country which he abandons in part because of its complicity in its own political and religious subjection: "I will tell you what I will do and what I will not do," says Stephen Dedalus. "I will not serve that in which I no longer believe, whether it call itself my home, my fatherland, or my church; and I will try to express myself in some mode of life or art as freely as I can and as wholly as I can, using for my defence the only arms I allow myself to use, silence, exile and cunning" (*A Portrait* 241). Eliot turns his back on the freedom of Joyce's private, polytheistic mythology in order to pay obeisance to home, fatherland and—most important, in Eliot's estimation—a national Church. Perhaps *Ash Wednesday* is unsettling because it renounces the artistic goals that the younger Eliot—following Joyce—so fervently espouses. Old Eliot is no longer the rebel, lighting out for the territories of surrealism, free verse and the red-light district of Paris. Instead, he's "sells out" to the establishment for what seems like a mouthful of mud.

There is no sense in *Ash Wednesday,* for instance, that Eliot plans to continue the struggle to create the uncreated conscience of his race in the smithy of his own soul, or even to move toward the establishment of a body of occult knowledge privy to the chosen few. (To give him credit, Eliot shifts such goals to the foundation of the Church of England). Rather, Eliot drops one of his characteristic poetic masks: he no longer poses as the anti-Romantic, the exiled cultural arbiter. In contrast to his early work, *Ash Wednesday* is embarrassingly free of guile, of subterfuge, of succinct impenetrability.

Eliot is no longer playing his contemporaries' game. Or if he is, he's doing it at a deeper, more cunning level, as he plays completely dead. His confession is a personal affront to a modern readership because it indicts not only his own artistic sins but those of his intellectual "generation." Eliot proudly proclaims his impotence as a triumph over the vain "glory" of his peers. The meek shall inherit the afterlife . . .

> Because I do not hope to know again
> The infirm glory of the positive hour
> Because I do not think
> Because I know I shall not know
> The one veritable transitory power
> Because I cannot drink . . .
>
> . . .
> I renounce the blessèd face
> And renounce the voice . . .
>
> And pray to God to have mercy upon us
> . . .
> May the judgement not be too heavy upon us
>
> Because these wings are no longer wings to fly
> But merely vans to beat the air . . .
> Pray for us sinners now and at the hour of our death
> Pray for us now and at the hour of our death. (CPP 60–61)

Eliot's "turns" appear perverse, even delusional, because of their literal bent. In his *Instaurations,* D. S. Carne-Ross explains Pound's allusive or elusive method of "explanation" in the *Cantos;* this figurative hinting at meaning might be put in direct contrast to Eliot's religious poetry. "[A]lthough Pound is didactic in a way no other important modern writer is," says Carne-Ross, "at his best he doesn't tell us what to believe"—as does Eliot, *at his worst,* we might add. "He presents the scattered elements of something," Carne-Ross says of Pound, "a belief or a usage or whatever, and leaves it to us to put the elements together—with the force of a personal discovery" (197). Eliot's literality prevents the reader the joy, or expectation, of this personal discovery. Carne-Ross might even say, as an aside to this discussion of the communion ritual and its pagan antecedents in Pound's Canto 81, that Eliot's *Ash Wednesday* is written in something like bad faith, since "[w]e don't have the words for this [concept of communion] now . . . That is why Pound has to be so indirect, why he can't simply tell us" (201) what he means. In other words, Eliot's method short-circuits the individual impression of, for example, the sacred marriage that Pound tackles so obliquely in Canto 81 and others, in favor of the cliché. In fact, Carne-Ross pits Eliot's *Waste Land* against Pound's fresh and leaping Cantos: "[S]tudents of the *Cantos* have been forced to take Pound's gods and myths as simply part of the machinery of the poem, matters we suspend disbelief in while we get on with the business of reading, like the vegetation ceremonies that provide part of the machinery of *The Waste Land*," he says (211). Carne-Ross seems to suggest, here, that a committed pagan, because unintelligible to generations steeped in 2000 years of desensitization to the mythic and the spiritual, is more "natural" than a Protestant-turned-Catholic like Eliot. For Carne-Ross, the fact that Pound's own personal tragedy lies at the center of the poem, "the center of consciousness" (212), makes him a better poet or even person than Eliot, whose beliefs were not tested by inhuman circumstances and calamitous mistakes as Pound's were. And so Pound's *Cantos* contain a simple complexity that, in Carne-Ross' estimation, makes it a more usefully "difficult" poem about belief and renewal than Eliot's *Waste Land* or *Ash Wednesday*. While Pound's approach and poem "offend against the ways that we read literature" by negating "the great principle of inwardness or internalization that has put man at the center of things and laid waste the visible world," by doing an end-around Eliot's abstractions and allusions, Eliot's return to the old beliefs flatters the modern senses. Eliot's *Ash Wednesday* is "difficult" after the fashion because "it's the kind of difficulty we enjoy. It flatters our self-esteem. Pound's simplicity is chastening" (Carne-Ross 216).

Strangely enough, what Carne-Ross has to say, lovingly, tenderly, about poor Mr. Pound can be applied to Old Possum: "[W]hen the test came Pound's 'pagan' beliefs did literally work" and this "points to something very important about these beliefs: they were always strangely, disconcertingly literal. We may have stumbled on a feature of his work which has put so many people off and perhaps holds the key to it" (213). "Pound honors the Church for preserving traces of the mysteries," Carne-Ross explains, "but it is the mysteries themselves he believes in. The Church has lost their true meaning, their true form, and that is what Pound wants to recover." Carne-Ross concludes that what Pound is/was missing is the sense of the sacred marriage in the communion ceremony; Christianity has reduced the myth of seasonal death and rebirth to a metaphor about wheat, "a figure for man's spiritual rebirth" (213).

In short, Eliot's religious faith is contrasted with Pound's. In the contemporary narrative, Eliot announces his faith in the same anti-rational and anti-intellectual terms as any other born-again penitent; he "renounces" the "blessèd face" and "voice" that he simultaneously claims to "construct" in order to "rejoice." (No wonder many readers accuse Eliot of wanting to have his cake and to eat it, too.) He constructs a new poetry—like God giving breath to an Adam made of clay—out of its death.

It is equally perverse to willfully renounce "will" as Eliot does when he proclaims that "these wings are . . . merely vans to beat the air" which is "Smaller and dryer than the will" (CPP 61). Eliot says that he would like to forget "these matters that which myself I too much discuss / Too much explain"—as if a *conscious* intellectual pursuit is indeed sinful—yet the entire poem is caught up in dissecting these matters. In other words, the poem, devoted to cataloguing and celebrating failure, is itself a failure in its stated goal.

Garbed in the self-destroying robes of this new poetic persona, Eliot eschews the attempt to uncover "the one veritable transitory power" that he once ascribed to art. Stripped of ironic artifice (though he seems to have swapped one set of artifices for another, providing us with a highly artificial rendering of the "natural"), Eliot's *Ash Wednesday* disavows the possibility of meaning in fragmentation, claiming the church as the single spiritual and artistic mediator. Northrop Frye, in his "Antique Drum," suggests that Eliot yearns after the "cultural synthesis" of society, religion and art characteristic of the Middle Ages: "All history since represents a degeneration of this ideal" for Eliot, writes Frye (19–20).

This move backward is repulsive to Frye and others because of its anti-progressive and anti-democratic flavor. In Eliot's work, Frye claims, "religion forms a third level above human society" (22)—Eliot's crime is thus a tyrannical snobbery, as he yearns after an aristocratic hierarchy and a feudal set of relationships that would install him in a patronage and ensure him of a "living." Eliot, "like other American writers with such names as Adams and Lowell, reflects the preoccupations of an unacknowledged aristocracy, preoccupations with tradition, with breeding, with the loss of common assumptions" (Frye 20). And Eliot can only second such motions when he reminds us that "in Dante's time Europe, with all its dissensions and dirtiness, was mentally more united than we can now conceive" (SE 202).

Lyndall Gordon describes Eliot's treasonous move as a return to a Victorian sensibility: "While most of the postwar generation liberated itself from faith," she writes, "Eliot moved in the opposite direction. The moderns rebelled against a Victorian version of faith, full of cant and hypocrisy. Eliot held on to an older faith—devouring, passionate, and mystical" (EEY 103).

Eliot's turn to religious sensibility is a turn away from the modernist ethic described—and promulgated—by such energetic New World salesmen as Ezra Pound. Herbert Schneidau describes Pound's tradition as "polymorphous, form-breaking, [and] exuberant . . . reveal[ing] his predilection for change, dynamism, activity" (236). In contrast, the saved Eliot argues for stillness, silence. The key to Pound's *Cantos*, Schneidau points out, is his "abandonment of the subjective, rambling harangue for the technique of letting things say themselves" (238). Even Eliot's singing bones claim that they cannot speak for themselves. In every case, an oppressive narrative voice breaks in, taking the name of God and speaking in Biblical tones, in order to dictate the terms of the relationship between speaker (subject) and spoken (tradition, art, Logos).

Eliot's artistic communion, then, is not constructive or empowering. Though Eliot frequently alludes to Christ's passion, crucifixion and resurrection, it would be sheer hubris to suggest that he identifies himself with Christ. Rather, Eliot stresses the poet's peripheral and dependent role in this rebirth. As *Ash Wednesday* reveals, Eliot is far more comfortable appealing to the Virgin in contemplation (that is, he seems to identify with his own wounded woman) than with the Christian messiah. So his submission to a higher authority is not regenerative. Quite the contrary—his bones are consumed and scattered by the leopards under the juniper-tree.

This repeated image might serve as an oblique reference to aspects of the Attis myths and rituals as described by Frazer. According to Frazer, Attis was either gored by a boar or "unmanned himself under a pine-tree" (V, 264). Rituals to celebrate Attis' death and resurrection involve processionals around pine trees decorated as corpses and lashed with effigies of the dead young god, wild music making and a triumphant, masochistic "Day of Blood":

> The third day, the twenty-fourth of March, was known as the Day of Blood: the Archigallus or high-priest drew blood from his arms and presented it as an offering. Nor was he alone in making this bloody sacrifice. Stirred by the wild barbaric music of clashing cymbals, rumbling drums, droning horns, and screaming flutes, the inferior clergy whirled about in the dance with waggling heads and streaming hair, until, rapt into a frenzy of excitement and insensible to pain, they gashed their bodies with potsherds or slashed them with knives in order to bespatter the alter and the sacred tree with their flowing blood. . . . Further, we may conjecture, though we are not expressly told, that it was on the same Day of Blood and for the same purpose that the novices sacrificed their virility. Wrought up to the highest pitch of religious excitement they dashed the severed portions of themselves against the image of the cruel goddess [Cybele]. These broken instruments of fertility were afterwards reverently wrapt up and buried in the earth or in subterranean chambers sacred to Cybele, where, like the offering of blood, they may have been deemed instrumental in recalling Attis to life and hastening the general resurrection of nature, which was then bursting into leaf and blossom in the vernal sunshine. Some confirmation of this conjecture is furnished by the savage story that the mother of Attis conceived by putting in her bosom a pomegranate sprung from the severed genitals of a man-monster named Agdestis, a sort of double of Attis. (V, 268–269)

Though Eliot may not have this particular passage of Frazer's *Golden Bough* in mind when he writes *Ash Wednesday*, his imagery (the mute Lady of the garden who sits "between the slender / Yew trees") recalls Frazer's account. In particular, the initiate's virility seems demanded by the "Lady" god who has been "offended" by "these bones":

> Lady, three white leopards sat under a juniper-tree
> In the cool of the day, having fed to satiety
> On my legs my heart my liver and that which had been contained
> In the hollow round of my skull. And God said
> Shall these bones live? shall these
> Bones live? And that which had been contained
> In the bones (which were already dry) said chirping:
> Because of the goodness of this Lady
> And because of her loveliness, and because
> She honours the Virgin in meditation,
> We shine with brightness. And I who am here dissembled
> Proffer my deeds to oblivion, and my love
> To the posterity of the desert and the fruit of the gourd. (CPP 61)

This is a bloodless Day of Blood, a destruction of personality and memory rather than body, a mutilation of mind. Schneidau argues that "[o]bjective predication . . . enabled [Pound] to believe that he had defeated the most insidious of human pretensions, the creation of the Cartesian gulf between mind and world, language and nature" (238). In *Ash Wednesday,* Eliot reestablishes the gulf between subject and God, glorying in the Father's ability to annihilate him. Masculinity, intention, will—virility—is definitely on the chopping block, as the narrative voice, a "withered apple seed," surrenders to the Lady and becomes one with the garden.

Eliot's *Ash Wednesday* takes on a series of dichotomies—in addition to the division between self and Other, or poet/creator and God, the poem tackles the gap between male and female, mind and body, divine and human, saved and damned. Eliot's ambivalence about his "fortunate fall"—the idea that in order to become "moral" the weak subject must first discover *himself* to be damned—appears in his portrayal of the silent Lady. Like the shadow in *The Hollow Men,* she troubles the usual boundaries between male-mind-saved-divine and female-body-human-damned. Represented as a silenced body, she is no longer Eliot's material Lamia, as in "Portrait of a Lady." Instead, she is a saint whose presence speaks of a divine yet absent Father. Her abstract sensuality—"natural" (connected to images of the natural world, that is and thus ephemeral)—is connected to vision and clarity in "the dreamcrossed twilight between birth and dying" (CPP 66). Her body is a mystical space, as it transforms sexual longing into eroticized intuition of God:

> And the lost heart stiffens and rejoices
> In the lost lilac and the lost sea voices
> And the weak spirit quickens to rebel
> For the bent golden-rod and the lost sea smell

Quickens to recover
The cry of quail and the whirling plover
And the blind eye creates
The empty forms between the ivory gates
And smell renews the salt savour of the sandy earth (CPP 66)

This Lady "who honours the Virgin in mediation," the "spirit of the river, spirit of the sea," becomes "all women" in this poem. As the poet's object of meditation, this "enlightened" virgin transforms his earthly longings into proper sensations, bringing him to the "place of solitude where three dreams cross." Eliot's poem describes a cosmic orgasm and ends in the promise of the crashing "union" that Eliot claims, in his *Four Quartets*, to be impossible: "suffer me not to be separated // And let my cry come unto Thee" (CPP 67). The poet re-enters the virgin Mother in order to reach the missing Father.

This move toward the "pure" light is a move away from the savage communion rituals Eliot alludes to in "Prufrock" and the *Waste Land*. In *T. S. Eliot, Wallace Stevens, and the Discourses of Difference*, Michael Beehler ascribes Eliot's conversion to changing ideas about difference, subjectivity and signification. Beehler uses Nietzsche's classifications in *Birth of Tragedy* (a volume which he claims influenced Eliot's thinking)—particularly the oppositional interaction between Dionysian and Apollonian impulses in Attic tragedy, the push-and-pull relation between intoxication and dreams, music and image or meaning—to show how Eliot eventually rejects the wild "music" of poetry for the safety of Apollonian discourse, ruled as it is by laws and seamless representations.

Eliot's increasing conservatism, Beehler says, as well as his conversion, can be attributed to fears of disorder, the abject. This is also the "mysterious primordial unity" and erasure of social boundaries that Nietzsche describes as the Dionysian in the *Birth of Tragedy*:

> Under the charm of the Dionysian not only is the union between man and man reaffirmed, but nature which has become alienated, hostile, or subjugated, celebrates once more her reconciliation with her lost son, man. Freely, earth proffers her gifts, and peacefully the beasts of prey of the rocks and desert approach. The chariot of Dionysus is covered with flowers and garlands; panthers and tigers walk under its yoke. . . . Now the slave is a free man; now all the rigid, hostile barriers that necessity, caprice, or "impudent convention" have fixed between man and man are broken. Now, with the gospel of universal harmony, each one feels himself not only united, reconciled, and fused with his neighbor, but as one with him, as if the veil of mâyâ had been torn aside and were now merely fluttering in tatters before the mysterious primordial unity. (37)

Nietzsche's description anticipates the way that Eliot's poetry conflates certain images and ideas. For both writers, women are part of an alienated, hostile or subjugated Nature (who, under the Bacchanalian influence of Dionysus, now wants to reconcile with her lost son), reproduced as one of the objects of *her* earth that she offers as gifts: food, beasts of prey, flowers. The suggestion is that *before* the advent of Dionysus and his chariot, Nature was hostile to her sons—she did *not* proffer her gifts freely, wild beasts devoured their prey, and flowers hid. Further, the "impudent convention" that Nietzsche fixes between man and man seems an artifact of the same rigid, hostile barriers of necessity and caprice: domesticity, in other words, or the veil of *mâyâ* (which, not surprisingly, reads as a hymeneal image). Thus, Nietzsche's Dionysian excess describes a "happy" rape of the unyielding earth by a "mysterious primordial unity."

As we see in the *Waste Land* and other sexually phobic poems, Eliot is as fearful of God's penis as of the torn *mâyâ*. In *Ash Wednesday*, the mystical moment transforms this fear into desire . . . implying, perhaps, that the two feelings have always been synonymous in Eliot's lexicon. Eliot seems to prefer the sedate, decorous, quality of this surrender to the phallic excess of Nietzsche's imagined chariot ride. In contrast, Eliot's union is summed up in the relatively simple female image of the multifoliate rose, "torn and most whole," a metonymic symbol for "the Garden / Where all loves end." There is nothing orgiastic about Eliot's conclusion: "Terminate torment / Of love unsatisfied / The greater torment / Of love satisfied" (CPP 62).

Beehler recalls the distinction Nietzsche charts out between Apollonian and Dionysian energies, showing the former's soothing attraction for Eliot. Nietzsche connects Apollonian imagery to philosophy and aesthetics, to art and poetry, to sooth-saying, to the interpretation of reality, and—perhaps most important to Eliot in his later years—to an unflappable calmness in the face of chaos:

> . . . [Apollo], who (as the etymology of the name indicates) is the "shining one,"
> the deity of light, is also ruler over the beautiful illusion of the inner world of
> fantasy. The higher truth, the perfection of these states in contrast to the incom-
> pletely intelligible everyday world, this deep consciousness of nature, healing
> and helping in sleep and dreams, is at the same time the symbolical analogue of
> the soothsaying faculty and of the arts generally, which make life possible and
> worth living. But we must also include in our image of Apollo that delicate
> boundary which the dream image must not overstep lest it have a pathological
> effect (in which case mere appearance would deceive us as if it were crude real-
> ity). We must keep in mind that measured restraint, that freedom from the
> wilder emotions, that calm of the sculptor god. His eye must be "sunlike," as
> befits his origin; even when it is angry and distempered it is still hallowed by
> beautiful illusion. (Nietzsche 34–35)

Though Eliot questions the subjective nature of the "beautiful illusion," substitut-
ing God for aesthetic perfection, the "measured restraint" which Nietzsche categorizes as Apollonian characterizes Eliot's impersonal poet. What's more, Nietzsche's
description troubles the border between divine intervention and delusion much as

Eliot's early poetry questions Prufrock's prophecy. Finally, Eliot's descriptions of the "impossible union," after 1925, are as bodiless as Nietzsche's Apollonian.

In fact, in *Ash Wednesday* Eliot partially rescinds his interests in the Dionysian, replacing untamed celebration with "worried repose." The poem asks of the divine that it "[t]each us to sit still" (61) rather than to dance in celebration of the mystical meeting. The poet's purpose becomes, simply, *to witness* a series of merged opposites that gesture at the impossible presence between them: the "[e]nd of the endless / Journey to no end / Conclusion of all that / Is inconclusible / Speech without word and / Word of no speech"(CPP 62). Eliot's divine unity is not Dionysus' sensual abjection but an emotional desert:

> Under a juniper-tree the bones sang, scattered and shining
> We are glad to be scattered, we did little good to each other,
> Under a tree in the cool of the day, with the blessing of sand,
> Forgetting themselves and each other, united
> In the quiet of the desert. This is the land which ye
> Shall divide by lot. And neither division nor unity
> Matters. This is the land. We have our inheritance. (CPP 62–63)

Eliot connects all kinds of human intercourse—sexual, conversational, intellectual—with false turns on the path to the divine dream. In Part III, he compares his protracted conversion process to a staircase; at each turn, he blinds himself to "distractions" set in his way.[4] For instance, he climbs past the "devil of the stairs who wears / The deceitful face of hope and of despair" (63), eschewing human emotions. Then, at the "second stair," he rejects sexual congress as he turns his back on a horrific gynecological image: "Damp, jaggèd, like an old man's mouth drivelling, beyond repair, / Or the toothed gullet of an agèd shark" (CPP 63). These images contain, again, Eliot's fears of a devouring female sexuality; his deliberate blindness to them is a celebration of male impotence and, in a perverse way, a celebration of the fact that such a wound is demanded of him. Finally, Eliot turns his back upon the Dionysian dance as an even more pernicious danger than the desiring woman. The dance promises the pregnant erotic, that is:

> At the first turning of the third stair
> Was a slotted window bellied like the fig's fruit
> And beyond the hawthorn blossom and a pasture scene
> The broadbacked figure drest in blue and green
> Enchanted the maytime with an antique flute.
> Brown hair is sweet, brown hair over the mouth blown,
> Lilac and brown hair;
> Distraction, music of the flute, stops and steps of the mind over the third stair,
> Fading, fading, strength beyond hope and despair
> Climbing the third stair. (CPP 63)

Pastoral images are further deceits, disguises for a fecundity that will detain the poet from his quest. Eliot blocks them all out with a self-deprecating prayer: "Lord, I am not worthy // but speak the word only."

In his next section, Eliot reinforces his move toward the "ancient rhyme" of Apollo: "Here are the years that walk between, bearing / Away the fiddles and the flutes, restoring / One who moves in the time between sleep and waking, wearing // White light folded, sheathed about her, folded" (64). Recalling Nietzsche's description of Apollo as the "shining one," Eliot substitutes a vision of the Virgin for the poetic god, whose silent walk through the garden "restore[s] / Through a bright cloud of tears, the years, restoring / With a new verse the ancient rhyme." This will, Eliot claims, "Redeem / The time" and "the unread vision in the higher dream" (CPP 64). Thus, Eliot fuses his unspoiled Hyacinth girl with the sun god, transforming her into pure fetish.

Eliot's choice of the "silent sister veiled in white and blue" over the music of the flute not only redeems the time (the past—perhaps his failed marriage with Vivien—"Eliot's early misfortune in his experience of human love," Gordon writes, "perhaps lay behind this monastic conception of divine love as utterly different in kind" [EEY 123]) but the woman as well. By installing her in his poetry as a "[t]he token of the word unheard, unspoken," who "sign[s] but [speaks] no word," Eliot masks her pathological potential, erases the taint of original sin from her. A sketch rather than a human being, she can no longer dictate the terms of the conversation, or insert herself in the poet's dream as the portrait of a laughing Medusa, a toothed gullet. She is veiled and thus more potent in the imagination, and as such the perfect image of God's power—what Lacan calls the phallus.

As the anti-Vivien, *Ash Wednesday*'s Lady forgives the "love unsatisfied" exacerbated by Eliot's marriage and allows him to escape his "sick" wife. "Eliot's marital and religious crises were inextricably mixed," Gordon says; "through his impulsive love of Vivien, Eliot made 'that frightful discovery of morality' when 'the not naturally bad but irresponsible and undeveloped nature [is] caught in the consequences of its own action' and 'becomes moral only by becoming damned.'"5 Thus Eliot celebrates his failure as the beginning of grace. "The sense of damnation," Gordon continues, "the remorse and guilt that Vivien evoked were essential to Eliot's long purgatorial journey. . . He could escape her, morally, only by embracing the ascetic Way of the Catholic mystics" (EEY 123). As a would-be saint, Eliot worships the woman but cannot touch her. Frye's estimation of Eliot's longing for the medieval mindset is perhaps dead on the mark; such chauvinism, Lacan reminds us, sutures over the lack of the sexual union by pretending that it is we who have put it there. The offended woman is converted, in the chivalric fantasy and in Eliot's confessional poem, from laughing Medusa's head to the Father's intercessor:

> Will the veiled sister between the slender
> Yew trees pay for those who offend her

And are terrified and cannot surrender
And affirm before the world and deny between the rocks
In the last desert between the last blue rocks
The desert in the garden the garden in the desert
Of drouth, spitting from the mouth the withered apple-seed. (CPP 65–66)

Her job is to affirm "the desert in the garden and the garden in the desert." This she does by "spitting from the mouth the withered apple-seed" that is not only the sign of original sin but of the withered man and his impotent seed. She "forgives" all Eliot's offenses, then.

Eliot's woman's turn—from self-interest and sexuality to self-sacrifice and sublimation, a move that creates the cult of true womanhood—is first completed, C. W. Sullivan suggests, as Christianity reconstructs the Great Mother as the Virgin Mary and thus idealizes maternity. Eliot repeats this conversion in *Ash Wednesday.* "I rejoice," Eliot writes, "having to construct something / Upon which to rejoice" (CPP 61). According to Sullivan, Christianity appropriates and recuperates the Great Mother through St. Anne, supposedly the mother of the Virgin Mary. This rescue is only partial, since St. Anne retains vestiges of pre-Christian mythology. Her dual nature—she represents the power of life and death, regeneration and destruction—evokes ambivalence (Sullivan 12–13). As the Christian Church reached ascendancy, Sullivan argues, it had to accommodate goddess worship while quelling the ambivalence connected to the figure, so the Virgin Mary was born, asserting a kind of independence (at least from her son, Jesus Christ), and acting as a sort of "Magna Mater, who is appealed to directly for protection, nourishment, and spiritual fulfillment" (14). This Mary seems the best model for Eliot's *Ash Wednesday* Lady.

As the Great Mother is transformed into pregnant Virgin, the goddess' primary life force, the womb/vulva, becomes the "pure vessel in which the new [Christian] god [is] first nurtured and out of which he [is] born" (Sullivan 14). Eliot's religious poetry works the same alchemy, as Eliot uses his new and improved Lady to represent the silent garden where the poet's Word is born. Thus Eliot recasts her as a portal to what we might call the before-and-after-life: she offers, through the simple contemplation of her luminous, voiceless body, the poet's means of escape or return to a lost unity. Some might interpret this as Eliot's longing after an unmediated relationship to the mother—what is called the abject, in some circles—a preconscious, prelingual, polymorphously perverse state of primary narcissism. Eliot portrays this "state," however, as a merging with pre-history or even pre-time, an infinite regression to a wordless Logos. If we can call it Eliot's dream of pure or perfect mothering, it must be a bodiless mothering, since we must admit that Eliot lusts after an unmediated relationship with the Father.

As the Mother of all mothers, Eliot finally puts his Lady where she can do him the least harm. As the Christian Great Mother (who is really the mother of none), she is least—or most—alienated from the reins of phallic power and so is unlikely to take revenge on the poet for what she sees as his original crime: his birth, for her a paradoxical love satisfied and unsatisfied. (Lacan reminds us that the woman, unable to *have* the phallus, wants to *be* the phallus, and the best way she can do this is to offer up a son to the social contract.) The Virgin Mary, Freud reminds us, operates as part of the most compelling family romance for the son; his human father has never touched her, that is. No one has really had her but God the Father. . . *and the son.*

Marina Warner points out a paradox in power central to Marian cults in Christianity, particularly Catholicism: "There is no more matriarchal image than the Christian mother of God who bore a child without male assistance," she writes (47). Yet Christianity transforms this potential agency into a patriarchal triumph by combining Aristotelian biological schemes with an emphasis on the mother goddess' Immaculate Conception and delivery:

> It is highly paradoxical that this parthenogenic goddess fitted into the Aristotelian biological scheme, and that it was a deeply misogynist and contemptuous view of women's role in reproduction that made the idea of conception by the power of the Spirit more acceptable. For many matrifocal societies also entertain erroneously exaggerated ideas about the material contribution of women in parturition and belittle the biological role of the man. But in their case the imbalance leaves mothers in the ascendant, while in Christianity identification of the womb with the lower, carnal order gives fathers precedence. Thus the self-same ideogram of the mother and child can be worshipped by both societies that respect and despise women for their maternity. (47)

One might suggest that Eliot's poetry contains both these attitudes—respect and despite—for maternity. The Virgin, still an ambivalent figure because of her pagan ancestry, is perhaps the best objective correlative for this impossible union. Christianity's insistence on the chastity of the mother goddess "utterly transform[s]" the symbol's content, Warner explains (47), broadening it to "embrace a fully developed ascetic philosophy. The interpretation of the virgin birth as the moral sanction of the goodness of sexual chastity [is] the overwhelming and distinctive contribution of the Christian religion to the ancient mythological formula" (48). By emphasizing restraint from "'lower' animal passions" as the necessary distinction between man and beast, Warner claims, Christianity ensures the mother's sacrifice: "It [is] this shift, from virgin birth to virginity, from religious sign to moral doctrine, that transform[s] a mother goddess like the Virgin Mary into an effective instrument of asceticism and female subjection" (49).

Barbara F. McManus illustrates how the Christian apochyrphal tale of St. Anne and the Virgin Mary, for example, replaces the myth of Demeter and Persephone, and a fundamental split between sexuality and maternity in the Greek myth is replayed in the Christian narrative. Aphrodite rises from the waves clutching the severed genitals of the sky-god Uranus, embodying the principle of female sexuality as desire rather than fecundity: "Herself motherless," McManus writes, "Aphrodite has little connection with motherhood" (2). In contrast, Demeter struggles to preserve her daughter Persephone from the clutches of sexuality and the underworld, and thus serves as a marker of "positive maternity without sexuality" (2).[6] St. Anne and her daughter, the Virgin Mary, as outlined in the apocryphal *Protevangelum of James,* mirror the Demeter and Persephone myth. According to McManus, St. Anne vowed to dedicate her child to God if he would make her fertile, and she "chose this attenuated relationship with her daughter in order to be a mother, thus embracing— rather than resisting—the circumscribed role of motherhood within patriarchy" (5). The crucial difference between Demeter and St. Anne, in McManus' estimation, is St. Anne's acceptance of patriarchal hierarchy and its institutionalization of maternal sacrifice. Demeter struggles to regain her daughter from the clutches of the underworld, that is, and so is the only goddess to defy Zeus' direct orders. Her refusal of the father's dictum has cosmic consequences as her yearly defiance results in fall and winter—Eliot's *Waste Land.*

McManus' description of the Demeter-Persephone myth recalls other aspects of Eliot's imagery and poetics, particularly regarding women and the "feminine." Eliot's construction of the idealized mother/sister/daughter—what the Hyacinth girl becomes in poems such as *Four Quartets*—borrows from the Demeter and Anne figures, and his insistence on a self-sacrificing poetic is echoed in Anne's dedication of her child to the Temple. And Eliot clearly troubles himself with the dichotomy between female sexuality and maternality, undercutting the woman who does not surrender her sexual desire to the patriarchal contract, like the wife in "A Game of Chess," or the mother who does not surrender her child to something greater than herself, or who procreates indiscriminately, like Lil. On one level, the *Waste Land* is simply a diatribe against the bad mother who won't let go of her daughter or, worse, her only son. The earth suffers a spiritual cataclysm whose fallout is a kind of nuclear winter.

Some readers see Eliot's conscious religious sacrifice, his privileging of intellectual or mental mysticism over sensual abandonment, as a will to power. His attempts to renounce the phallus, they claim, are in reality bids for the opposite. One of Eliot's casual acquaintances once diagnosed his nervous condition, in the midst of *Waste Land* composition, as the desire to become God—a diagnosis on the fly that drove Eliot into a frenzy of offense and alienation, and that ended in breakdown at Margate. In contrast to readers such as Leavell, who find in *Ash Wednesday* a poignant primal longing and joyful surrender to the elements, Marc Manganaro sees a willful incantation at work in a poem "full of totemic figures" ("Beating" 406). Manganaro argues that Eliot uses *Ash Wednesday* to establish himself as a modern shaman: "In effect the poet is acting as primitive magician, formulating a series of words meant to call the realm of spirits toward the completion of some earthly action . . . In the anthropology of Eliot's day the shaman is the master namer in 'primitive' society, he who is granted the power to give names and thus have access to their spiritual connections . . ." (406–7). Manganaro bases his claim on the images that Eliot uses to "signify" the unsignifiable: the *Waste Land*'s thunder, for example, and the "infant word" that develops out of the mists of *Ash Wednesday* are both "versions of the utter sanctity that has no verbal equivalent" (410). Manganaro asserts that Eliot's project is not to deny meaning or our ability to approach the divine but to imply the possibility of mystic union (by authorized service representatives): " . . .in an age of dissociation," Manganaro concludes, "when sacred and profane emerge as distinctly divided, and signifier and signified are forever separate though chained, it is the poet-magician who gives at least the powerfully nostalgic illusion of return to that seamless whole that is the first word" (412). Manganaro implies, then, that Eliot's claim for "Our peace in His will" smacks of masculine self-assertion.

If so, Eliot chooses a back-door approach to this podium. Like the woman in Lacan's scenario, we might say, Eliot's "bid" is not to possess the phallus—he knows that is impossible, or so he says—so much as to *be* it. (The thesis of "Tradition and the Individual Talent," if it exists, is something like: 'The good poet doesn't not want to possess the tradition but to be possessed by it.') If Eliot aligns himself with the "perfect" woman, then he must be subject to all of her contradictions. Joan Riviere argues, in "Womanliness as Masquerade," that the powerful woman who plays for the big daddies in the front row, supposedly exaggerating her "femininity" in order mitigate against punishment at their hands (castration), is an affront to all women. They see through her act immediately.[7] Eliot's crime is his obvious masquerade; he poses as God's representative in a culture that claims to have stripped itself of such pathetic disguises.

What is perverse about Eliot's conversion, according to the powers that be, is not his announcement of faith. That is, after all, a rather pedestrian part of the ritual. Rather, his insistent celebration of a peculiarly Catholic fetishism proves unsettling to a skeptical audience, and his flamboyant performance of this fetishism is truly abject. The Eliot after 1927 is an uncanny eunuch, transvestite. As he offers himself to the tradition, and then to God, Eliot metaphorically pokes his eyes out and demands to be eaten. So he appears "contaminated" or altered by some sort of prehistorical or preverbal narcissism, and the "religious" poetry born of this contact with the "divine" is deemed radioactive.

Perhaps that's why he's so often and easily misread. Whatever else he's guilty of plotting or completing, Eliot does not represent himself—in *Ash Wednesday* or other poems—as capable of joining with the seamless whole that Manganaro sees behind occult modernism. It would be more accurate to suggest that Eliot performs as the seem-less hole between the yew trees that he conflates with his Lady.

Ash Wednesday anticipates a performance that Eliot continues, and attempts to refine, in *Four Quartets*. As he closes "Little Gidding," the last of his poems before he turns completely to performance, Eliot describes the demand for Love as "the unfamiliar Name / Behind the hands that wove / The intolerable shirt of flame / Which human power cannot remove" (CPP 144). This demand, Eliot suggests, leads to poetry—it impels the alienated male poet on an unceasing exploration for the proper words to express or remove this flaming desire from his back. The impossible union requires the impossible demand, Eliot implies: the right incantation, the perfect power over or under the Other. And so Eliot exhorts his readers (particularly himself—the late poetry has the quality of intense solipsism, where the reader is an accidental auditor to the poet's private, and pleasurable, pain) to accept their inability to consume the Other and to submit to their own consumption in It/Him: "Every phrase and every sentence is an end and a beginning," he writes, "Every poem an epitaph. And any action / Is a step to the block, to the fire, down the sea's throat / Or to an illegible stone . . ." (144).

For Eliot, death serves as the ultimate God, the phallic mother, "source of the longest river" and "voice of the hidden waterfall / And the children in the apple-tree" (CPP 145). His spiritual and poetic epiphany, if we can call it that, is not simply a distanced fantasy or vision of the primal womb. Instead, to "arrive where we started / And know the place for the first time" (CPP 145) is, in Eliot's scenario, to be properly possessed, transformed into the pure fetish, the wombless/woundless mother:

> A condition of complete simplicity
> (Costing not less than everything)
> And all shall be well and
> All manner of thing shall be well
> When the tongues of flame are in-folded
> Into the crowned knot of fire
> And the fire and the rose are one. (CPP 145)

5.
Return of the Repressed

[Eliot's] pronouncements attained, both in his lifetime and no less since his death, an authority that has been received with awe. How this absolute and enduring authority came to be, in so cynical a century, is still a mystery.
—Lyndall Gordon, *Eliot's New Life*, 226

A CURSORY EXAMINATION OF THE CRITICAL SCENE SURROUNDING ELIOT THESE days might give the reader the impression that Eliot is indeed a latter day pariah, an example of what *not* to do if you want to be remembered by the academy fondly. As a case in point: Christopher Ricks just published Eliot's juvenile notebooks under the title *Inventions of the March Hare*, another slim volume of Eliot's (thankfully) unpublished ruminations blown out of proportion with 300–plus pages of Ricks' notes. The release of Eliot's unsurprisingly racist, sexist and classist poetic "unconscious" (or the dusty attic for his standard works), coming on the heels of Michael Hastings' *Tom and Viv*, has launched quite a few angry ships, condemnations of Eliot's politics and subject positions, rejections of his religious conversion, apologies for his "humanity," economiums for his poetry. The upshot of it all is that Eliot lives again, both in the critical and the popular imagination. Just as he threatens to retire permanently from the scene, embalmed as required reading in English core courses or hung in effigy at the center of heated debates about a dead, white, patriarchal Canon, we roll back the rock from his tomb. His reanimated corpse and corpus dance across the critical horizon, the razor sharp edge of the abyss.

Could it be that Eliot is once again fashionable, or fascinating, as we approach the turn-of-the-century and find ourselves wrestling with the same old questions about moral and aesthetic responsibility, public and private, eternal and commercial? Perhaps we exhume and crucify Eliot in an attempt to express the inexpressible: the (absent or questionable) "soul" of a current academic, social and/or political "class" or climate. Certainly, we are guilty of singling out particular aspects of Eliot's poetics and personality as representative of the "whole" we wish to celebrate or condemn. Our ghoulish return to the garden/graveyard of modernism reveals more about our Frankensteinian projects to cobble together a "postmodern" critical consciousness than it does about Eliot's misbegotten politics and personality.

The academy isn't the only arena where Eliotic dramas take place, though the critical establishment would like to think so. Music, stage, film, television, and even the press lay claim to various parts of Eliot's anatomy, using such fetishes to exalt or denigrate his political/social ideology, his "identity" or personality, and thus his poetry. Attempts to separate the mind that creates from the body that made us suffer fail. It turns out there is no way to amputate one from the other. Anthony Julius, whose central claim to fame is his role as Princess Di's divorce lawyer, has just warmed up his dissertation and put it out on the table, "exposing" Eliot's anti-Semitism. *T. S. Eliot, Anti-Semitism, and Literary Form* tells us nothing new about Eliot's predictable prejudice but it does pique our social consciences and impel us to re-examine the subject of Eliot's ideology and its connection to his work. Is Eliot a regrettable eccentric or is he representative of the mythological consciousness of a generation, as his fans claim? If we find Eliot's poetry pleasing, does that mean that we should count ourselves as anti-Semites?

More nuanced studies of Eliot's work and racial consciousness, such as Christopher Ricks' *T. S. Eliot and Prejudice*, may help us to ponder these questions. In the meantime, Hollywood grabs up Michael Hastings' mean-spirited drama, *Tom and Viv*, and indulges in fashionable feminist advocacy, suggesting that Eliot profited, in more ways than one, from his wife's supposed mental illness. Fresh rock bands, popular with college listeners, immortalize Eliot's Prufrock in their refrains, drawing from his turn-of-the-century ennui and making much of his performative impotence: "I have measured out my life in coffee spoons," the Crash Test Dummies wail. Such long popular tag lines as "not with a bang but a whimper" are supplemented by Tommy Lee Jones' rendition of a vengeful Irish terrorist in *Blown Away*, a mainstream action-adventure piece. Jones menaces the hero's girlfriend and young daughter as he prances down the beach doing an impromptu rendition of "I should have been a pair of ragged claws."

Thirty-one years after his death, Eliot's trademark pessimism—his visions of a tattered Europe and a civilization defined by its discontents—serves as the proper tone for the encroaching "postmodern" millennium, when, we imagine, a proliferation of information, media and methods will culminate in an hopeless snarl. Given such an array of communication, it will be impossible for us to say just what we mean or to mean what we say. Eliot's legendary and, as such, mysterious breakdown and retreat to Margate Sands—a mental deconstruction that ended in the whimpers of his *Waste Land*—provides us with an objective correlative for postmodern angst in the age of the information superhighway: "I can connect / Nothing with nothing," intones Eliot, known for speaking in tongues. "The broken fingernails of dirty hands. / My people humble people who expect / Nothing"—except, perhaps, the proper dose of MTV.

As the academy struggles to fit Eliot into his proper place (which, for most younger critics, would be at the back of the bus or, better, underground), the public converts him into an institution of Broadway musical theater, *Cats*. Most theatergoers could care less that the Andrew Lloyd Weber brouhaha they pay forty dollars to consume was created (in a set of silly moments) by Tom Eliot over 50 years ago. This is, perhaps, a fitting finale for the most playful and, some would say, most uncharacteristic legacy of a man who once said that Marie Lloyd's popularity with working-class audiences was "not merely evidence of her accomplishment" but "evidence of the extent to which she represented and expressed that part of the English nation which has perhaps the greatest vitality and interest" (SE 405). "[N]o other comedian succeeded so well in giving expression to the life of that audience, in raising it to a kind of art," Eliot comments in his homage to the celebrated music hall performer. "It was, I think, this capacity for expressing the soul of the people that made Marie Lloyd unique. . ." (SE 406).

If *Old Possum's Book of Practical Cats* is popular because it somehow expresses, in turn, the soul of the people who pay to watch the spectacularly cliched musical performed, what is the essence of that collective soul? Eliot's jolly opener, "The Naming of Cats," suggests, in a strange way, the invasive and narcissistic projects of public and academic audiences as they confront his profoundly nonsensical meditations. Scholars caught up in what Stephen Medcalf calls the "fallacy of extended reference" are as determined as Hastings and Gilbert are, in their pretentious *Tom and Viv*, to uncover "the name that you will never guess" that the "cat himself . . . will never confess."

Eliot's puerile ruminations mock our assiduous attempts to lay bare his peculiar private life, eccentric desires and egotism by suggesting that such forays are, in fact, evidence of cultural narcissism. We look at the cat and name him after ourselves. In his most recent incarnations, Eliot plays a kaleidoscopic array of cultural roles: the harmless neighborhood eccentric, the mystical philosopher, a nonsensical cat lover who dresses in three-piece suits and green face paint for his jaunts to the music hall, a vampire of high modernism, the anorexic aesthete, a fin-de-siècle fop, the failed romantic and trembling gynephobe, the impotent lover and deadbeat husband, the self-flagellating would-be saint, and the Pope of Russell Square. Eliot was indeed a man of disguises, contradictions, secrets and late-in-the-game conversions. But most of this change-up work seems imposed on him after the facts of his biography. Was

Eliot really an early-century Madonna, selling image over substance, or is he a Rorsasch blot for our own self-image?

Eliot knew that he had to give the people what they want in order to be remembered. As readers and then consumers of Eliot, we focus on his inconsistencies and masks. Our attempts to re-value and historicize his work hinge on discovering or uncovering whatever it is we think serves as his "essence" at the current moment or in given a theoretical context. And so we see Eliot's dandified dead-man pose as an alibi for misogyny, gynephobia, anti-Semitism, fascism, puritanical zeal, egotism, suppressed homosexuality, and neurosis. Current Eliot criticism swirls around this mysterious and mystifying investigation—mystifying because it is ever occluded, incomplete, hesitant, itself shrouded in masks of propriety or shocking overexposures—of the very quantities or qualities which Eliot worked so hard to keep out of his critical discussions. Even those critical volumes ostensibly dedicated to an investigation of Eliot's philosophical or scientific thinking can be read as attempts to salvage Eliot as a mythical figure, a messiah or pariah. His individual foibles serve as cultural markers, as universalized signs for widespread or international malaise, and his accomplishments become the high water marks of the first half of the century.

While Marie Lloyd's mimicry made her working class audiences "not so much hilarious as happy" (Eliot, SE 406) as they watched themselves recreated on stage, we drag Eliot out of the closet as evidence of a moth-eaten past that should be sent straight to the incinerator. Self-congratulatory celebrations of "difference" are not confined to the academy. Popular culture has appropriated the same role as cultural arbiter. A recent newspaper report detailing work on genetics and disposition, for instance, uses Eliot as an example of someone who is constitutionally dour. Jonathan Eliot, the hip New York hero of an NBC sitcom, "The Single Guy," misquotes lines from Prufrock as a way to impress a babe in the bookstore. On his own mission of revenge, Jonathan searches for his new novel on the bookshelves of a trendy bookstore; his work has been poorly reviewed by the owner of this store, a surly "Charlie" who Jonathan plans to confront with proof of his creative greatness. As he lingers by the stacks, lamenting the scarcity of copies, a stunning woman looks over his shoulder.

"Interested in T. S. Eliot?" she asks.

"Oh yes—," Jonathan doesn't lose a beat. "'The Love Song of J. Alfred Prufrock' was my favorite poem in college." He pushes the pose a little. "'Let us go then, you and I,'" he muses, hands on hips, eyes on the ceiling, voice breathy— "'while the evening is laid out against the sky like a patient anesthetized upon a table . . .'"

"It's etherized," the blonde cuts him off.

Jonathan quickly scans a copy, his mouth a round O. As he tries to cover his mistake, he digs his grave a little deeper. It turns out that the woman he's failed to impress is the aggressive Charlie, author of the hostile review. Thus Jonathan Eliot becomes the hapless Prufrock, unable to say what he really means before the bored woman cuts him off with a look. We are meant, of course, to identify with Jonathan's resentment and distress, his need to be accepted. In this scene, T. S. Eliot acts as a marker for a particular literary snobbishness that we see as castrating, female and (because Jonathan makes his living as a sports writer) vaguely un-American.

Cynthia Ozick, in "Eliot at 101," may not see Eliot as feminized or feminizing (she may question that sitcom assumption) but she certainly calls into question Eliot's cachet as she describes how Eliot held her undergraduate generation, and more than a few subsequent incarnations, in thrall:

> Eliot's voice, with its sepulchral cadences, came spiraling out of student phonographs . . . That tony British accent—flat, precise, steady, surprisingly high-pitched, bleakly passive—coiled through awed English Departments and worshipful dormitories, rooms where the walls had pinup Picassos, and where Pound and Eliot and 'Ulysses' jostled one another in higgledy-piggledy in the rapt late-adolescent breast. (119–120)

Ozick's acerbic exposé of Eliot's ruinous personal life, his naked ambition and political savvy, his business-like approach to and exultation of the arts, and his use and abuse of the few women central to this life proves the norm, rather than the exception, in mainstream critical commentary. The man who in 1928 declared his general point of view to be "classicism in literature, royalist in politics, and anglo-catholic in religion" alienated more than a few friends and supporters. A review of *For Lancelot Andrewes* in the *Times Literary Supplement* expressed "increasing perturbation" at the turn in Eliot's pronouncements; Eliot appeared to have "rejected modernism for mediaevalism" (qtd in Behr 35). The fact that, in 1956, Eliot filled a football stadium with 14,000 fans reflects, as Ozick points out, the arch-conservative soul of his McCarthy-era audience.

Even Ezra Pound, who was responsible for discovering and promoting Eliot as a force in modern poetry, criticized his friend for his elitism. According to Pound, the man "who [had] arrived at the supreme Eminence among English critics largely through disguising himself as a corpse" retained little respect for the intelligence of his target audience(s) ("Credo"). "[Mr. Eliot's] contempt for his readers has always been much greater than mine," Pound says in 1933,

> by which I would indicate that I quite often write as if I expected my reader to use his intelligence, and count on its being fairly strong, whereas Mr. Eliot after enduring decennial fogs in Britain practically always writes as if for very very feeble and brittle mentalities, from whom he can expect neither resilience nor any faculty for seeing the import instead of the details or surfaces. ("Prefatio" 389)

Years later, Ozick sums up prevailing critical and popular winds:

It may be embarrassing for us now to look back at that nearly universal obeisance to an autocratic, inhibited, depressed, rather narrow-minded, and con-
siderably bigoted fake Englishman—especially if we are old enough (as I surely
am) to have been part of the wave of adoration. In his person, if not in his poetry, Eliot was, after all, false coinage. (121)

No dummy, Eliot anticipated our late-century scorn and rejection, as well as
our attempts to assert our distance from him and his "principles." "How unpleasant
to meet Mr. Eliot!" he proclaims of himself,

> With his features of clerical cut,
> And his brow so grim
> And his conversation, so nicely
> Restricted to What Precisely
> And If and Perhaps and But. (CPP 93)

Better to avoid this chap, Eliot suggests, "whether his mouth be open or shut."
We like to imagine Eliot as the vengeful father who zealously guarded his place at
the head of the table at weekly Faber editorial meetings, where he silently filled in
the blanks of his crossword puzzles and snipped hopeful young poets dead with a
dismissive flick of the wrist. "The tiger in the tiger-pit / Is not more irritable than
I," Eliot reminds us in his self-parody—

> The whipping tail is not more still
> Than when I smell the enemy
> Writhing in the essential blood
> Or dangling from the friendly tree. (CPP 95)

Our current adversarial relationship to Eliot makes a serious case of his flippant
self-portrait; we smell the enemy as he writhes in the essential blood. We lynch him,
as in *Tom and Viv*, on the friendly tree.[1] Our emotional violence as we confront Eliot
and his corpus mimics the sacrificial subjects of Eliot's poetry—it's as if our conversions from Eliot fans to foes, like Ozick's, represent a peculiar stab at redemption.
We want to redeem the time, to turn to account the destructive self-loathing that
Eliot's poetry, politics and personal life has come to evoke and embody for us.

Ozick sees the cost of Eliot's time in the sun as evidence of a corrosive cultural
loathing, a critical self-hatred that spills out of the Academy and into the streets. We
continue to consume Eliot, Ozick argues, because we "buy" his anti-American zeal.
The result? We inhabit Eliot's waste land of the heart. Rejecting Eliot is a good cultural therapy, since the act involves rejecting his desert of the mind, his conservatism, his corrosive pessimism, and his sly, aristocratic act. Eliot's "unalloyed self-
alteration," Ozick muses, "suggests a hatred for the original design," the blueprint
to the developing America that Eliot rejected in his twenties:

> Certainly Eliot condemned the optimism of democratic American meliorism; certainly he despised Unitarianism, centered less on personal salvation than on the social good; certainly he had contempt for Jews as marginal, if not inimical to his concept of Christian community. But most of all he came to loathe himself, a hollow man in a twilight kingdom. (122)

When we reject Eliot, we assert ourselves as original Americans, Ozick suggests. Crudely put, we get in touch with our inner child.

Perhaps the most extended examination of the negative capability of Eliot's life and work is Michael Hastings' stage play, "Tom and Viv." In 1995, the play was revamped and released as a Hollywood movie, starring Miranda Richardson and Willem Dafoe. For two hours, Dafoe's Eliot perpetuates the passive abuse of his "ill" wife, using her family name and funds to finance his effete art. (It appears to be one of the film's contentions that Vivien contributed in no small way to the conception of the *Waste Land*, not only as his manic muse but as his personal secretary, nurse, neurotic repository and creative consultant. Brief scenes suggest that Vivien, who really suffered from a minor menstruation problem that could have been solved with hormone therapy,[2] was probably responsible for large portions of the poem; in one such moment, the chain-smoking Viv waves Eliot off to an afternoon lunch with his pedantic Bishop, as she squints over the chaotic pages of his manuscript and blasts away at the typewriter.) Miranda Richardson's plaintive portrayal of Vivien, who supports her treacherous husband even after decades in the padded cell of an upperclass mental institution, shames Dafoe's cigar-store Indian Eliot with his emotional frigidity, his intellectual and social pretensions, and—ultimately—his Anglophile servility.[3]

Tom and Viv presents itself as a high-brow examination of the lower impulses, a psycho-biographical thriller in which every titillating moment of Bloomsbury voyeurism is heightened by arch glances, period costumes and a soundtrack laden with crescendos. Eliot has something to say, of course, about our interest in such spectacles—even our need to invent them. "Those who have lived before such terms as 'high-brow fiction,' 'thrillers' and 'detective fiction' were invented," Eliot comments, "realize that melodrama is perennial and that the craving for it is perennial and must be satisfied. If we cannot get this satisfaction out of what the publishers present as 'literature,' then we will read—with less and less pretense of concealment—what we call 'thrillers'" (SE 409). Though *Tom and Viv* doesn't satisfy all our cravings, it certainly rakes up the muck surrounding Eliot's life and work. The film's celebrants see it as a much-needed revision of Eliot's myth. Ed Kelleher and Cynthia Lucia, in a *Cineaste* review, for instance, laud the film's exploration of the Eliots' sexual struggles; we should read Eliot as a representative of repressive medical, religious and academic establishments and should diagnose his treatment of Vivien as the projection of his own hysteria onto another. Kelleher and Lucia insist on Vivien's crucial role in Eliot's composition: Vivien deals quite patiently with her husband's neurotic headaches and superstitions, serving as his wet-nurse and amanuensis: "Viv points out a certain self-destructive undercurrent in Tom's neurotic belief that he must be sick in order to write but can't write when he's sick. . . . Viv has the 'sickness' he needed in order to create, but once his position as a major poet was assured, the 'sickness' got in his way . . ." The juxtaposition of a distraught Vivien sequestered in the honeymoon suite, scrubbing futilely at the bloodied bed sheets, with Eliot's solitary amble along the overcast beach is emblematic of the roles assigned these characters in the social contract, Kelleher and Lucia argue. Viv is "consigned to the role of hysterical female trapped by her own biology, and Tom is permitted the role of suffering poet cleansed, even transformed, by nature." Kelleher and Lucia complain that though "the film struggles to create a critical cinematic dialog which will acknowledge Eliot's negligence as husband," it "recuperates his image as poet" and "endorses his need to be part of a patriarchal social order from which an unstable presence like Viv must be exiled." Kelleher and Lucia lament the fact that Eliot is not further exposed and maligned. "[T]he film's reluctance to address Eliot's rather 'slippery' politics cannot be ignored," they write.

Richard Alleva, of the *Commonweal*, critiques *Tom and Viv* for the very reasons that Kelleher and Lucia claim it falls short. "Michael Hastings and Adrian Hodges," the film's writers, "proceed for some time as if they were treating both participants in a conjugal catastrophe with equal compassion, but all the while they're sharpening their knives to skin Old Possum," Alleva comments. As far as he's concerned, the film is a grotesque morality play. "If the filmmakers had really been attuned to Eliot, really curious about the many-sided spirit that dwelt behind his detached demeanor (V. S. Pritchett called the poet 'a company of actors inside one suit, each twitting the other . . .'), monotony would not have doused Dafoe's performance," he claims. This ends in a dull movie that can only be saved by the "adrenaline of blame": "At the (virtual) last minute a villain is found on whom the audience can fasten as the source of the woe that is this marriage. And, of course, that villain, in our age of pedestal pulverization, has got to be T. S. Eliot." Indeed, Eliot serves as a last-minute villain for many readers—not only for the woe in his marriage, but for the woe perceived to be part and parcel of modernism and its adherents. Eliot's archetypal sin, Alleva implies, is his elitism: "Mrs. Haigh-Wood, presenting herself and her family as the cream of England's gentry, exposes Eliot as a calculating American snob breaking into England's cultural establishment."

Stanley Kaufmann, of *The New Republic*, on the other hand, faults the movie as a feeble representative of its genre: "Slips and all, what we get is another story of an unbalanced wife and her patient but finally frazzled husband, of the love between them that never disappears but finally has to bow to circumstances." In short, Kaufmann dismisses *Tom and Viv* as yet another woman's weepy, centered around a squeamish poet who no one really likes. Jonathan Romney argues that any film striving to explore an artist's inner life is doomed—such a life can only be expressed in what he calls iconic imagery. Thus *Tom and Viv* "can't quite deal with [Viv] as a writer, rather than as the impassioned Repressed of her husband's grim-lipped stuffiness. She's simply his avenging angel, the throbbing, bloody Problematic Feminine."

Anthony Lane is the most emphatic in his condemnation of the film's hatchet job. In "Etherized," he argues that the film exists merely to vilify Eliot and to sympathize with Vivien as an obscured heroine (the genuine article to Eliot's bad reproduction). All this, Lane infers, might stem from another female plot. After all, Lane sneers, Dafoe's Eliot sounds like Ashley Wilkes. Hastings' stage and screenplay are based on "almost nothing at all, apart from a smattering of blind prejudice and a thick ear for English verse" (125). To counteract this prejudice, Lane takes pleasure in reporting the biographical emendations made for the sake of Eliot's vilification:

> I am glad to report that the film . . . loses none of the rich nonsense of the original play, although I was sorry not to hear the interesting line in which Vivien reports that her husband 'adores the Fascists.' A daring little slander, not least because it was Vivien herself who joined the British Union of Fascists, in 1934. That would not suit the playwright's plan—wronged woman versus cold fish— so he made the switch. By way of compensation, there is plenty of new nonsense; try as I might, I just couldn't get my brain around the idea of T. S. Eliot hugging the Bishop of Oxford, resting his weary head against the reverend waistband. Nobody minds liberties being taken with the facts, but one doesn't expect those liberties to be pressed into the service of a hardline willfulness; the film is more intolerant than the man whom it surveys with such distaste. (126)

As Lane sees it, the movie and its audience "resents Eliot's need for seclusion and ritual and is set on disturbing his peace"; *Tom and Viv*'s mean-spirited Eliot-bashing is what results when "the snob section of the movie industry meets the sleazy end of the biography trade" (126).

Finally, Lane argues, the movie dramatizes a postmodern envy, "raising the dismal prospect that our age has become offended by genius" (126). "Devotees of the poet . . . will leave the theatre in suitably controlled fury; he is now so unfashionable that the act of reading him has itself become a monastic, Eliot-like operation, and the film can only drive us deeper underground," Lane says (127). The film's final image—Eliot descending in the iron elevator cage—is, in Lane's point of view, a blatant assertion of smug postmodernism:

> . . . we see Willem Dafoe standing in the cage of an elevator, doing his familiar impersonation of a dyspeptic sphinx; the camera stares back at him, and then returns for one last closeup, just to hammer home the point that Eliot was a prisoner of his own self. The effect, of course, is to lull us into superiority; we've seen through this guy, we know why he wrote, we know how he treated others, and, frankly, we're not surprised that he got on better with cats.

"The movie is not just lacklustre but irresponsible," Lane concludes, "because it will foster more Eliot haters than there are Eliot readers; people will come away knowing for certain that they dislike him, without feeling the need to discover whether they like his work" (127). Indeed, as Lane suggests, the movie works to define the "Eliot-like operation" as a quintessential etherizing—a monastic attempt to drive passion "deeper underground."

Indeed, an element of unabashed envy motivates *Tom and Viv*'s repudiations of Eliot's self-promoting, "establishment" philosophies. It's no mistake that Eliot serves as a convenient pariah for contemporary media moguls with artistic ambitions. After all, Eliot got his licks in on filmmakers long before Hastings got hold of him. Eliot was never shy about publishing imperatives for poetry and drama writers, nor was he very circumspect in his attack on readers and viewers alike. In "Marie Lloyd," for example, Eliot describes the dangers of film. It is an inferior medium, he asserts, glad that Marie Lloyd "never descended to this form of money-making" (SE 406). In drafts for the *Waste Land*, Eliot suggests that cinema-going has replaced worship as a collective consciousness: "So the close rabble in the cinema / Identify a goddess or a star," he writes. "In silent rapture worship from afar."[4]

To Eliot's mind, this "rapture" is a middle-class phenomenon and (as such) should be excoriated: "Thus art ennobles even wealth and birth," he concludes, "And breeding raises prostrate art from earth" (WL 29). Eliot claims that Marie Lloyd is "the expressive figure of the lower classes," while "the middle classes have no such idol" because they are "morally corrupt"—"their own life fails to find a Marie Lloyd to express it; nor have they any independent virtues which might give them as a conscious class any dignity" (SE 406). In the same essay, Eliot describes the cinema as the "catalyst" for a pernicious social democracy: "The middle classes, in England as elsewhere, under democracy, are morally dependent upon the aristocracy, and the aristocracy are subordinate to the middle class, which is gradually absorbing and destroying them," Eliot writes. This might be where Eliot loses us. The soulless middle class, Eliot argues, uses the cinema to devour the rest:

> With the decay of the music-hall, with the encroachment of the cheap and rapid-breeding cinema, the lower classes will tend to drop into the same state of protoplasm as the bourgeoisie. The working man who went to the music-hall and saw Marie Lloyd and joined in the chorus was himself performing part of the act; he was engaged in that collaboration of the audience with the artist which is necessary in all art and most obviously in dramatic art. He will now go to the cinema, where his mind is lulled by continuous senseless music and continuous action too rapid for the brain to act upon, and will receive, without giving, in that same listless apathy with which the middle and upper classes regard any entertainment of the nature of art. (SE 407)

This mind-numbing "civilization," Eliot suggests, converts the working class into corpses, destroying the possibility for community or cultural consciousness. This is

Eliot's twentieth-century apocalypse: the hooded hordes are "dying from pure bore-dom." Eliot sounds as if he's repeating a familiar conservative party line. His rheto-ric in "Marie Lloyd" chimes in quite well, for example, with the continuing refrain about "family values" and violence in the media. Given these doleful pronounce-ments, Eliot seems akin to one of 1996's most prominently Prufrockian presidential candidates, Bob Dole.[5]

Perhaps Hastings' exposure of the "great" poet, then, is motivated by a killing boredom of his own, composed of equal parts envy and spite. Hastings' portrayal of Eliot's "backward" social ambition deflects scathing repudiations of middle class "values" by assigning them to a convenient villain. In the light of Eliot's assertions about middle class culture and its filmic expressions, negative reviews for *Tom and Viv* could be read as expressions of similarly dismissive principles. The film should be rejected because it doesn't offer Eliot as a figure with independent virtues or dig-nity of class: instead, he is manipulated as the icon of a self-centered social impera-tive that uses women and then the Church of England to claw its way to English nobility.

On the popular front, Eliot's work and persona expresses a cultural depression. Across the street, the academy uses Eliot to work a wedge between those who expect nothing and those right-minded readers who expect everything. The on-going crit-ical debate about modernism's backward-looking elitism and, in particular, Eliot's role in it—as well as the expected grumblings about Eliot's impact on contemporary literary studies—is all about the disconnection and humbling of this infamous "Other." In a 1992 review of Eliot scholarship, George and Cleo McNelly Kearns dismiss a "currently fashionable rhetoric of aspersion on Eliot" (*American Literary Scholarship* 124), attributing it to the theoretical reader who uses the hapless Eliot to make a political point (and who, according to the Kearns, is nearly always blind to the operation of the same principles in his/her own work). Two years later, Michael Coyle and Laura Cowan argue that "the year's best work [on Eliot] resists either the merely contentious dismissal of his political or ideological commitments, or the uncritical veneration of [his] poetic accomplishments" (*American Literary Scholarship* 1994: 127), implying that modernist criticism suffers from its associa-tion with the New Criticism, where rootless readings fail to take into account a work's lineage and context. Like Eliot, Cowan and Coyle seek to ground readings of his poetry and politics in the tradition that allowed him to come into being (or that comes into being as a result of his propaganda), rather than in the cult of the per-sonality or around the readers' private emotions. They argue that literary criticism "becomes increasingly and genuinely critical" only as it "at last becomes historical" (*American Literary Scholarship* 1994: 127).

In "The Shaman's Secret Heart," another survey of current Eliot studies, Stephen Medcalf describes the advocacy and enmity that Eliot evokes in contemporary readers and the "madness" that results. In the spirit of Cowan, Coyle and the Kearns, Medcalf is made particularly uneasy by what appear to be subjective interpretations of Eliot's work and persona—appropriations of Eliot's priestly masks. In particular, Medcalf lambastes Ted Hughes' sweeping claims for Eliot in *A Dancer to God*. Comparing Eliot to Shakespeare, Hughes exalts Eliot as a visionary who "contained within himself 'the spiritual tragedy of his epoch'"—"the shaman or "prophet of our time." Hughes's unqualified admiration reveals more about himself than Eliot or his/our times, says Medcalf: "Just though this sense of Eliot as a prophet is, it is clearly related to Hughes' peculiar sense that any poet is a kind of shaman, to his sense, as shown lately in his Laureate poems, of his own vocation as a tribal poet, and to his understanding of Shakespeare as having a poetic self, a god within, whose fate he expressed in the myth of Adonis" (10). Yet, as Medcalf sees it, more critical readers discover themselves equally flummoxed as they fall prey to "the fallacy of distended reference: if there is a reference to one line of the *Aeneid* in Eliot, then everything for a hundred lines each way from that line can also be assumed to be relevant" (10).

Medcalf suggests that Eliot studies are plagued by voodoo approaches—popular and critical interpreters alike turn into zombies in their attempts to resurrect and control the modernist figure in their own image. Interpreters, in a perverse move, refuse to read Eliot on his own terms: "Not a scrap of evidence from Eliot's mouth about the meaning of his poems, nor from the mouths of others about his private life, goes unused," Medcalf laments (12). Such excursions are red herrings, as critics "construct from their own responses an Eliot without a sense of humor"; if we were to see Eliot as the perennial fool and much of his work a cosmic joke, then "much that is implausible or misplaced in the hermeneutics of *The Waste Land* would vanish," Medcalf claims. Instead, critics ignore or dismiss evidence of Eliot's humorous complexity, such as *Old Possum's Book of Practical Cats,* which Medcalf sees as "perhaps the only one of his works in which Eliot succeeded in being a poet for the whole community, as he wanted to be" (12).[6]

The madness about (or for) Eliot goes to extremes—either of subjectivity or objectivity. In assiduous attempts to historicize Eliot's achievements, some of his critical readers obliterate questions about his private life from their pseudo-scientific examinations of the corpus and so avoid confronting their own investment in the research. Historically grounded readings, such as Richard Crawford's painstakingly documented study of Eliot's use of anthropological material in his urban poetry, *The Savage and the City in the Work of T. S. Eliot,* attempt to rescue Eliot from the dungeon of postmodernism by suggesting that Eliot's foibles stem from fashionable intellectual debates rather than a private agenda. This advocacy can only be read between the lines, of course. Richard Skaff's metaphysical examination of Eliot's development, *The Philosophy of T. S. Eliot: From Skepticism to A Surrealist Poetic,* treats Eliot like the fascinating neurotic on the academician's sterile couch, reading his academic interests as symptoms of his peculiar pathology. Both Skaff and Crawford avoid their own central issues through a painstaking (or painful) attention to detail and historical "framework." While Crawford's textual "preconscious" contains an apology for Eliot's personal peculiarities, Skaff's holds a disavowal of Eliot's religous conversion.

On the other side of the fence, Eliot's biographers' investment in him as saint or sinner shifts with the critical tides. In the 1970s, Eliot served as the subject of both supportive and prurient interest in the forefathers of Beat and then Black Mountain poetry, fueled by pop readings of psychology. T. S. Matthews' *Great Tom: Notes Towards the Definition of T. S. Eliot* portrays Eliot as a fascinatingly complex namesake, whose repressive childhood explodes into an enduring poetic. In 1977, James E. Miller, Jr., suggests that Eliot derived his poetic energy and eccentricity from a suppressed homosexuality. The next decade is marked by an interest in Eliot's commodification. Peter Ackroyd's definitive *T. S. Eliot*, published in 1984, focuses on Eliot's enigmatic and contradictory self-promotion, suggesting that his "objective" poetry served as a come-on for generations of autograph hounds and peeping Toms (how Ackroyd manages to stay above such a madding crowd is yet another mystery). As the 80s draw to their close, Cynthia Ozick uses Eliot's mythic life as a diving board, launching into a critique of her generation's veneration of a bigoted, self-involved woman-hater and the perpetuation of such attitudes as "art."

Perhaps Lyndall Gordon, one of Eliot's most complicating critical biographers, provides the best model for this evolution in perception and personal investment. In 1977, Gordon published her first critical study of Eliot, *Eliot's Early Years*. She devotes the volume to describing Eliot's seminal role in the construction of modern poetry, poring over Eliot's warts and beauty marks with reverence, deeming his social and psychological quirks incidental by-products of his mystical poetry. By the time Gordon publishes *Eliot's New Life*, in 1988, she is not as lavish with her praise. Here, Gordon takes issue with what she sees as the costs of Eliot's public persona and exalted poetics, arguing that he used—regrettably—at least three key women as he worked through private issues of damnation and redemption. In a 1991 essay derived from *Eliot's New Life*, Gordon reiterates her critical thesis: "His passion for immortality was so commanding that it allowed him to reject each of these women with a firmness that shattered their lives. At the same time, his poetry and plays transformed them as the material of art" ("Eliot and Women" 20). "Every poem an epigraph," indeed. In a move that many of her contemporaries avoid like the plague, Gordon connects (if only in passing) this condemnation of Eliot's poetic method to her position as a female reader. This impulse to confess personal motives, however, is easily overshadowed by the plenitude of Gordon's historical documentation, and by the fact that this admission is a single sentence buried in an anthology entitled *T. S. Eliot: The Modernist in History*.

Despite a plethora of diversionary tactics, Eliot's contemporary readers grudgingly acknowledge the centrality of his personal life to any further understanding of his work, as well as to our increasingly suspicious reactions to his poetic projects. Increasingly, the consensus is that Eliot is one of the first "confessional" poets. In retrospect, Eliot dismissed his *Waste Land* as the mistaken voice of a generation, describing it as a personal grouse. Gordon puts it this way: "What begins to emerge here is a poet preoccupied with self who, as it were by accident, intersects with his age" (*Eliot's New Life* 232).

Medcalf's insistence that we read Eliot on his own terms, then, is itself a red herring. As Louis Menand argues in *Discovering Modernism: T. S. Eliot and His Context*, it is impossible to trace a coherent line of intellectual or philosophical development in Eliot's prose; essays such as "Tradition and the Individual Talent" are contradicted by later essays. (Hence the need to read Eliot as a deliberate Fool, or ironist.) By the same token, Eliot's rejection and advocacy of particular literary figures—as well as his reasons for creating the "in" crowd—shift as his own poetic projects and personal ideas develop. In the 1920s, Milton is the enemy; in the 1940s, he is the unacknowledged model. Menand suggests that Eliot, a creature of fashion, used prevailing critical winds to promote his own work. Thus, no reader can take the tenets set out in "Tradition and the Individual Talent" or even *The Idea of a Christian Society* as gospel. Each of Eliot's emphatic statements must be seen as a calculated self-promotion.

This view is nothing new. Eliot's contemporaries and friends were the first to point the finger. In 1933, Ezra Pound accuses Eliot of participating in an elitist "puffing up" of American letters. "Mr. Eliot's flattering obeisance to 'exponents of criticism', wherein he says that he supposes they have not assumed that criticism is an 'autotelic activity,'" Pound says,

> seems to me so much apple-sauce. In so far as the bureaucracy of letters has considered their writing as anything more than a short cut to the feeding trough or a means of puffing up their personal importances, they have done little else for the past thirty years than boost the production of writing about writing, not only as autotelic, but as something which ought to receive more attention from the reading victim than the great books themselves. ("Prefatio Aut Cimicium Tumulus" 389–390)

Eliot contributes, in Pound's estimation, to the decline and fall of international letters, as he is more interested in promoting his "position" than in any program of genuine artistic appreciation. "In the course of his eminently professorial volume," says Pound of Eliot's *Selected Essays*, "he must have mentioned at least forty-five essayists whom tomorrow's readers will be most happy not to hear mentioned, but mention of whom must have contributed enormously to Mr. Eliot's rise to his deserved position as arbiter of British opinion" (390).[7]

As far as Pound is concerned, an essay like "Tradition and the Individual Talent" is written in bad faith. First of all, it "assumes the existence of a culture that no longer subsists and does nothing to prepare a better culture that must or ought to come into being." Such an essay maintains "a system wherein it is possible to receive fifteen guineas for an article of approximately 3,000–4,000 words, in a series to which Mr. Eliot's sensitivity and patience will give lustre and wherein his occasional eminence will shed respectability on a great mass of inferior writing" (393). Finally, Pound suggests that his good friend Eliot uses literature to assert his superiority as an intellectual commodity, just as the mercenary "system" uses him in return—if only to award itself a little invented glory and authority. The best critics, Pound says, "are those who actually cause an amelioration in the art which they criticize," while the worst, no doubt full of passionate intensity, are "the pestilential vermin" who "distract attention *from* the best, either to the second rate, or to hokum, or to their own critical writings. Mr. Eliot probably ranks very high in the first of these . . . groups," admits Pound," and deserves badly of us for his entrance into the last" (391).

These days, those of us who tout ourselves as "revisionary" readers leap to view Eliot in Pound's terms: as the quintessential hollow man, the figurehead of a middle-class (that refuses to see itself so) "modernist" movement so entrenched in selling the status quo that he "quite easily drive[s] a man to the movies" (Pound, "Prefatio" 390). Like Pound, however, we skirt the issue of our own self-promotion as, in the never-ending game of public relations and image bartering, we pick and choose the face Eliot wears to meet the faces that he meets. "It is . . . becoming apparent that a new set of shibboleths have come into play that reinforces the New Critic's Eliot," writes Ronald Bush in "T. S. Eliot and Modernism at the Present Time," "this time not to praise the poet but to bury him." Bush questions this move in much the same terms that Pound questions his old buddy Possum:

> Simplifying, we may identify the source of these pressures with that wing of post-structuralist theory that has come to ascribe to postmodernism more and more of the oppositional values that were once seen as the essence of modernism and consequently has depicted the modernists themselves as homogeneous and reactionary. . . . Eliot is a sitting duck because he himself prepared the ground in the latter phase of his career. Thus we find Fredric Jameson in his book *Fables of Aggression: Wyndham Lewis, the Modernist as Fascist*, blithely identifying Eliot's "aesthetic and political neoclassicism" with Lewis' celebration of Hitler and cautioning us that our admiration of the modernists indicates we live in a time "when new and as yet undeveloped forms of protofascism are in the making around us." (197)

Just as Pound accuses Eliot of blinding himself (and us) to his pernicious influence over and implication in the very low-brow middle-class society he claims to disavow, postmodern readers imply that modernists are, at best, naïve in their investment in

Eliot's philosophy and poetics. Dare to admire Eliot's work and you are guilty of the same paternalist prejudices.

During my preliminary examinations, I confronted a question that, though brief, implied that this set of shibboleths poses an ethical imperative for any modernist scholar. No reader of Eliot can ignore his unpleasant personality—his self-created social position, his conservative politics, his personal life and motivations, or the impact of any one of these has on the methods of critical reading and writing he promotes. No reader can ignore the dangers of being implicated in Eliot's unpleasantness, either. The question reads:

> If modernism is sometimes characterized in recent revisionary criticism as the literature of "dead white males," Eliot is often regarded as the whitest and deadest (though not the malest). How would you go about justifying the teaching and valorizing of Eliot in such a critical climate?

Immediately, I found myself caught on a double-edged sword, as teaching is conflated (at least in this context) with valorizing. My tentative answer to the question mirrored Coyle's and Cowan's call for the proper historicizing of modernism and its proponents. At the same time, my response was—by necessity—personal; the persuasive dangers of Eliot's scientific analogies and metaphors are plain to me, as a female reader and a graduate student subordinate to a complex academic hierarchy, and as a would-be writer hoping to make her own place in what appears to be an environment hostile to such endeavors. Clearly, I must differentiate my methodology and readings from Eliot's, making it clear that Eliot is the object, rather than the subject, of my critical studies and that he will remain so in the classroom. And I must assert that, though I may have been influenced by his work while developing as a writer, I have suffered my own awakening along the way. I do not identify, in any way, with Eliot's poetic project or persona. No one wants to be identified, even as an unwitting participant, in a new and improved protofascism.

And so I argued that we must re-evaluate Eliot's work (and, by implication, Eliot's life) in the light of developments in critical and philosophical thinking—that we must draw crucial lines between critical reading and valorizing, investigation and advocacy. Eliot orders a writer to position him/herself in a critical and historical framework, and to be aware that his/her attempt to refashion or recreate that tradition represents only another voice in the wilderness. Taking the post-structuralist party line, I suggested that critical readers must be subject to the same demands. It is not only critical to review and re-evaluate Eliot's poetry and criticism against the detailed backdrop of the debates and concerns of his own time, but to carry on this re-reading using current methodologies and readings. It is also crucial, I added, that we acknowledge our own stake in such methodologies: that we take account of our own investment in the subject.

This project of anthropological or archaeological sifting sounds easy enough. But, as I acknowledged in my preliminary exam, the practice of it is strewn with land mines. My own attempts to encourage students to look at Eliot's assumptions about the divine nature of tradition and the supposedly universal culture it under-writes—and to see the dead forefathers who underlie it—proved as threatening as the voracious character of Beloved in Toni Morrison's novel of the same name, a work which the students rejected as "incomprehensible" and just plain "bad." (In contrast, they accepted Eliot's *Waste Land* as "literature," despite their inability to "get it.") *Beloved* does some of the same work of the post-structuralist reading: it fractures the academic calm that lingers in Eliot's substantial wake. By compelling us to expose and review cultural motives, methods and results, Morrison's novel throws into relief the constructed nature of Eliot's naturalized tradition or genealogical schema and—even more frightening—questions the very same "nature" of our own subjectivity and authority. Thus, reading a novel like *Beloved* against Eliot's *Waste Land* and the prose that prepares us for it unravels Eliot's fantasies about the divine Word of poetry and the Ideal Order that it creates. In a sense, then, *Beloved* and other post-structuralist readings signal the demise of Eliot's God.

Here's where our own critical blindness or prejudice enters in. Even as we insist on a particularized reading of ourselves and Morrison in contemporary classrooms and academic discussions, we generalize about Eliot and his "generation" of writers—forgetting that works like the *Waste Land* and "Tradition and the Individual Talent" are, by our own admission, expressions of private desires and prohibitions. Eliot's God and Eliot's hell are not synonymous with modernism's or fascism's God, or even with postmodernism's Satan—in fact, such singularity is impossible from our enlighted perspective. It is necessary, Pound reminds us, "to distinguish between Eliot registering his belief *re* a value, and Eliot ceding to the bad, not to say putrid habits of the bureaucracy which has surrounded him" ("Prefatio" 397). Yet in current critical debates Eliot's peculiar beliefs and values are more often than not seen as exemplary of the "putrid habits" of the middle-class ideology that supported and surrounded him. (Pound, on the other hand, a self-proclaimed protofascist, is less often impaled on the postmodern spike. Ronald Bush prefaces his remarks about postmodern revisions of modernism, in fact, by listing some of the latter genre's res-cued figures; Pound is prominent among them.)

It is impossible to ignore Eliot's private life, his regrettable eccentricities and neuroses, because they not only help to fashion his poetic and the social imperative he eventually derives from it, and influence the course of his work, but (apparently) result in a "type" of reading and critical reaction which we are now attempting to kill for the last time. We resurrect Eliot in order to make an example of him, to eschew the attitudes and habits he "represents." Indeed, he is the Guy Fawkes of the millennium, as his personality becomes the emptied soul of a despised American middle-class.

It would appear that what we "hate" most about Eliot is how he handled his mid-life crisis. We cannot forgive him for his religious "conversion" and the implications it had for his poetic and social criticism. Our investigations of Eliot's queer masculinity and masochistic Christianity, as well as our exhumations of his disastrous marriage and sexual relations, end up in a loathing for Eliot's self-abnegating rebirth that feels quite a bit like the infidel's defensiveness. Milan Kundera's wry portrayal of the young lyric poet, Jaromil, in *Life Is Elsewhere,* captures cogently the potential source of our revulsion and (perverse) abandonment as we confront Eliot's series of conversions, especially his last. We read in Eliot's lyrical masochism and pessimism, as might Kundera, an overwhelming egotism: "An obsessive longing for admiration is not a vice appended to the poet's talents (as may be true of a mathematician or an architect); rather, it is part of the very essence of the lyrical temperament, it virtually defines the lyrical poet: the poet is he who shows his self-portrait to the world in the hope that the face projected upon the screen by his poetry will be loved and worshipped" (214).

We see Eliot's conversion and self-abasement as cries for attention, attempts to escape from the sexual "difficulties" of his private hell, just as Kundera describes young Jaromil's attempts to write lyric poetry as attempts to mitigate sexual inexperience and revise reality. Jaromil's masturbatory fantasies of power are transmuted into semi-ecstatic visions that rival Eliot's image of the Hyacinth girl: "He didn't long for the nudity of a girlish body; he longed for a girlish face illumined by the nudity of her body. He didn't long to possess a girl's body; he longed to possess the face of a girl who would yield her body to him as proof of her love. The body was beyond the bounds of his experience, and for that very reason it became the subject of countless poems" (111). Like Eliot, Jaromil uses poetry to transform the womb "into an airy conceit of fanciful dreams" (111).

Eliot's religious fantasies about the bodiless Lady in white in *Ash Wednesday* and the *Four Quartets* fulfill the same functions as Jaromil's fanciful adolescent poetry. But we react against these fantasies with more vehemence than we do against, say, Pablo Neruda's equally idyllic fantasies of the dismembered woman in his *Twenty Love Poems* or D. H. Lawrence's infamous, self-denying women in "love." Perhaps, as the reactions against *Tom and Viv* suggest, we find ourselves implicated in Eliot's gynephobia and misanthropy. We translate his embrace of the Anglican church into a loathing for what is outside of that "purity"—for what he implies (as in the essay on Marie Lloyd) that *we* represent as members of an amorphous "middle class" . . . i.e. as Americans.

Our vehement rejection of the place Eliot seems to have set up for us in the poetic contract reveals, ironically, the power of his—and others'—poetic pronouncements. If poetry is a moribund art in contemporary society (as Eliot fears it is becoming), then his conservative pronouncements in the 1940s and 50s are now moot/mute points. Yet Eliot's impersonal poetic and visions of intellectual holocaust continue to haunt current discussions. In fact, as Kundera might argue, a poet like Eliot uses his private emotions to create a fantasy which he intends to be representative of reality. Though this fantasy is intended, primarily to make up "for the lack of dramatic action" in his own life (Kundera 213), we tend to see these confessions as universal reflections or even imperatives. There is something intensely manipulative in the poet's incarnation: "We suspect that the poet sometimes squeezes his heart with the same detachment as a housewife squeezing a lemon over her salad" (Kundera 212–213). The result is depressing. Kundera's Jaromil, like Eliot at the end of the twentieth century, turns out to be "a person who [is] uninterestingly odd rather than oddly interesting" (214).

What we find compelling, at the present moment, is Eliot's closely guarded private life. We suspect him of personal motives and eschew his attempts to universalize or depersonalize them even as we admit their power over our cultural imagination.[8] Lyndall Gordon, for instance, argues that Eliot used three pivotal women— Vivien Haigh-Wood, Emily Hale and Mary Trevelyan—to work through private demons. "Looking back on his life," she says, "there had been two attitudes to women: grim contempt and reverence for an ethereal Lady" (*Eliot's New Life* 242). "He could be 'stirred up' by a lovable woman," Gordon writes, "but, because of his state of mind, was unable to develop this feeling into a stable commitment. His attraction to a particular woman warred with his general idea that all women are 'unclean creatures'. His solution is to find refuge in an 'ambiguous relation'" (49).

We view the terminal point of that "ambiguous relation" as Eliot's commitment to the Church of England. Gordon suggests that Eliot identified each of the women in his life with a phase of his religious journey or transformation. "Only through the poetry do we see the whole man," she writes, "for whom the important ties were those that served religious emotion by generating some feeling—it might be horror, it might be ardour—strong enough, extreme enough, to open him to 'vibration beyond the range of ordinary men'" (ENL 101). Eliot used women, Gordon argues, and particularly Vivien, to continue the martyr's dance of "reckless surrender" to the flame. Vivien served to embody his notions of sin and temptation. Eliot finally sloughs off Vivien through conversion: "As Eliot's works put aside the distractions of worldliness for self-contemplation, real women are replaced by abstractions, ideal beneficence or hellish torment" (ENL 68). Certainly, that seems to be Hastings' thesis in *Tom and Viv*.

After Vivien, Gordon says, Eliot turned to Emily Hale to experience a pure state of platonic worship. Emily serves as Eliot's sacrificial virgin (and thus as his strongest point of identification). When Vivien dies and Eliot is once again, even according to his own stringent spiritual standards, free to marry, Eliot terminates his relationship with Hale—which she has begun to see as heading (through long years of obedience and patience) toward marriage. This rejection calls into question the motivations behind Eliot's social and religious poetry: "He had to atone for his abandonment of Vivien and try to expunge the taint left by their marriage," Gordon says. "There was an increasing conviction that nothing must impinge on this ordeal. What Emily perhaps did not fully measure was Eliot's concern with pain, his need, more pressing than the need to love, to recast pain as a dark night of the soul" (ENL 50).

Finally, Eliot turns to Mary Trevelyan. If Eliot is, as Gordon says, the "master detective" of the human soul and "the incarnation of Holmes: aloof, solitary, trusting no one but the faithful Watson," then Mary plays Eliot's faithful Watson, "the uninspired but worthy confidante, rather worldly in outlook, to whom could be trusted the more mundane details of a great enterprise" (Gordon, ENL 196). When Mary violates the strict boundaries of their platonic "contract," Eliot chastises her severely. Twice she asks Eliot to marry her, only to be rebuffed through the mails. Coldly, Eliot arranges to marry his second wife (secretary Valerie Fletcher) without telling Mary or long-time roommate, John Haywood.

As Americans, we like to read this personal usury as individualistic rather than cultural. It is Eliot's sin to use women to play out his own spiritual fantasies, not ours. As we re-evaluate his impact on American and international modernism, we are careful to stress Eliot's perversities and self-imposed exile. Our readings dwell on, even create, Eliot's difference from the American norm. His famous snobbery becomes our redemption.

On the other side of the Atlantic, Gordon calls attention to Eliot's particularly American approach to life and work as she compares him to Henry James, another eccentric American expatriate. Tellingly, Gordon calls Eliot "a loner in the American tradition of cranky loners" who "wished to express feelings that were savage and strange, like the mystical hatred that is close to madness" (ENL 235).

> The dominant forms of American writing, soul history and sermon, give a curious backing to Eliot's impenetrability. He shares with Emerson, Thoreau, Whitman, and Dickinson a guarded mode of confession. . . . Their confessions, like *The Waste Land*, are fragmentary, and, left so deliberately incomplete, demand a reciprocal effort. The point lies not in their content so much as in the act of self-discovery and judgement. Its ultimate purpose is not to expose the speaker but to create the reader. (234–35)

Gordon describes Eliot's vision of friendship as Emerson's: "The notion of friendship based on use . . ., the notion of a man inwardly alone, essentially independent of all ties . . . a state of mind that verges on oblivion to all others" (199). And Gordon contends that Eliot inherits Hawthorne's pessimism when it comes to investigating the human spirit: "Both share the Calvinist presumption—Hawthorne regretfully, Eliot savagely—that man's nature is fundamentally depraved" (ENL 32). This sense of Eliot's emotional savagery, as well as his uncanny American heritage, condemns him for us.[9] While we are put off by Eliot's ambivalent relation to the role/right of the prophet, his reliance on the "classic American sermon, the Jeremiad" as he deplores the decline and fall of civilization (often at the hands of the woman) condemns us in turn (Gordon, ENL 41).

The idea that Eliot plays out his personal dramas on a large scale annoys us; more hideous is the thought that such private traumas are read as public. Eliot's Puritanical dealings with women reveal a set of neuroses that we refuse to identify as cultural. Further, Eliot's ongoing project—to write a poetry of "witness," a poetry that unifies rather than divides the people it "represents"—inflames a series of American generations raised to reject Eliot's proto-modernist moves as exclusionary and foreign. Yet, at least through his conversion, Eliot resists his exile as he strives, particularly through his drama, to reconnect himself with what Czeslaw Milosz calls "the human family" (28). If it does nothing else, Eliot's embrace of the church ensures that he will be (at least in the afterlife) rejoined with a timeless human family.

Milosz ascribes the enduring schism between modern poets and this human family to "the issue of the poets' anxiety," which has everything to do with masculinity and social power, he says. According to Milosz, this poetic anxiety seizes poets such as Eliot as soon as they encounter "the man in the street": "at such moments they have sensed their own refinement, their 'culture,' which has made them incomprehensible; thus they have felt potentially subject to the mockery of the common man, who found their occupation unmanly" (30). Eliot's Prufrock is the modern poet who cannot ingratiate himself with the common man or woman because the result is "not good, for poetry does not accord with such forced operations" (30).

Contemporary poets, critics and readers want to see anxieties about masculinity and social class as peculiar to Eliot; we rush to separate themselves from the taint of association. But Milosz claims we're still experiencing this "phenomenon" in the United States, particularly as we make poetry an academic institution. The explosion of MFA and Ph.D. programs devoted to poetry writing produce both writers and readers for the genre, but this has not improved the status of verse in popular culture.

> The proliferation of poets and students' interest in poetry should not veil the fact that behind all of this there is a mutual hostility between the elite and the ordinary citizens, one that perhaps has not diminished since the time of the French *poètes maudits*. (Milosz 30–31)

Eliot's early poetry, most salient in anthologies of modern literature, emphasizes his anxiety about masculinity, power and the lower class. The Sweeney poems, for instance, make graphic Eliot's fears about "primitive" sexuality; paired with "The Love Song of J. Alfred Prufrock," Eliot's stereotypical fears as the "unmanly" poet are difficult to ignore. It is not until he writes *Old Possum's Book of Practical Cats*, and then his drawing-room dramas (such as *The Cocktail Party*) that Eliot tries to "lower himself" to his audience's level. Admittedly, critics of the plays find Eliot's attempts to ingratiate himself with such audiences condescending at best. But in poems such as *Ash Wednesday*, we see Eliot groping for connection, as opposed to those moments of deliberate disconnection which characterize the Sweeney poems, "Prufrock" and "Hysteria."

We might see the "common" reader's anxiety as opposed to the poet's uneasiness about masculinity and power. In an elemental zero-sum game, power is a singular commodity; one man's or woman's seizure of that power is predicated on another man's or woman's loss of it. For Eliot to assert his connection "the human family," there must be some loss. Perhaps we view his attempts to reconnect as an attack on our own uncertain "subjectivity" as American citizens, as a threat to our borders. His overt denial of masculinity and power, then, threatens the illusion of American machismo—if we accept him as part of our "human" family, that is. Thus we don't hesitate to call attention to Eliot's expatriate status, or to read his plays as peculiarly faux-British in flavor. What's more, we make much of the fact that Eliot converts to the Church of England, rejecting his Unitarian heritage (for Unitarian, read "reasonable" or "practical"; for Anglican, read "Anglo-Catholic").

We object, surely, to Eliot's religious program, reacting to it as vaguely anti-American, more than a little coercive, and unequivocally suspect as far as the individual, "pull-yourself-up-by-the-bootstraps," democratic way is concerned. The unspoken accusation of much contemporary Eliot criticism is against Eliot's reliance on religion (rather than reason, sexuality or idealism) in order to recreate an essential communication between poet and audience. Eliot's infamous surrender to the Word and God—his "romantic" imposition, couched in "objective" terms—seems to us an oppressively conservative imperative. Ironically enough, Eliot takes it for a revolutionary stance: "For Eliot, to invoke the Order of Things in the midst of twentieth-century chaos, to insist on self-discipline in the face of a permissive society, to be, in short, a Critic (in poetry no less than in speeches) was to take a revolutionary line" (Gordon, *Eliot's New Life* 236).

Milosz, like Eliot, writes about the purpose of poetry from the pulpit of the Charles Eliot Norton Lecture series at Harvard. But he contrasts his own post-World War II aesthetic with what he sees as Eliot's and Pound's idealistic representations of the past, which he sees as representative of modernist assumptions and fantasies. This past, exemplified by nineteenth century French social structure, separates art from the public. As Milosz describes it, once "neither workers nor peasants were counted among the consumers of art,"

> what remained was the bourgeoisie with its bad taste . . . For the bohemians that class became an object of hatred, and they regarded writing as an activity directed against it. . . . The separation of art and the public has been an accomplished fact ever since. In various schools and manifestoes of the twentieth cen-

tury there was a division into two camps: on one side those who earn and spend, with their cult of work, their religion and patriotism, and, on the other, the bohemians whose religion is art and whose morality is the negation of all values recognized by the other camp. . . . In Europe, since the middle of the nineteenth century, the poet has been an alien, an asocial individual, at best a member of a subculture. (27–28)

This trend, Milosz suggests, we see repeated now in the United States as an elite corps of artists strive to recreate a "pure" poetry (Milosz counts Eliot among this group). Thus, at least according to Milosz, we are guilty of the same anxieties and imputations of difference that we accuse Eliot of indulging. Simply put, we have transformed Eliot's and Pound's supposedly idealistic representations of the past into negative terms. The past, in our equations, is dark and monstrous. Thus, though we question the nature of culture and its imperatives, expose and deconstruct its careful "monuments," and pick apart the ideology of what we call the ruling elite, we read Eliot as an uncomplicated member of the bourgeoisie. His cult of work, his devotion to religion, and his patriotism are all moral outrages for new bohemians.

Clearly, we do not want to be connected or even reconnected with T. S. Eliot— there is not even a monument to him in St. Louis, the city of his birth. In fact, his childhood home has been razed to make way for a parking lot.

Douglas describes the evolution of religious ritual and recoil in *Purity and Danger*: "The long history of Protestantism witnesses to the need for continual watch on the tendency of ritual form to harden and replace religious feeling," she writes (61). She could be writing about our rekindled sense of Eliot's criminality, his rigidity and anal obsessions with control, which we attempt to tie to his renunciation of American citizenship and his conversion to the Church of England. Douglas explains:

> So long as Christianity has any life, it will never be time to stop echoing the parable of the Pharisee and the Publican, to stop saying that external forms can become empty and mock the truths they stand for. With every new century we become heirs to a longer and more vigorous anti-ritualist tradition.
> . . . The Evangelical movement has left us with a tendency to suppose that any ritual is empty form, that any codifying of conduct is alien to natural movements of sympathy, and that any external religion betrays true internal religion. (61)

As *Tom and Viv* so vividly testifies, we see Eliot as exactly this "alien," this unnatural ritualist. As he walks, alone, on the beach, leaving his distraught bride to wail and rend her garments in the devastated hotel room, we are presented with the image of a man emptied of human feeling: a form which he commemorates and immortalizes in "Prufrock." And when, in a memorably loaded scene, Eliot embraces his

Bishop friend around the surplice and sobs "Oh what shall I do, what shall I do?" into the man's groin, we are certain Tom has betrayed his "true internal religion" for an empty form.

Douglas attributes our recoil from this rigid ritualizer, this seeker after masculine purity and the Ideal Order, to our perhaps unearned sense of rational superiority. We count ourselves immune to what we perceive as Eliot's neuroses. As Douglas describes it, we see rituals of pollution and purification—such as those we ascribe to Eliot's conversion—as unthinking reactions against reality. She writes:

> [I]t may seem that in a culture [here we could insert the word "individual"] which is richly organised by ideas of contagion and purification the individual is in the grip of iron-hard categories of thought which are heavily safeguarded by rules of avoidance and by punishments. It may seem impossible for such a person to shake his own thought free of the protected habit-grooves of his culture. How can he turn round upon his own thought-process and contemplate its limitations? (5)

Yet self-questioning appears to be one of Eliot's most enduring projects, as his visions and revisions, even in the contested essays, reveal. Why then do we insist on redefining Eliot as a blind bigot? Why are we unable, at the same time, to question our own motives and thought processes as we make Eliot into a rigid villain, or to see how we repeat some of the same moves of pollution and purification as we expel Eliot from consideration? In a very real sense, Eliot poses as a literary Hitler in our discussions and revisions of the twentieth-century literary canon: his quirks are compelling, fascinating, annihilating; his prejudices are mythological and thus frightening; his figure distorts the critical lens. (Douglas is quick to point out that we are often guilty of the same blindnesses as those we claim afflict the poor souls we deem to be outside of our system.)

Douglas' thesis is that we, too, are caught up in the same symbolic systems as the "primitives" Eliot and his cohorts studied—divisions between primitive and modern, or modern and postmodern (or even post-postmodern) are just further ways of "tidying" a system that is certainly chaotic, even at war with itself. As she puts it:

> ideas about separating, purifying, demarcating and punishing transgressions have as their main function to impose system on an inherently untidy experience. It is only by exaggerating the difference between within and without, above and below, male and female, with and against, that a semblance of order is created. (4)

A culture reacts against ambiguity or anomaly—anything outside of the accepted norm—by representing it as "dirt" or pollution. In *Tom and Viv*, Eliot is the definitive dirtbag, the bottom-feeder who rises to the top of the pond on the backs of the more worthy. Perhaps he is even the cause of Vivien's persistent illnesses. In Cynthia Ozick's terms, Eliot can only be remembered as the bourgeoisie contaminant of modern poetry, an adolescent brain fever.

Douglas describes how a culture creates a set of particular "provisions" designed to control pollution, to keep it within (or without) boundaries. We might settle on one or another interpretation of an ambiguous quantity or physically control anomaly through, for example, extermination. On the other hand, we might make it a habit to avoid anomalous things by cementing definitions and categories, thus establishing how they do not conform. Finally, we might label anomalous events as taboo or use ambiguous symbols in ritual "for the same ends as they are used in poetry and mythology"—to amplify existing meaning or to open up other levels of existence, as in Eliot's mystical poetry (Douglas 39–40).

In fact, we deal with Eliot in many of these ways, as he serves as a pollutant that must be purified through exposure and/or extermination. We "interpret" Eliot's ambiguous relations and behavior according to iron-clad rules of social conduct; we attempt to exclude Eliot—or his anomalous behavior—from our schema; we avoid thinking about, writing about, or replicating Eliot's politics and label them "dangerous"; and we use Eliot himself as an ambiguous symbol in complex rituals related to history, poetry, aesthetics, and critical theory.

If we turn to Julia Kristeva's sense of the abject as "what disturbs identity, system, order"—what Douglas calls pollution—and as such what we call the "feminine," we can see how movies like *Tom and Viv* are attempts to deal with Eliot's ambiguity or anomaly by re-creating identity, order and system over and against him (*Powers* 4). We do not want to be associated with Eliot's brand of death and worship, with his femininity, his maternality. But our revulsion is fueled by our very likeness to him, as Kristeva explains. The abject

> is experienced at the peak of its strength when that subject, weary of fruitless attempts to identify with something on the outside, finds the impossible within; when it finds that the impossible constitutes its very *being*, that it *is* none other than abject. (Powers 5)

In order to purify ourselves of this taint, we must either destroy ourselves or project that impossibility onto another . . . and destroy her/him.

René Girard explores the cultural or collective persecution of the "victim" for the group's sins in *The Scapegoat*. We persecute the victim who commits crimes that serve to eliminate difference, he says. "Despite what is said around us persecutors are never obsessed by difference," Girard writes, "but rather by its unutterable contrary . . ." (22). Do we really persecute Eliot as we expose (rightly, in many cases) his own persecutions of such "victims" as Vivien and Emily Hale, or the Jews, or the working and middle classes? And do all of us call Eliot onto the carpet and attempt to exterminate his mythological status? Obviously not, since readers such as Anthony

Lane accuse *Tom and Viv* of taking an innocent Eliot, and his legion of admirers, to a mean-spirited slaughter.

Girard's discussion of the scapegoat mechanism accounts, in part, for Eliot's ambiguous status as a victim/villain: "Medieval and modern persecutors do not worship their victims, they only hate them. They are therefore easy to identify as victims. It is more difficult to spot the victim in the supernatural being who is a cult object," he says (38). Though Eliot is not, by any measures, "supernatural," he is accorded the status of a cult object (whether positive or negative) in discussions of literary culture. Cynthia Ozick's visceral reaction to Eliot's fame and fortune, for instance, poses as evidence of his continuing notoriety.

Girard accounts, as well, for the unconscious (or unexamined) nature of our own persecutions. We are fighting the good fight as we pillory Eliot as a hollow man. As Girard explains,

> persecutors believe in the guilt of their victim; they are imprisoned in the illusion of persecution that is not a simple idea but a full system of representation. Imprisonment in this system allows us to speak of an unconscious persecutor, and the proof of his existence lies in the fact that those in our day who are the most proficient in discovering other people's scapegoats, and God knows we are past masters at this, are never able to recognize their own. Almost no one is aware of his own shortcoming. We must question ourselves if we are to understand the enormity of the mystery. Each person must ask what his relationship is to the scapegoat. I am not aware of my own, and I am persuaded that the same holds true for my readers. We have only legitimate enmities. And yet the entire universe swarms with scapegoats. The illusion of persecution is as rampant as ever. . . (40–41)

Girard goes on to describe how, in the Middle Ages, saints such as St. Sebastian (who modeled for Eliot's Narcissus) served as the magnet for pestilence and disease, sparing the people who acknowledged or worshiped him. "There is affinity between Saint Sebastian and the arrows," explains Girard, "or rather the pestilence; the faithful hope that his presence in their churches will attract the wandering arrows to him and spare them. Saint Sebastian is offered as the preferred target for the malady; he is brandished like the serpent of brass in front of the Hebrews" (60–61). Like Saint Sebastian, Saint Eliot "protects" contemporary audiences from contamination "as long as he monopolizes and incarnates the plague" (Girard 61).

What is the plague that Eliot carries? Is it gynephobia? Fascism? Anti-Semitism? Royalism or conservatism? Religious fervor? Delusions of aristocratic grandeur? Impotence? Modernism? All of the above? It would appear, at least to this reader, that Eliot's plague is essentially American. In this way, Eliot plays his favorite role— the pose he dared never speak aloud. As readers, we demand Eliot's crucifixion.

Yet Eliot is continually read as an American, and his symptoms catalogued as peculiar to this country. Gordon's apologetic moves are fairly familiar. We have to admire Eliot, she says, as one in the tradition of the American Jeremiad. Even in *Tom and Viv*, Eliot is never quite assimilated into the "old world" that we would like to see him inhabiting. England, too, disavows a permanent connection to him. Instead, his difference from Vivien, her brother and other European characters such as Virginia Woolf is asserted through his obvious masquerade: his fake accent, his stiff-legged walk and zombie poses (at times, it seems as if he's reading from a teleprompter). Vivien may be crazy, the movie suggests, but at least she's real. She has the energy to throw her hat into the air, to lie back in a boat in a fevered embrace, to threaten Virginia Woolf with a rubber knife, to fly off at the proverbial handle. Maurice Haigh-Wood may be an inveterate dummy, a doofus in cricket uniform and khaki, but at least he loves sister and country. At least he's capable of guilt. The British find their own rituals of exclusion and scapegoating, in other words.

Over a recent dinner, David Antin, an American "talk" poet, identifies what he considers the key to reading and understanding Eliot: "You have to remember that he was always just a boy from St. Louis," he says. Eric Sigg anticipates this contextualization of the often difficult and eccentric poet for his Cambridge audience. Sigg sets up his study of Eliot's work *before* 1927 by calling it exemplary of *The American T. S. Eliot*. Sigg claims to bring to the forefront precisely this aspect of Eliot's famous personality and personal poetry—"my remarks assume about Eliot, his career, and his writing what ought to be obvious about them but which has received insufficient attention despite Eliot's own acknowledgements on this score." Sigg elaborates:

> I refer to his American—distinctly, self-consciously, irrevocably American— heritage. The ambivalence pervading his writing, his surprising and sometimes bizarre opinions on diverse subjects, his theoretical inconsistencies, and the relations—both continuities and gaps—between his critical dicta and poetic practice: these troublesome matters, and perhaps less demonstrably many of the beautiful and striking qualities of his poetry, partake of American facts and traditions insofar as Eliot preserved or overthrew them. (viii)

Apparently, it takes a "foreign" consciousness to see what is essentially American in Eliot. Sigg implies that Eliot's early expatriation is itself quintessentially American, an American response to an intolerable situation in the arts and intellectual life. "Such exiles represent the casualties of the country's nervously experimental nature, of its sense of social incompletion, of its unexamined sense of what it is," Sigg concludes (viii). Sigg's reading of Eliot becomes, in these final introductory paragraphs, a wide-screen interpretation, even analysis, of the "youthful" America itself. As the self-styled exile, Eliot represents his country: "That it rebels against its own past and against its own identity," Sigg says of the United States, "wishing to keep its future open-ended, makes American culture unique, but also uniquely vulnerable and perhaps uniquely ill at ease. Into this permanently paradoxical society Eliot matured, and out of it his ambivalences grew" (viii).

The thought that Eliot might represent us is chilling at best for any reader at the present moment. As furor about Eliot's recently published notebooks whips mainstream critics into a frenzy of editorial writing, the "facts" about the case boil down to a catalogue of Eliot's most embarrassing cultural sins. As Michiko Kakutani comments in a March 1997 *New York Times* piece, youthful jottings reveal Eliot's early development as well as "what previously published poems have already made perfectly clear: that Eliot was a bigot who regarded Jews, blacks, women and the working class with fear and contempt."

The best of all worlds would be to cast Eliot, permanently, as the man without a country, the Guy Fawkes of the modernist's unfettered (unmoored) world. Or to put a definitive stop to his cyclical resurrection and lynching. Then his conservatism, his conversions, his anxieties and neuroses, his tendency to suck up to the powers that be in the hopes of catching a few scraps, his impotent attempts to fit into high-brow society, even his unmanly masquerades and foppish poses, wouldn't define us. He could exist or die outside of our zealously guarded boundaries and we would be free, finally, of his American plague.

Afterword

W HEN I DEFENDED THIS WORK IN 1997, HEATED CRITICAL DEBATE ABOUT Eliot's life—his conservative political and social views, his so-called "impersonal poetics," his potential fascism, his misogyny and racial prejudice—consumed the popular imagination. Now, as the last millennium fades into the next, "Eliot subsists mostly as a toppled icon: the source of a handful of indelible phrases, a venerable addition to academic bibliographies, reliable sustenance for the literary jackals who practice the indelicate art of diminution-through-biography," Roger Kimball writes.

Yet Eliot's image, or at least his work, receives new institutional veneration. In a 1998 *Time* article, noted Harvard literary critic Helen Vendler announces Eliot as the Poet of the Century. Certainly, Eliot remains a highly vexed figure in our popular and critical imaginations, the cathexis of a cluster of charged and contradictory emotions, especially in the American academy. If, as I suggest in my last chapter, Eliot serves us as a cultural scapegoat, we have not yet cleansed ourselves of the contagion we see in him.

Eliot's anti-Semitism takes a front seat in debates about the poet's declining reputation and serves as compelling evidence in a case to dismiss Eliot from a new university canon. Since Anthony Julius's guilty verdict, critics and readers find themselves called upon to side with or against Eliot on the issue of racial hegemony. Most of Eliot's readers, even his adherents, admit that his work is, at times, frankly anti-Semitic, but those who want to recuperate Eliot emphasize his work as the "voice of a generation." As such, it reflects, unflinchingly, the attitudes of his intellectual contemporaries, of Anglo-Catholic cohorts, of modern Western consciousness. Thus Eliot is an amalgamation of the best and the worst in his generation, and of our own; he cannot be held accountable for sins that we (still) share.

Eliot's sin in this case seems to be his lack of repentance, his failure to be accountable. Eliot never says he's sorry. "There are many instances of anti-Semitism in literature that seem to me best forgotten," says John Gross in *Commentary*, and "if, in Eliot's case, a guilty verdict still seems called for, it is largely on account of his failure to make amends . . ." Lee Smith, of *The Village Voice*, reminds us that Anthony's study brings nothing new to our critical consciousness, and criticizes, rather, the critical silence that has surrounded Eliot's racial prejudice for so long. Again, accountability seems to be the issue.

The publication of Eliot's early notebooks in *The Inventions of the March Hare* fuels the on-going debate over Eliot's cultural crimes. The wider availability of Eliot's early drafts, doggerel and notes exposes the rootedness of Eliot's less appealing philosophies and politics and provides for them, unfortunately, an American setting and impetus. Though some find Eliot's embryonic work fascinating and delightful, most agree with Michael Donaghy of the *New Statesman* that the recovered work is "wretched" enough to call for a reassessment of the poems "on which the great man's reputation rests" (59). Perhaps Eliot's infamous reticence, his attempts to destroy or sequester these drafts, proves a canny strategy to secure an "immaculate" reputation for as long as possible. Now that the "truth" about Eliot is out, poststructuralist critics of all sorts question Eliot's continued stature as a leading modernist and suggest that further study of his work will simply feed the elitist machine he and his expatriate friends created.

Following on the heels of the film *Tom and Viv*, Carole Seymour-Jones takes as her project Eliot's first, troubled marriage. In a lengthy *Painted Shadow: The Life of Vivienne Eliot, First Wife of T. S. Eliot, Their Marriage, and the Long-Suppressed Truth about Her Influence*, Seymour-Jones obviously acts as Vivien's advocate. Taking Eliot's lead, she argues, critics underestimate Vivien's crucial role in the poet's work, even exaggerate her "madness" to discredit her substantial influence. Seymour-Jones maintains that Eliot's suppressed homosexuality serves as a significant motive for him to incarcerate (and thus eliminate) his much maligned Muse.

Eliot still has his share of fans, of course. Lyndall Gordon has merged and revised *Eliot's Early Years* and *Eliot's New Life* into a comprehensive reflection on Eliot's "single-minded career," *T. S. Eliot: An Imperfect Life* because, she says, "we are now ready to view Eliot from the vantage point of the next century . . . with a keener sense of his strangeness, his prejudice, and extremism" (ix). Gordon hopes that critical readers will learn to see Eliot as a reflection of a familiar collective conscience as she "follow[s] the trials of a searcher whose flaws and doubts speak to all of us whose lives are imperfect" (ix). Ultimately, Gordon hopes to salvage a love for Eliot's work from the understandable outcry against his hatreds. Perhaps, Gordon suggests, the works are "all the greater, in fact, for their admission of failure to match the perfect life" Eliot to which aspired (3).

In *Eliot's Dark Angel: Intersections of Life and Art*, Ronald Schuchard grapples with Eliot's tortured creation process, identifying Eliot's motivating force as an internal "fury" and "muse" who both "caus[es] and conduct[s] the internal drama of shadows and voices that inhabit his acutely personal poems and plays" (3). Schuchard reads Eliot's enduring fascination with St. John of the Cross, Saint Sebastian and other Christian mystics as evidence of the poet's attempts "to represent and control in his art the intensity of his internal conflicts," attempts that inevitably fail, as Eliot is "able to create poems but unable to sublimate passions" (13), and finally unable to escape "that demonic wilderness of the self" (17). This struggle, Schuchard argues, grounds Eliot's poetic in the temperament, spiritual burden and work of late Romantics such as Davidson, Symons, Wilde, and Baudelaire.

Meanwhile, Schuchard justifies the aims of biographical criticism against the lingering stigma cast on the enterprise by New Critics and the corrosive cynicism of postmodernists and poststructuralists. Our disinclination to explore the transformation of life into art "makes criticism of Eliot less humanistic and arresting than it might be," Schuchard asserts, "for our strongest intimation from the first reading is that all [Eliot's] work is intensely personal" (21-22). Ultimately, Schuchard hopes his "cartography" (22) of the intersections between Eliot's art and private life will yield a richer understanding of his work.

Donald J. Childs tackles Eliot's literary reputation, philosophy, ambivalent fascination with mysticism, and private life in *T. S. Eliot: Mystic, Son and Lover*. Childs first situates Eliot in poststructuralist debates as the "seminal influence" in New Criticism, and so necessarily eclipsed by the shadow of the "new new criticism" (x). Childs focuses his study on Eliot's mysticism and describes it as an offensive "unorthodoxy" for poststructuralist readers: "T. S. Eliot's reputation as something of a mystic . . . spells nothing but trouble for his standing in the stock market of literary reputation" (x) since it seems to gather "power in a priesthood guarding the logos within the literary canon" and thus to cement "the tyranny of a logocentric culture that represses difference" (xi). Eliot's proponents and detractors tend to agree, Childs says, that the poet's mystical impulse "represents a version of the logocentric impulse so suspect in a poststructural world" (xv). Childs wants to explore and, to a certain extent, refute this assumption in his study, showing how Eliot's work can be seen as proto-poststructuralist.

Childs describes another strand of inquiry into Eliot's poetics performed by scholars and critics such as Cleo McNelly Kearns, Sanford Schwartz, Walter Benn Michaels, Harriet Davidson, Richard Schusterman, Michael Beehler and James Longenbach. These writers explore Eliot's early work in philosophy, particularly his dissertation, to identify the "latently poststructuralist dimension of his sensibility" (xv) and, one gathers, to recuperate Eliot for the new critical orthodoxy. Childs frames his own discussion with these readings, and begins by discovering in Eliot's first philosophical inquiries a divided consciousness: "Apparently offering intimations of the absolute that resolves all contradictions, Eliot's mystical moments inevitably recall in their very effort to express such intimations . . . the inescapability of difference" (xix).

Childs rounds out his discussion of Eliot's philosophy with the psycho-biological aspect, as he calls it, of Eliot's lived experience. In order to completely understand the development of Eliot's mind, Childs argues, one must investigate the mother-complex Eliot claimed he shared with D. H. Lawrence and also appreciate the "visionary experiences that attended the almost pathological misogyny that developed during his first troubled marriage" (xix).

Colleen Lamos' *Deviant Modernism* explores canonical male modernism as a site of "errancy," arguing that Eliot's works "struggle against identifications and desires that he considered perverse yet that found symptomatic expression within his own texts" (1), such as homoerotic and same-sex desire, or feminine identification. "Eliot is the straight man of modernism, Joyce is its 'ladies' man,' and Proust is its queer fellow" (16), Lamos says, as she seeks to re-examine the "monolithic entity" male modernism poses in the critical imagination by exposing "unresolved struggles" (2) in the writers' works. In an attempt to stitch together poststructuralist and close readings, Lamos suggests that a constructive approach to canonical modernists is "to attend carefully to the particular complexities of their texts in order to gain an understanding of the larger crisis of gender and sexual definition in the early twentieth century" (3). The male modernists Lamos chooses for her study "share the modern problem of a loss of confidence in the status and meaning of masculinity, and consequently of what one might call male hysteria," illustrated by a fear of female power and a "peculiarly modern version of homophobia" that appears as a dread of feminization (9).

"Although Eliot rarely hints at sexual perversion," Lamos writes, "the types of error that he censures are closely implicated with errant sexuality and, more broadly, with transgressions of the social order" (17), and so "Eliot's critical texts are grounded in a disavowal of the very forces that energize them" (18). "Eliot disavows his gender and sexual anxieties, like his Americanness," Lamos says, "subsuming them within a European, patriarchal and anti-Semitic literary tradition; abjuring feminine and queer alterity, he positions himself as the adoptive heir of his self-appointed fathers" (9). Lamos argues that Eliot's early poetry is marked by a kind of matricidal struggle, no doubt because Eliot's attempts to become a poet entailed both a battle with and an identification with his mother, Charlotte Stearns Eliot, herself a poet. Ironically, Eliot does away with the mother by taking her place, Lamos says, and this "inversion" becomes the condition for his poetry. Further, this inversion supplies a "revolutionary" position in Eliot's conservative, early twentieth century milieu: "In a world turned upside down by male effeminacy and female virility, sexual inversion became, and remains, a powerfully charged symbol of social disorder" (Lamos 15).

Richard A. Kaye, in "'A Splendid Readiness for Death': T. S. Eliot, the Homosexual Cult of St. Sebastian, and World War I," deals with Eliot's potential "inversion" as he reads "The Love Song of Saint Sebastian." Kaye suggests that Eliot weaves experiences with his sisters, mother and other women into mortification and eroticism in the abandoned poem. I depend on Kaye's careful study to explore this draft in "'Torture and Delight: T. S. Eliot's Love Song for St. Sebastian," and argue that the difficulty in the poem's point of view comes, perhaps, from a repeated mis-reading. The second stanza in the poem actually represents a second speaker, I sug-gest—the woman who rescues and rehabilitates the half-dead Sebastian—and the poem further illustrates Eliot's fear of female sexuality, his fascination with sadistic and masochistic sexuality, and his identification with the passive (female) partner in such exchanges. Though the poem describes a heterosexual encounter, that is, the role Eliot's speaker adopts is feminine, and so goes against the grain of reading. This may be why the poem proves so difficult to follow.

In "T. S. Eliot's 'Uranian Muse': The Verdenal Letters," James E. Miller, Jr., revisits the subject of *T. S. Eliot's Personal Waste Land.* Miller reads letters from Jean Verdenal, collected in *The Letters of T. S. Eliot,* Volume I, to reiterate that Eliot's *Waste Land* is a confessional, or desiring, poem directed to a male other. Miller uses the *Waste Land* drafts, Verdenal's letters, and biographical information to argue that the poem is an elegy for Verdenal. Miller proposes that the desire expressed in the Hyacinth girl section, as well as the "awful daring of a moment's surrender," should be read as Eliot's homosexual longing for his lost friend.

In contrast, Sebastian Knowles argues that a great part of the *Waste Land* is motivated by Eliot's identification with, and desire for, a woman—specifically Marie Lloyd, the London music hall star. Citing Eliot's use of music hall song lyrics in the poem, as well as comments Eliot makes in his "London Letters" for the *Dial,* Knowles argues that Eliot sees himself in Lloyd and makes her a central player in the poem. Lloyd's legendary bawdiness by inference, her seeming placelessness, her "winks and silences," Knowles says, inform not only the *Waste Land* but Eliot's leg-endary persona. "The *Waste Land's* display of freaks and queens and psychics and hyacinth girls and cockney vaudeville acts gives the opening two sections of the poem, particularly, the format of a variety show," Knowles writes. Knowles's argu-ment fits into a new collection of readings that focus on Eliot's connection to music and popular culture.

In response, perhaps, to the general outcry against Eliot and his politics, some contemporary critics regroup around new critical ideas of the text's supremacy. Roger Kimball, critical of Eliot's literary empire and the culture he attempted to sal-vage, asserts that Eliot's poetry and criticism live on in our imagination without him. His poems serve, Kimball says, as "existential signposts" for his generation and a few following, as "landmarks in modernity's spiritual battle for a survivable culture," and the New Criticism that Eliot helped to launch "once seemed—and perhaps still is—

the most supple, serious, and responsive of any [literary theories] formulated in the twentieth century."

Mary Karr, of Syracuse University, pleads with readers of the *Chronicle of Higher Education* to focus on the vivid *experience* of reading Eliot's *Waste Land* rather than its arcane references or the echoes of elitism it creates in the academy and beyond. "[T]he poem exists as a kind of seminal instant for the aesthetic (and, in some circles, moral) values we espouse," Karr argues, and, as such, offers "totemic powers" to the initiated and new reader. We mustn't let academic squeamishness or laziness prevent us from sharing the poem with students. "[N]ot to read [the *Waste Land*]," Karr says, "is to pretend that we of this 21st century have drawn ourselves whole . . . from our own heads." We should embrace Eliot's complexity as part of his music, of his attempt to capture a disorienting life experience that we are still living, Karr concludes, and "to construct a bulky apparatus of scholarship over the poem can actually obscure it, throw its language out of balance."

Without losing sight of cultural history, new New Critical readers such as Jewel Spears Brooker suggest that we acknowledge all of Eliot—his regrettable prejudices and fears as well as his significant contribution to poetic philosophy—and yet consider the merit of his enduring work. Brooker's T. S. *Eliot and Our Turning World* collects a series of essays covering such topics as Eliot's senses of loss and spiritual hunger, his studies of philosophy and religion, his involvement in the arts, the influence of Dante and Shakespeare on his work, his ties to popular culture (particularly the music hall and radio), the problem of authorship and gender in his work, and recent charges of anti-Semitism. Brooker wants not only to bring our attention back to the poems, and thus to reanimate our appreciation for Eliot's legacy, but to rethink some of the "baggy" tenants of postmodernism that authorize critics to "make moral judgements on the most complex situations in the lives of artists and, moreover, to attach these evaluations to the art itself" (xvi).

Brooker stresses that the critics collected in her volume are quite aware of history and important shifts in critical readings; all of the writers take into account the newly published documents relevant to Eliot's poetry and criticism, and several of them also pay attention to "revised theoretical paradigms in cultural studies" (xvi). Finally, one of the goals of Brooker's project seems to be to refute moralistic rejections to Eliot, including Julius's, by demonstrating the weak and perhaps biased nature of the cases against him.

A group of critics continues to argue that Eliot's poetry represents the voice of a particularly *American* generation. In T. S. *Eliot and American Poetry*, Lee Oser fits Eliot securely into American literary history, close-reading the poet's work through *Four Quartets* to emphasize his connection to Emerson, Whitman, Poe, and Lowell. Oser also points out Charlotte Eliot's significant influence on her son's poetry. To make his argument, Oser stresses the dialogic nature of American poetry as it strives to constitute citizenship; Oser is particularly concerned with what he sees as a shift in American poetics away from a public-oriented medium to "a highly process-oriented, metalinguistic poetry" (xii). Perhaps Oser sees Eliot and American forefathers as correctives to this diversion in poetic consciousness. In hopes of redressing this "wrong," Oser intends his study for "younger readers in particular, who are dissatisfied with our corporate-academic culture, and who want to explore what is good and serviceable in our literary past" (xii).

Like Oser, Denis Donoghue wants to move the discussion of Eliot away from his life and back to his work, and thus to spark renewed respect for the poet's artistry as well as a more sophisticated understanding of the work's shortcomings. If anyone's life should be explored, he implies, it's the reader's. In *Words Alone: The Poet T. S. Eliot*, a study that combines memoir with critical analysis, Donoghue weaves his own experiences with Eliot's work into a description of their imagistic force on the reader. Donoghue takes up Eliot's later religious poetry and examines it for quality of belief, including Eliot's struggles to reconcile physical and spiritual desire, often confessed as disgust with himself and others. Donoghue suggests that Eliot identifies, to a certain extent, with the martyrs and mystics in his early work. Like St. Narcissus, Eliot chooses the desert.

What's clear from even a cursory reading of recent Eliot scholarship is that the discussion has grown larger than the man. The debates that swirl around Eliot and his regrettable personal life and opinions often ignore Eliot's poetry; they seem to be battles between intellectual camps, between fashionable or less-fashionable ways of interpreting what we call reality. As New Criticism struggles to survive on the fringes of poststructuralism, a new millennium—ushered in by the unforgettable cataclysm of September 11, 2001—brings with it a new set of pressing ethical, cultural, and material imperatives. Perhaps Eliot's life will soon cease to amaze and disturb us.

And though some readers declare themselves ready to pitch Eliot from the canon, none can successfully claim that his work has no importance in the current critical and artistic moment. Though Eliot's doctrinal attitudes toward God and others are at times hurtful or repulsive, the poems that echo these attitudes survive despite shifts in critical consciousness, academic power upheavals, new theories of subjectivity, divinity and psychology, changes in government, and terrorist attacks. Eliot's work demands attention, stresses the painful job of stitching meaning from fragments, of moving beyond the self into other realms of experience through images, and at the same time suggests to a careful reader the our need for such striving.

On September 11, 2001, I feared there was no place in the world for poetry. What does poetry do? I asked. What does it make happen? How can it force us to recognize each other as valuable individuals in an interdependent web of existence? How can it teach us transcendence? A few days later, however, I found myself reading aloud from *Four Quartets*, finding solace in Eliot's words as they swirled through the classroom, in his assertion—coming now from my mouth—that "the end is

where we start from," that "we die with the dying" and "are born with the dead: /
See, they return, and bring us with them" (CPP 144), because "[w]ords, after
speech, reach / Into the silence" (CPP 121).

Indeed, there is enduring beauty and reverence in Eliot's poetry, despite the
fears and hatreds that sometimes obsess and motivate the man who writes them.
That man is gone and yet his work lives on and, I hope, will continue to do so
despite academic politics, theoretical fashion, and human fear. Ultimately, Eliot's
suffering *is* art, and thus is not private. His poetry gives us a vision of the Love
"[b]ehind the hands that wove / The intolerable shirt of flame / Which human
power cannot remove" (CPP 144). It reaches into the silence and brings us with it.

September 2002

Notes

NOTE TO THE INTRODUCTION

[1] Eliot spells his wife's name as Vivien. Some of his biographers and critics, Lyndall Gordon among them, spell it as Vivienne. For the sake of clarity, I have adopted Eliot's spelling throughout the dissertation, including passages by Gordon and others. It would be worthwhile—though not germane to this project—to investigate the variation.

NOTES TO CHAPTER 1

[1] Eliot's readers and writers are always gendered male. It is certainly instructive to read Eliot's work against the grain—that is, as a woman—but for the purposes of this close-reading I will use the masculine pronoun as a way of getting closer to Eliot's vision of the poet and his reader as, inherently, male.

[2] It is worth mentioning that Kaja Silverman and Eliot focus on the same image: Mantenga's arrow-infested St. Sebastian. Silverman uses a reproduction of the painting on the cover of her study, repeating the image at the start of her chapter entitled "Masochism and Male Subjectivity," a section devoted to a discussion of moral or Christian masochism. Harvey Gross shows, in "The Figure of St. Sebastian," that the figures Eliot says that he studied include, and center on, Mantenga's portrait.

[3] See Tom Matthews' brief discussion of the poem's significance in this respect in his biography *Great Tom: Notes Toward the Definition of T. S. Eliot*. Matthews uses the poem, particularly the image of the caught fish—"slippery white belly held tight in his own fingers, / Writhing in his own clutch" and the fact that Narcissus is "stifled and soothed by his own rhythm"—as evidence that Eliot masturbated in his adolescence and felt excessive guilt about it. Matthews suggests that Eliot's sexual experimentation is not eccentric so much as his reactions to those experiences, com-

paring Eliot to the "typical" male teenager as he comments on Eliot's excessive guilt and impulse for atonement.

[4] Notes to *Poems Written in Early Youth* reinforce our sense of the poem's uncertain and/or ambiguous genesis, positing the time of composition quite roughly—between 1911 and 1915. This implies, at the very least, that Eliot agonized for a good four years over the poem's composition and content—or that he was loathe to let go of it, despite negative or indifferent reactions from his readers.

[5] I am indebted to Herbert Schneidau for this ascetic vision of Pound's *Waste Land*, as well as for the idea that one could read the long poem itself as typical Eliotic "bizarrerie": a strained, surrealistic confession.

[6] Hereafter, references to Lyndall Gordon's *Eliot's Early Years* will be designated by EEY.

[7] As this is an unfinished draft, published in Eliot's *Letters*, I have included all of his editorial marks and marginal comments. In some cases, his slips are revealing.

[8] This part of the myth not only introduces the "narrator" or collective consciousness of Eliot's *Waste Land*, Tiresias, but also anticipates some of the water and rape imagery in the long poem. Lirope is a "naiad of the river / . . . whom the river-god, Cephisus / Embraced and ravished in his watery dwelling" (III, 342–44), and Narcissus is their "love" child. This genealogy recalls the river's broken tent in "The Fire Sermon," as well as the departed nymphs. Near the end of "The Fire Sermon," a disembodied nymph recounts her rape on the river: " . . . By Richmond I raised my knees / Supine on the floor of a narrow canoe." Though this passage has often been interpreted as an allusion to Eliot's unsatisfactory marriage to Vivien Haigh-Wood (and his supposed "guilt" over a sexual encounter with her before that marriage), it could also be interpreted as another of Eliot's confessional moments. Like "The Death of Saint Narcissus," the *Waste Land* mingles didactic social commentary with personal angst, often confusing the two. It's unclear when Eliot is accusing and when he's confessing. Narcissus, in both Ovid's Eliot's poems, is victim and victimizer, rapist and ravished. In the *Waste Land*, sexual encounters are characterized by such ambiguous status.

[9] See *Josiah Royce's Seminar, 1913–1914*, for Eliot's somewhat enigmatic commentary on the value of a descriptive methodology over an explanatory approach. Eliot praises Frazer for avoiding the impulse to explain primitive rituals, citing such exercises as delusional in nature. It is impossible for the modern theorist, Eliot argues, to understand the primitive mind. Any modern explanation for primitive behavior, ritual or artifact, Eliot concludes, is in fact an explanation of the modern mind and so completely misses the mark.

NOTES TO CHAPTER 2

[1] One could argue that Eliot fills his city with an equal number of male crudities, such as the brutal sexuality of Sweeney or the mercenary desire of the young man

carbuncular, or the implied homosexuality of the vaguely predatory Mr. Eugenides. (Given this character's name, a reader has to wonder, too, at Eliot's implication for the production—or reproduction—of a "master race." Is Eliot making an ironic comment on eugenics here?) Furthermore, one could point out that Eliot seems attracted to the image of the young virgin as victim, identifying with figures like Ophelia and Philomel, and even with his beleagured typist or the downtrodden Lil. On the other hand, each of these male characters appears under the "spell" of some form of perverted femininity or female ambition. Sweeney visits prostitutes who seem to infect him with their own syphilitic epilepsy and hysteria. The young man carbuncular is a means to the typist's ends. Mr. Eugenides is frightening because he is the amalgamation of male and female ambition—a merchant who approaches the poet/speaker as if he were a prostitute. Certainly, Eliot identifies with women who are the victims of aggressive, male desire; but he identifies with virginal victims rather than sexually knowledgeable women such as Cleopatra, Vivien's stand-in. I will explore this identification and its implications for Eliot's poetics in the next chapter.

² Gordon describes one of Eliot's early visions of God, recorded in his notebook, as the image of a syphilitic female spider sitting in the midst of a massive web.

³ Only ghostly virgins like the Hyacinth girl, Philomel, and their spiritual equivalent, *Ash Wednesday*'s Lady of Silences, present no threat to the poet's ability to witness. Significantly, they are all unable to speak.

⁴ The motivating purpose of Eliot's letter seems to be to comment, critically, on Pound's "Preliminary Announcement of the College of Arts."

⁵ For a thorough description and analysis of this "phenomenon" in American literature—as seen through the eyes of influential nineteenth and twentieth century male writers, see Ann Douglas' ground-breaking study, *The Feminization of American Culture* (New York: Knopf, 1977).

⁶ In his notes for *The Philosophy of T. S. Eliot*, William Skaff criticizes Lyndall Gordon for calling Eliot's mystical experiences hallucinations. Eliot makes a distinction, Skaff argues, between a genuine, intellectual experience of the divine and the "inversion" of the mystical moment, or the hysteric's hallucinations. Like many, Eliot sees female-dominated religiosity as the enemy of his Absolute—of "true," unbodied vision. Skaff notes that Eliot agrees with William James that hallucinations are a "malfunction of our physiology, as the visions of hysterics in psychiatric clinics are an inverted mysticism" and thus a "disease of memory" (217). Genuinely mystical visions, on the other hand, stem from the religious impulse, "a normal function of our physiology for Eliot which, at more intense and heightened moments, will produce mystical visions" (217). Clearly, Eliot connects such inversions of the mystical impulse with female talk, suggesting that hallucinations are connected with egotism—or the projection of individual desires onto the world. In contrast, he posits the mystic's insight as the opposite; such "seeing," he would have

argued, springs from a deliberate sacrifice of the self. Put crudely, Eliot would have said that God somehow projects his will or desire onto the mystic.

7 Thus, the triumph of Eliot's *Ash Wednesday* is that he manages to abstract the Lady into complete silence. All witness is filtered, now, through the poem's poetic consciousness.

8 On December 9, 1905, the opera *Salomé* opened at Dresden's Hofoper, with music by Richard Strauss, and a libretto based on Oscar Wilde's 1898 play. According to *The People's Chronology*, "Soprano Marie Wittich . . . originally refused to sing the title role's sensuous song to the imprisoned John the Baptist praising his body, his hair, his mouth, saying, 'I won't do it, I'm a decent woman.'" Eliot might have been aware of the controversy stirred by this frankly sexual rendition of the biblical tale and Salomé's role in it. After the opera's first performance at New York's Metropolitan Opera House in January of 1907, J. P. Morgan forbids further performances. (*Salomé* was not revived at the Met until 1934.)

9 My reading takes into account the admittedly autobiographical content of this moment. Biographers, critics, and even Tom and Vivien themselves, point out that this scene mimics a characteristic evening at home for the Eliots. Though some might interpret the passage as, simply, evidence of the Eliots' mutually dependant sexual and social neuroses, I think it reveals a glimpse of their obscure sexual relationship (a relationship that has been the cause of extended speculation, culminating in the recent Hollywood film, *Tom and Viv*. See my concluding chapter for a reading of this film and its value for a cultural critique). I would argue that Vivien's neurotic questioning, compared to Cleopatra's imperious rule, and the poet's answering silence, reveal the passive-aggressive nature of this "platonic" marriage. The poet has taken a typically "female" stance: he acts as the offended, and frigid, wife. In contrast, the woman makes invasive demands, trying to "get into" her husband's head. His refusals to speak only spur her into a further frenzy of asking. The entire tableau, paired with the image of Philomel, suggests the emotional (if not physical) rape of the husband.

10 This interlude also serves as a self-deprecating joke on his own name, and an allusion to his interests in primitive religious rituals

11 See, for example, Josef Breuer and Sigmund Freud's *Studies on Hysteria*, and Freud's *The Interpretation of Dreams*.

12 Incarnations—and disembodiments—of Emily Hale appear in Eliot's poetry as signs of mystical purity, a doorway to the divine that the mystic enters in his mind. Emily Hale and other virginal women, with whom Eliot identifies, will be the focus of my next chapters.

13 If *The Odyssey* serves as the foundation for Joyce's *Ulysses*, the *Orestia* might serve as the same for Eliot.

14 Because the poem stands out from the rest, stylistically and ideologically, a reader could argue that Eliot did not, in fact, write it—and that it is thus *unauthorized*.

A convincing argument might be made that Eliot inserted one of Vivien's poems into the volume under his own name. Vivien was, after all, widely known to be engaged in writing short prose pieces that indicted marriages such her own, which Eliot published in *The Criterion*. (See, for instance, Lyndall Gordon's *Eliot's Early Years*, 75.) Another reader might argue that Eliot's prose poem is a merely a mistake in the "proper order," an error not of omission but of inclusion, and that Eliot inserted the poem in order to make clear, in a bitter moment, some of the under-currents of heterosexual and marital revulsion circulating in his more ambiguous poetry. "There is no use denying," writes Gordon, "that many of Eliot's early poems suggest sexual problems—not lack of desire, but inhibition, distrust of women, and a certain physical queasiness. . . . Vivien's slightly vulgar manner perhaps liberated [Eliot] momentarily from his genteel constraint, but he was soon put off by it, and it was clear to friends who observed them early on that he felt ashamed of her" (75).

[15] Oddly enough, the Spanish *embarrasar*, often confused (by English speakers), with "to embarrass," means "to impregnate." This association is particularly telling when we consider that Eliot's poem uses the verb to rather poignantly rhyme with "in-vulve." Thus, being "invulved" is truly embarrassing.

[16] This image suggests that Eliot's narrator confuses the laughing woman with the mother, as he begins to see her entire body—as well as her laugh—as collected in her shaking breasts.

[17] Though Freud stresses our inability to "interpret" a dream without the associa-tional input of the dreamer, he reminds us that literary dreams follow a slightly dif-ferent logic. Freud links "*symbolic* dream interpretation" to the earliest attempts to see dreams as metaphors for waking desires, comparing such reconstruction to para-ble and biblical instruction; this tradition, Freud argues, is what lies behind the con-struction of literary dreams. "Most of the artificial dreams constructed by imagina-tive writers," Freud writes, "are designed for symbolic interpretation of this sort: they reproduce the writer's thoughts under a disguise which is regarded as harmonizing with the recognized characteristics of dreams" (*Interpretation* 129).

[18] Eliot married at about the same time that he published "Hysteria" ("a new poem," *The Letters of T. S. Eliot*, 103n) in the *Catholic Anthology*.

[19] This, of course, could be said of much—if not all—of Eliot's poetry.

[20] The drawing looks, suspiciously, like a set of breasts.

[21] The Oxford English Dictionary defines Priapism as, first, a "persistent erection of the penis" (pathological), and then as "an obscene mental image . . . licentious-ness; intentional indecency," "prostitution to what is low and base." Priapus is not only the Greek and Roman god of procreation, his effigy placed in gardens and vine-yards to ward off depredators, but also "a representation of the male generative organ; a phallus" and "a drinking vessel of phallic shape." Priapism thus combines Eliot's interests in perverse sexuality, penetration and oral copulation.

[22] This means, roughly, "the main station."

[23] As he writes this letter, Eliot has not only already read such religious and philosophical theorists as Frazer, Evelyn Underhill, W. R. Inge and William James, but has incorporated methods, images and ideas from their work into his poetry and written more than a few reviews of such scholarship for literary journals. In addition, note cards and transcriptions of Eliot's participation in Josiah Royce's seminars (1913–14) reveal his ongoing investigation into an experience of the Absolute. In 1911, Eliot attended seven of Bergson's lectures in Paris and, though disapproving of Bergson's philosophy, he borrowed aspects of Bergson's methodology of indirection (Gordon, EEY 38).

[24] In a later letter to his father, Eliot makes his intentions for Pound clear: "I am sorry that you cabled to him," Eliot writes, "because he is not the sort of person whom I wish to be intimate with my affairs. He has shown a keen interest in my career; and has been and will be useful; but my acquaintance with him is primarily professional"(L 117).

[25] In much the same way, Freud describes his grandson's game of *fort-da*, where the child "pretends" that a toy (which he can control) is the mother, and that he can so control the mother's coming and going, destroying her and bringing her back at will. This is, in effect, the child's "revenge" for his powerlessness in the relationship.

[26] Freud's description of the beating fantasy and its analysis—which he initially connects to female patients—are as involved as Eliot's poem. The fantasy has, according to Freud, three phases. The child imagines that "a child is being beaten," another child, the analyst discovers, who the imagining child "hates." In the third phase of the fantasy, the child is absent or perhaps merely looking on while representatives of the father's authority (such as teachers) beat faceless groups of children. The second phase is unconscious, "a construction of analysis, but . . . no less a necessity on that account" (114); it is the phase that connects these two distorted wishes. The first phase can be translated as "my father is beating the child, who I hate" because "my father loves only me." The second phase substitutes the fantasizing child for the "child who I hate": "my father is beating me because he loves only me." Thus, Freud argues, the masochistic fantasy makes an incestuous desire for genital sex with the father and, at the same time, metes out punishment for this forbidden wish.

[27] Cf. John 6:27: "Do not work for the food that perishes, but for the food that endures for eternal life, which the Son of Man will give you. For it is on him that God the Father has set his seal," says Jesus, after working the miracle of the fishes and the loaves.

[28] Harrison claims that: "Totemism . . . stands for fusion, for *non*-differentiation. Man cannot project his individual self, because that individual self is as yet in part undivided; he cannot project his individual human will, because that human will is felt chiefly as on with the non-differentiated *mana* of the world; he cannot project his individual soul because that complex thing is as yet not completely compound-

ed" (122). Later, she adds: "Totemism . . . is to our mind a habit of collective thinking based on collective emotion. The main characteristic of such thinking is union, or rather lack of differentiation, of subject and object" (128). Christian communion rituals repeat, symbolically, the "primitive" rituals of incorporation and community Harrison describes—through the course of his poetry, Eliot moves toward Christian communion as an "objective correlative" for the proposed action of his poetry and plays: a symbolic feast on the divine body.

[29] Eliot elaborates on this incarnation further in "Tradition and the Individual Talent." My next chapter will take up the implications of this sacrificial role as Eliot describes and enforces in this "seminal" essay.

NOTES FOR CHAPTER 3

[1] This is ironic, considering Eliot's earlier prejudices (contained most saliently in the Sweeney poems) against Irish Catholic immigrants.

[2] In the "personal" life that he so assiduously attempted to keep separate from his public or poetic life, Eliot struggled with fears of the afterlife. Perhaps his move toward orthodox Christianity, and his poetry "about to do something" to address that lack in his—and others'—life, was brought about in part by this fear. In *The Pound Era,* Hugh Kenner describes a moment in 1919 when Eliot confesses this fear to Pound at Excideuil (336).

[3] The next chapter will take up Eliot's use of Mary as a figure of mystic maternity and as a point of identification, using a close reading of *The Hollow Men* and *Ash Wednesday.*

[4] Readers point out Eliot's attempt, in this essay, to repudiate Emerson's "Self-Reliance." Eliot's diatribes against the "Inner Voice" and his repeated order that poets submit to a higher authority serve as jibes against Emerson's romantic treatise and, in general, the Protestant "mistake" that he represents for Eliot—the idea that every man serves as his own priest. Emerson's accusations could be addressed to Eliot's monumental theory of literature, however. "If . . . a man claims to know and speak of God and carries you backward to the phraseology of some old mouldered nation in another country, in another world, believe him not," Emerson says (66). In fact, Emerson's opening directly contradicts Eliot's: "[M]an postpones or remembers; he does not live in the present, but with reverted eye laments the past, or, heedless of the riches that surround him, stands on tiptoe to foresee the future. He cannot be happy and strong until he too lives with nature in the present, above time" (67).

[5] One could argue that Eliot's "Hamlet" is filled with ironic self-criticism—that Eliot is thinking of himself as he lambastes poets with "some weakness in creative power" who feel compelled to divert poetry into criticism. While this may be true, it appears equally true that Eliot's fear of the marauding mother or lover and her "artistic" ambitions is at war with his ability to "read" and respond to his own ambi-

tions. This is not the first time that a writer expresses contradictory ideas or emotions in the same piece.

⁶ It is interesting to note that Eliot's father, Henry Ware Eliot, died on January 8, 1919. In July of the same year, Eliot published "Reflections on Contemporary Poetry" in *The Egoist,* arguing that a young writer may "suddenly fall under the spell of an older one" and through imitation become part of the same literary tradition. Commenting implicitly on his own discovery of Jules Laforgue in 1908, Eliot describes "a feeling of profound kinship, or rather of a peculiar personal intimacy, with another, probably a dead author'" (Behr 17). In September 1919, Eliot published the polished version of this credo as the first part of "Tradition and the Individual Talent," again in *The Egoist.* In all of these transactions, Eliot seems bent on replacing his mother's poetic influence with that of a father, or father figure. This "profound kinship" or "peculiar personal intimacy," as a male-to-male mode of artistic transmission, transcends the reproductive bond that Eliot associates with women.

⁷ In "The Music of Poetry," in *On Poetry and Poets,* Eliot returns (again) to touch on the underlying subject: "Whether poetry is accentual or syllabic, rhymed or rhymeless, formal or free," he writes, "it cannot afford to lose its contact with the changing language of human intercourse" (21).

⁸ In 1942, Eliot softens his view of what he sees as an adolescent fascination with Romantic egotism, "invasion," and imitation: "When we imitated Shelley, it was not so much from a desire to write as he did, as from an invasion of the adolescent self by Shelley, which made Shelley's way, for the time, the only way to write" ("The Music of Poetry," OPP 19). What a way of putting it—the rape of the senses by the older, more "fascinating" boy at school.

⁹ See Ben Barker-Benfield's essay, "The Spermatic Economy: A Nineteenth Century View of Sexuality," for a detailed description of this economy and its consequences for a man caught in a patriarchal society bent on preserving the distinctions between the sexes. Barker-Benfield uses popular texts from the time to show how men represented their work (to themselves and others) as diving for gold or pearls, or mining valuable material from the earth. This was male "progress." Similarly, men feared "sticking" in the depths, or drowning in the sea, and these metaphorical fears expressed their gynephobia, "the fear of not passing through the dangers of being born, of not being distinguished from woman, from the mass" (346).

¹⁰ Again, Eliot appears to be countering Emerson's philosophy of self-reliance and other nineteenth century Romantic cant. Emerson pits the individual against chaos and the dark (society, conformity, God), while Eliot pits the social structure, as a luminous order, against the chaotic individual. "Society everywhere is in conspiracy against the manhood of every one of its members," says Emerson. "Society is a joint-stock company, in which the members agree, for the better securing of his bread to each shareholder, to surrender the liberty and culture of the eater. The virtue in most

requests is conformity. Self-reliance is its aversion. It loves not realities and creators, but names and customs" (51–52). "I am ashamed to think how easily we capitulate to badges and names, to large societies and dead institutions," he says (52). As far as Emerson is concerned, society castrates the individual in the name of "custom" and dead ancestors are the "corpse of your memory" that you have to "drag about" in order to be "consistent" in social situations. Eliot strives to reinstate this amputating judgment in "Tradition and the Individual Talent."

[11] For extended studies of Marionology and historical perspectives on her as an icon, see Marina Warner's *Alone of All Her Sex* and Maurice Hamington's *Hail Mary?* The use Eliot makes of Mary as an ideal mother will be explored in detail in the next chapter.

[12] The Eumenidies are reprised, later, in Eliot's play *Family Reunion*. Here, they track down a husband, Harry, who might be guilty of pushing his neurotic and demanding wife overboard during a sea crossing. Contrasted with the neurotic wife is Mary, Harry's second cousin, who acts as a companion and secretary for Harry's dowager mother, Amy. The play seems more than obliquely autobiographical as it explores the kinds of women—virgins and viragos—who surround and manipulate a befuddled and self-flagellating Harry.

[13] Ironically, Eliot ends this discussion by dismissing Tourneur's misanthropy with pity: "[I]n reading Tourneur we can only think, 'how terrible to loathe human beings so much as that.' For you cannot make humanity horrible merely by presenting human beings as consistent and monotonous maniacs of gluttony and lust" (SE 167). In a sense, Eliot condemns much of his own early work at the same time, particularly the Sweeney poems.

NOTES TO CHAPTER 4

[1] An informal survey of contemporary poetry readers, even those relatively unfamiliar with the historical context for modernism and/or the history of the genre of poetry, reveals that many think of "The Love Song of J. Alfred Prufrock" as a "great" poem. It is certainly one of the most widely quoted—inside and outside of academic circles—twentieth century literary texts. Apparently, many readers identify with Prufrock's damaged or impotent vision. Compare this sympathetic relationship to Eliot's anti-hero to Eliot's and Pound's scathing commentary on versions of "Portrait of a Lady" and "Prufrock." Perhaps Eliot and Pound protested too much to be taken at their word(s).

[2] See Koestenbaum's extended reading of this trope, "The Waste Land: T. S. Eliot's and Ezra Pound's Collaboration on Hysteria." Unfortunately, Koestenbaum assumes, throughout his reading, that Eliot is some sort of *idiot savant*, raw material—like Freud's Dora—to be molded into lyric poetry. He does not take into account the deliberate and mercenary nature of Eliot's association with Pound during this period. Eliot played the fool for Ezra's editor; his convenient "nervous break-

down" ended in a "rest cure" that rather resembles the contemporary writer's "retreat." Perhaps Eliot knew that he had to be strange and exciting (and damaged) in order to garner Pound's undivided attention and literary patronage. Of course, one could read Freud's relationships with "hysterical" women in the same terms; the "talking cure" becomes a way for the marginalized "voice" to be reproduced (under the aegis of a fatherly or phallic power) and published abroad.

³ One might read the "shantih shantih shantih" ending of the *Waste Land* as a hopeful approximation of benediction. However, given the pessimistic flavor of the closing stanzas, all tinged by the assertion that "these fragments I use to shore up my ruins," this failed union with the metaphysical realm of experience seems pleasurable (to the writer) precisely because of its ineffectual or impotent plea for divine penetration.

⁴ It might be interesting to note that Freud, interpreting the "dream of a young man inhibited by his father-complex" in his *Interpretation of Dreams*, suggests that climbing up or down a staircase, even in his own dreams, expresses "sexual intercourse in the vagina." This dreamer, once sexually active with women, had given up such activities "on account of inhibitions" but, through Freud's therapy, "now hoped to be able to resume it" (400–401). Later, Freud describes a patient "whose sexual abstinence was imposed on him by a severe neurosis, and whose [unconscious] phantasies were fixed upon his mother"; this patient "had repeated dreams of going upstairs in her company" (406). Does Eliot engage in the same (admittedly clichéd) expression of sexual desire? Or is *Ash Wednesday* a religious/mystical dream that fulfills the opposite desire—the desire to turn his back on sexual intercourse, the woman's vagina, and (as Freud suggests) his mother? Certainly, Freud's advice for the severe neurotic with a mother fixation could do Eliot little harm: "I once remarked to him that a moderate amount of masturbation would probably do him less harm than his compulsive self-restraint. . ." (406).

⁵ See Eliot's essay on Baudelaire for this examination of the fortunate fall and the beauty derived from horror or misfortune that Eliot suggests as the motivating energy behind the French poet's work.

⁶ This struggle is doomed, of course: Zeus arranges a trap for the unsuspecting Persephone in the form of a lovely narcissus flower, which she is compelled to pick. As soon as she touches the phallic bloom, it is transformed into "a dark and powerful male who rushe[s] upon her and carrie[s] her off" to the dark underworld (McManus 3).

⁷ Riviere goes on to conclude that the masquerading woman (necessarily in a position of power) is not trying to circumvent her father's anger so much as her mother's—she plays the flirting fool, the object of male desire, in order to pay obeisance to the resentful (because socially castrated) mother. Thus, some theories of subjectivity are based on this fundamental distrust of the mother; the poet must kill her in order to come into his/her own. This clearly has implications for future readings of

Eliot's will to poetic power as its inverse, since his insistent submission might be a bid to avoid his mother's artistic resentment.

NOTES FOR CHAPTER 5

[1] This is no doubt a playful inversion of Eliot's original fantasy of the dying god, since Attis was reputedly hung on the laurel or pine tree.

[2] The implication is that Vivien was deemed "crazy" and institutionalized because her (greedy) family and husband didn't want to put up with her PMS. The film further implies that Vivien's mood swings were as creative (if not more so) as Eliot's alcoholic bouts of self-loathing and sexual disgust.

[3] The film explains Eliot's Anglophilia, in fact, as a means to disguise (badly, apparently) his inner emptiness behind British reserve.

[4] Yet Eliot drew heavily from the effects of (silent) films as he composed such poems as the *Waste Land*. We should never take his frontal attacks at face value. Consider, for instance, the implications of self-criticism and acknowledged irony in his essay on *Hamlet*.

[5] Once again, we should read Eliot's rhetoric on this occasion as just that—perhaps he is, as Pound fondly suggests, once again playing possum.

[6] The denial of Eliot's (and Pound's) repeated attempts to write a poetry with communal impact, "the tale of the tribe," is a particularly insistent impulse in critical and popular tracts of late. Undergraduate seminars stress Eliot's and Pound's supposed alliance with "the privileged," just as *Tom and Viv* suggests that Eliot rejected his plain, upstanding American childhood by chasing after British nobility. No doubt deluded and doomed to failure, Eliot nevertheless hoped to appeal to the same "working class" audience as Marie Lloyd. Since this purpose is key to understanding Eliot's poetics, this critical reversal is emphatically perverse.

[7] Herbert Schneidau adds that we must read Pound with the proper distance and historical perspective at this point. After all, this diatribe is also the disappointed "raving" of a former allay and (still) faithful friend, a man who wanted all to follow him into Douglasite economics. Pound lived to regret these harsh words, Schneidau reminds us.

[8] At the risk of offending members of my reading public, let me add that (underneath all this critical outrage) our interest in Eliot's private demons and personal politics stems from another problem in contemporary literary studies and debates: we are enjoined to teach only literature that embodies the "proper" political values and operate as if these values can be deduced from the writers' lives. As in Eliot's case, these arguments and pedagogical imperatives are grounded on/in questionable premises.

[9] It is important to note that though we think the savage can save us (i.e. that a return to or investigation of the unconscious will regenerate the tribe by explaining the genesis of its subjectivity through social imperatives and propaganda), we do not

identify this "savage" with Eliot's supposed cruelty. As *Tom and Viv* implies, Eliot's savagery is highly civilized.

Bibliography

Abdoo, Sherlyn. "Woman as Grail in T. S. Eliot's The Waste Land." *The Centennial Review* 28.1 (1984): 48–60.

Ackroyd, Peter. *T. S. Eliot.* London: Hamish Hamilton, 1984.

Aldington, Richard. *Stepping Heavenward: A Record.* London: Catto & Windus, 1931.

Alleva, Richard. "Tom and Viv." Review. *Commonweal* 27 Jan 1995: 24–25. Online. Expanded Academic Index ASAP. 24 Sept. 1996.

Bagchee, Shyamal, ed. *T. S. Eliot: A Voice Descanting.* London: Macmillan, 1990.

Barker-Benfield, Ben. "The Spermatic Economy: A Nineteenth Century View of Sexuality." *The American Family in Social-Historical Perspective.* Ed. Michael Gordon. New York: St. Martin's, 1973. 336–372.

Bataille, Georges. *Death and Sensuality: A Study of Eroticism and the Taboo.* 1964. New York: Walker and Co., 1984.

Baudelaire. *The Complete Verse, Volume I.* Ed. and trans. Francis Scarfe. London: Anvil Press Poetry, 1986.

Baym, Nina. "Melodramas of Beset Manhood." *The New Feminist Criticism: Essays on Women, Literature and Theory.* Ed. Elaine Showalter. New York: Pantheon, 1985. 63–80.

Beaumont, Francis and John Fletcher. *The Maid's Tragedy.* 1619. Ed. T. W. Craik. Manchester: Manchester UP, 1988.

Beehler, Michael. *T. S. Eliot, Wallace Stevens, and the Discourses of Difference.* Baton Rouge: Louisiana State UP, 1987.

Behr, Caroline. *T. S. Eliot: A Chronology of His Life and Works.* London: Macmillan, 1983.

Bell, Vereen and Laurence Lerner, eds. *On Modern Poetry: Essays Presented to Donald Davie.* Nashville, TN: Vanderbilt University Press, 1988.

Bell, Vereen. "Grace Dissolved in Place: A Reading of *Ash Wednesday.*" *On Modern Poetry: Essays Presented to Donald Davie.* Eds. Vereen Bell and Laurence Lerner. Nashville: Vanderbilt UP, 1988. 1–14.

Berg, Temma F. *Engendering the Word: Feminist Essays in Psychosexual Poetics.* Urbana, IL: U of Illinois P, 1989.

Bergson, Henri. *Matter and Memory.* Trans. Nancy Margaret Paul and W. Scott Palmer. London: George Allen & Co., 1913.

Bettelheim, Bruno. *Symbolic Wounds: Puberty Rites and the Envious Male.* 2nd Ed. New York: Collier, 1962.

Birrell, T. A. "A Reception of T. S. Eliot: Texts and Contexts." *English Studies* 69.6 (1988): 518–533.

Blom, J. M. Rev. of *Eliot's New Life,* by Lyndall Gordon. *English Studies* 69.6 (1988): 539–540.

Bloom, Harold. "Reflections on T. S. Eliot." *Raritan* 8.2 (Fall 1988): 70–87.

Brett, R. L. "Mysticism and Incarnation in *Four Quartets.*" *English* 16.93 (Autumn 1966): 94–9.

Breuer, Josef and Sigmund Freud. *Studies on Hysteria, 1893–1895.* Trans. James Strachey. NY: Basic Books, 1955.

Brooker, Jewel Spears and Joseph Bentley. *Reading* The Waste Land*: Modernism and the Limits of Interpretation.* Amherst: The U of Massachusetts P, 1990.

Brooker, Jewel Spears, ed. *Mastery and Escape: T. S. Eliot and the Dialectic of Modernism.* Amherst: U of Massachusetts P, 1994.

———, ed. *The Placing of T. S. Eliot.* Columbia: U of Missouri P, 1991.

———. "Substitutes for Christianity in the Poetry of T. S. Eliot." *T. S. Eliot: Essays from the* Southern Review. Ed. James Olney. Oxford: Clarendon, 1988. 39–54.

———. *T. S. Eliot and Our Turning World.* New York: St. Martin's, 2001.

Brown, Ashley. "T. S. Eliot in the Postmodern Age." *The Virginia Quarterly Review* 65.4 (Autumn 1989): 693–701.

Bush, Ronald, ed. "But is it Modern?: T. S. Eliot in 1988." *The Yale Review* 77.2 (Winter 1988): 193–206.

———. "T. S. Eliot and Modernism at the Present Time: A Provocation." *T. S. Eliot: The Modernist in History,* ed. Ronald Bush. Cambridge: Cambridge UP, 1991. 191–204.

———. *T. S. Eliot: The Modernist in History.* Cambridge: Cambridge UP, 1991.

Carne-Ross, D. S. "The Music of a Lost Dynasty: Pound in the Classroom." *Instaurations.* Berkeley: U of California P, 1979. 193–217.

Childs, Donald J. "Metamorphoses, Metaphysics, and Mysticism from The Death of St. Narcissus to Burnt Norton." *Classical and Modern Literature* 13.1 (Fall 1992): 15–29.

———. "Risking Enchantment: The Middle Way Between Mysticism and Pragmatism in *Four Quartets.*" *Words in Time: New Essays on Eliot's* Four Quartets, ed. Edward Lobb. London: The Athlone P, 1993. 107–130.

———. "T. S. Eliot's Rhapsody of Matter and Memory." *American Literature* 63.3 (September 1991): 474–88.

———. *T. S. Eliot: Mystic, Son and Lover.* New York: St. Martin's, 1997.

Childs, John Steven. "Eliot, Tradition, and Textuality." *Texas Studies in Literature and Language* 27.3: 311–323.

Chinitz, David. "T. S. Eliot and the Cultural Divide." *PMLA* 110.2 (March 1995): 236–247.

Christ, Carol. "Gender, Voice and Figuration in Eliot's Early Poetry." *T. S. Eliot: The Modernist in History.* Ed. Ronald Bush. Cambridge: Cambridge UP, 1991. 23–37.

Clark, Stephen H. "Testing the Razor: T. S. Eliot's *Poems 1920.*" *Engendering the Word: Feminist Essays in Psychosexual Poetics.* Ed. Temma F. Berg. Urbana, IL: U of Illinois P, 1989. 167–189.

Costello, Harry T. *Josiah Royce's Seminar, 1913–1914.* Ed. Grover Smith. New Jersey: Rutgers UP, 1963.

Cowan, Laura, ed. *T. S. Eliot: Man and Poet, Volume I.* Orono, ME: National Poetry Foundation, 1990.

Coyle, Michael and Laura Cowan. "Pound and Eliot." *American Literary Scholarship 1994.* Ed. David J. Nordloh. Durham, NC: Duke UP, 1996. 127–147.

Crawford, Robert. *The Savage and the City in the Work of T. S. Eliot.* Oxford: Clarendon, 1987.

Dally, Ann. *Inventing Motherhood: The Consequences of an Ideal.* London: Burnett Books, 1982.

Dante. *Inferno: First Book of the Divine Comedy.* Trans. Allen Mandelbaum. New York: QPB Club, 1980.

Davidson, Harriet. *T. S. Eliot and Hermeneutics.* Baton Rouge: Louisiana State UP, 1985.

Dawson, J. L., P. D. Holland, and D. J. McKitterick, eds. *A Concordance to* The Complete Poems and Plays of T. S. Eliot. Ithaca, NY: Cornell UP, 1995.

DeKoven, Marianne. *Rich and Strange: Gender, History, Modernism.* Princeton: Princeton UP, 1991.

Donaghy, Michael. Rev. of *Inventions of the March Hare. New Statesman* 27 Sept. 1996: 59.

Donoghue, Denis. "Donald Davie on T. S. Eliot." *Partisan Review* 67.1 (2000): 10–38.

————. *Words Alone: The Poet T.S. Eliot.* New Haven: Yale U Press, 2000.

Douglas, Ann. *The Feminization of American Culture.* NY: Knopf, 1977.

Douglas, Mary. *Purity and Danger: An Analysis of the Concepts of Pollution and Taboo.* 1966. London: Routledge, 1988.

Durkheim, Émile. *The Elementary Forms of the Religious Life.* 1915. Trans. Joseph Ward Swain. London: George Allen & Unwin, 1957.

Eliot, T. S. Rev. of *The Ascent of Olympus,* by Rendel Harris. *The Monist* 28: 640.

————. "The Beating of a Drum." *The Nation and the Athenaeum* 34(1923): 11–12.

————. *The Complete Poems and Plays, 1909–1950.* New York: Harcourt Brace Jovanovich, 1950.

————. Rev. of *The Elementary Forms of the Religious Life,* by Emile Durkheim. *The Monist* 28: 158–159.

————. Rev. of *Elements of Folk Psychology,* by Wilhelm Wundt. *International Journal of Ethics* 27: 252–254.

————. Rev. of *Elements of Folk Psychology,* by Wilhelm Wundt. *The Monist* 28: 159–160.

————. Rev. of *Group Theories of Religion and the Individual,* by Clement C. J. Webb. *International Journal of Ethics* 27: 115–117.

————. Rev. of *Group Theories of Religion and the Individual,* by Clement C. J. Webb. *The New Statesman* 29 July 1916: 405.

————. *Inventions of the March Hare: Poems 1909–1917.* Ed. Christopher Ricks. London: Faber and Faber, 1996.

————. *Knowledge and Experience in the Philosophy of F. H. Bradley.* 1964. New York: Columbia UP, 1989.

————. *The Letters of T. S. Eliot.* Vol. I. Ed. Valerie Eliot. New York: Harcourt Brace Jovanovich, 1988.

————. "London Letter." *Dial* 71(1921): 452–55.

————. *On Poetry and Poets.* New York: Farrar, Straus and Cudahy, 1957.

————. *Poems Written in Early Youth.* New York: Farrar, Straus & Giroux, 1967.

————. "Recent British Periodical Literature in Ethics." *International Journal of Ethics* 28: 270–77.

————. *The Sacred Wood.* 1920. London: Methuen, 1969.

————. *Selected Essays.* New Edition. New York: Harcourt Brace & World, 1960.

————. *Selected Prose of T. S. Eliot.* Ed. and Intro. Frank Kermode. New York: Harcourt Brace Jovanovich, 1975.

————. Rev. of *The Study of Religions,* by Stanley A. Cook. *The Monist* 27 : 480.

————. *To Criticize the Critic.* London: Faber and Faber, 1965.

————. *The Use of Poetry and the Use of Criticism.* London: Faber and Faber, 1933.

————. *The Waste Land: A Facsimile and Transcript of the Original Drafts.* Ed. Valerie Eliot. New York: Harcourt Brace Jovanovich, 1971.

Ellmann, Maud. *The Poetics of Impersonality: T. S. Eliot and Ezra Pound.* Sussex: Harvester P, 1987.

Emerson, Ralph Waldo. "Self Reliance." *Essays: First and Second Series.* Boston: Houghton, Mifflin and Co., 1883. 45–87.

Fathman, Anthony E., M. D. "Viv and Tom: The Eliots as Ether Addict and Co-Dependent." *Yeats Eliot Review* 11.2: 33–36.

Fiedler, Leslie. *Love and Death in the American Novel.* 1960. New York: Anchor Books, 1992.

Fleissner, Robert F. *T. S. Eliot and the Heritage of Africa.* New York: Peter Lang, 1992.

Frazer, Sir James George. *The Golden Bough: Adonis Attis Osiris.* Part IV, Vol. 1. 3rd Ed. New York: MacMillan, 1935.

———. *The Golden Bough: The Dying God.* Part III. 3rd Ed. New York: MacMillan, 1935.

Freud, Sigmund. "On Narcissism: An Introduction." 1914. *General Psychological Theory.* Ed. Philip Rieff. New York: Collier Books, 1963. 56–82.

———. *Beyond the Pleasure Principle.* 1959. Ed. and Trans. James Strachey. New York: Norton, 1961.

———. *Civilization and its Discontents.* 1930. Ed. and Trans. James Strachey. New York: Norton, 1961.

———. *Dora: An Analysis of a Case of Hysteria.* 1905–09. Ed. Philip Rieff. New York: Collier Books, 1963.

———. *Sexuality and the Psychology of Love.* Ed. Philip Rieff. New York: Collier Books, 1963.

———. *The Interpretation of Dreams.* 1900. Ed. and Trans. James Strachey. New York: Avon Books, 1965.

———. *Totem and Taboo.* 1913. Ed. and Trans. James Strachey. Intro. Peter Gay. New York: Norton, 1950.

Froula, Christine. "Eliot's Grail Quest, or, The Lover, the Police, and *The Waste Land.*" *The Yale Review* 78.2 (Winter 1989): 235–253.

Frye, Northrup. "Antique Drum." *T. S. Eliot.* Ed. and intro. Harold Bloom. New York: Chelsea House, 1985. 19–30.

Gallop, Jane. *Reading Lacan.* Ithaca, NY and London: Cornell UP, 1985.

Gallup, Donald. "The Eliots, and the T. S. Eliot Collection at Harvard." *Harvard Library Bulletin* 36.3 (1988): 233–247.

Gibert-Maceda, M. Teresa. "T. S. Eliot on Women: Women on T. S. Eliot." *T. S. Eliot at the Turn of the Century.* Ed. Marianne Thormählen. Sweden: Lund UP, 1994. 105–119.

Gilbert, Sandra M. and Susan Gubar, eds. *The Female Imagination & the Modernist Aesthetic.* New York: Gordon and Breach Science Publishers, 1986.

Girard, René. *The Scapegoat.* Trans. Yvonne Freccero. Baltimore: The Johns Hopkins UP, 1986.

Gish, Nancy K. "Eliot and Marianne Moore: Modernism and Difference." *Yeats Eliot Review* 11.2: 40–43.

Gordon, Lyndall. "Eliot and Women." *T. S. Eliot: The Modernist in History.* Ed. Ronald Bush. Cambridge: Cambridge UP, 1991. 9–22.

———. *Eliot's Early Years.* New York: Noonday P, 1977.

———. *Eliot's New Life.* New York: Noonday P, 1988.

———. *T. S. Eliot: An Imperfect Life.* New York: Norton, 1998.

Gross, Harvey. "The Figure of St. Sebastian." *T. S. Eliot: Essays from the* Southern Review. Ed. James Olney. Oxford: Clarendon P, 1988. 103–114.

Gross, John J. "Was T. S. Eliot a Scoundrel?" *Commentary* 102 (1996): 26–31. Online. EBSCOhost. 26 Aug 2002.

Hamerton-Kelly, Robert. G, ed. *Violent Origins: Walter Burkert, René Girard, and Jonathan Z. Smith on Ritual Killing and Cultural Formation.* Stanford: Stanford UP, 1987.

Hamington, Maurice. *Hail Mary?* New York: Routledge, 1995.

Harmsen, T. H. B. M. "T. S. Eliot's Poetic Testament: the Personality of the Impersonality Seeker." *English Studies* 69.6 (1988): 509–517.

Harrison, Jane Ellen. *Themis: A Study of the Social Origins of Greek Religion.* Cleveland: Meridian Books, 1912, 1927.

Hawkins, Desmond. "The Pope of Russell Square." *T. S. Eliot: a symposium.* Eds. Richard March and Tambimuttu. Freeport, NY: Books for Libraries P, 1968. 44–47.

Helmling, Steven. "The Success and Failure of T. S. Eliot." *Sewanee Review* 96.1 (Winter 1988): 55–76.

Howarth, Herbert. *Notes on Some Figures Behind T. S. Eliot.* London: Chatto & Windus, 1965.

Inge, W. R. *Mysticism in Religion.* Chicago: U of Chicago P, 1948.

Irmscher, Christoph. "Anthropological Roles: The Self and Its Others in T. S. Eliot, William Carlos Williams and Wendy Rose." *Soundings* 75.4 (Winter 1992): 587–603.

James, William. *The Varieties of Religious Experience.* New York: Random House, 1902.

Janet, Pierre. *The Major Symptoms of Hysteria.* 1907. 2nd ed. New York: MacMillan, 1924.

Jevons, Frank Byron. *An Introduction to the History of Religion.* London: Methuen, 1910.

Johnson, Loretta. "A Temporary Marriage of Two Minds: T. S. and Vivien Eliot." *Twentieth Century Literature* 34.1 (1988): 48–61.

Jones, Ernest. "A Psycho-Analytic Study of Hamlet." *Essays in Applied Psycho-Analysis.* London: International Psycho-Analytical P, 1923.

Joyce, James. "Ireland, Island of Saints and Sages." 1907. *The Critical Writings of James Joyce.* Ellsworth Mason and Richard Ellman, eds. New York: Viking, 1959. 153–174.

———. *A Portrait of the Artist as a Young Man.* 1916. New York: Bantam, 1992.

———. Letter to Lady Gregory. N. D. [November 1902]. *Letters of James Joyce.* Ed. Stuart Gilbert. New York: Viking, 1957. 53.

Julius, Anthony. *T. S. Eliot, Anti-Semitism, and Literary Form.* Cambridge, England: Cambridge University Press, 1996.

Kaiser, Jo Ellen Green. "Disciplining the Waste Land, or How to Lead Critics into Temptation." *Twentieth Century Literature* 44.1 (1998): 82–99.

Kakutani, Michiko. "Bigotry in Motion." *The New York Times Magazine* (nat'l ed.) 16 March 1997: 24.

Kane, Richard. "From Loins of Darkness to Loins of Pork: Body Imagery in Lawrence, Eliot, and Joyce." *Recovering Literature* 17 (1989–1990): 5–18.

Karr, Mary. "How to read 'The Waste Land' so it alters your soul." *Chronicle of Higher Education* 23 Feb 2001: B7–B11. Available online. ProQuest. 26 Aug 2002.

Kaufmann, Stanley. "Tom and Viv." Review. *The New Republic* 23 Jan. 1995: 30. *Expanded Academic Index ASAP.* Online. 24 Sept. 1996.

Kaye, Richard A. "'A Splendid Readiness for Death': T. S. Eliot, the Homosexual Cult of St. Sebastian, and World War I." *Modernism/Modernity* 6.2 (1999): 107–34. Online. Project Muse. 23 Jan 2001.

Kearns, Cleo McNelly. *T. S. Eliot and Indic Tradition: A Study in Poetry and Belief.* Cambridge: Cambridge UP, 1987.

Kearns, George and Cleo McNelly Kearns. "Pound and Eliot." *American Literary Scholarship 1993.* Ed. Gary Scharnhorst. Durham, NC: Duke UP, 1995. 101–112.

———. "Pound and Eliot." *American Literary Scholarship 1992.* Ed. David J. Nordloh. Durham, NC: Duke UP, 1994. 117–129.

Kelleher, Ed and Cynthia Lucia. "Tom and Viv." Rev. of *Tom and Viv. Cineaste* 21.3 (Summer 1995): 40–42. *Expanded Academic Index ASAP.* Online. 24 Sept. 1996.

Kenner, Hugh, ed. *T. S. Eliot: A Collection of Critical Essays.* Englewood Cliffs, NJ: Prentice-Hall, 1962.

———. *A Homemade World.* New York: William Morrow and Co., 1975.

———. *The Invisible Poet: T. S. Eliot.* New York: McDowell, Oblensky, 1959.

———. *The Pound Era.* Berkeley: U of California P, 1971.

Kimball, Roger. "A Craving for Reality: T. S. Eliot Today." *New Criterion* 18.2 (October 1999): 18–27. Online. EBSCOHost. 26 Aug 2002.

Kipling, Rudyard. *Kim*. London: MacMillan and Co., n. d.

Kirk, Russell. "The Politics of T. S. Eliot." *The Heritage Foundation,* Lecture 182. 9 Feb 1989. Online. Internet. 24 Sept. 1996.

Knowles, Sebastian. "'Then You Wink the Other Eye': T. S. Eliot and the Music Hall." *ANQ* 11.4 (Fall 98): 20–33. Online. EBSCOhost. 26 Aug 2002.

Koestenbaum, Wayne. "*The Waste Land*: T. S. Eliot's and Ezra Pound's Collaboration on Hysteria." *Twentieth Century Literature* 34.2 (1988): 113–139.

Kristeva, Julia. "Stabat Mater." *The Kristeva Reader*. Ed. Toril Moi. New York: Columbia University Press, 1986. 160–186.

———. *Powers of Horror: An Essay on Abjection*. New York: Columbia UP, 1982.

Kundera, Milan. *Life is Elsewhere*. Trans. Peter Kussi. New York: Penguin, 1986.

Lacan, Jacques. *Feminine Sexuality*. Eds. Juliet Mitchell and Jacqueline Rose. Trans. Jacqueline Rose. New York: Norton, 1982.

Laforgue, Jules. *Selected Writings*. Ed and trans. William Jay Smith. New York: Grove P, 1956.

Lamos, Colleen. *Deviant Modernism: Sexual and Textual Errancy in T. S. Eliot, James Joyce, and Marcel Proust*. Cambridge, England: Cambridge UP, 1998.

Lane, Anthony. "Etherized." Rev. of *Tom and Viv*. *The New Yorker* 21 Dec. 1994: 125–128.

———. "Writing Wrongs." *The New Yorker* 10 March 1997: 86–92.

Leavell, Linda. "Eliot's Ritual Method: *Ash Wednesday*." *T. S. Eliot: Essays from the Southern Review*. Ed. James Olney. Oxford: Clarendon P, 1988. 145–152.

Leavis, L. R. "T. S. Eliot and the Poetry of the Future." *English Studies* 69.6 (1988): 481–496.

Leon, Juan. "'Meeting Mr. Eugenides': T. S. Eliot and Eugenic Anxiety." *Yeats Eliot Review* 9.4 (1988): 169–177.

Lesser, Wendy. "The T. S. Eliot Problem." *The New York Times Book Review* 14 July 1996: 31.

Lévi-Strauss, Claude. *The Raw and the Cooked. Introduction to a Science of Mythology: I*. Trans. John and Doreen Weightman. New York: Harper and Row, 1969.

Lévy-Bruhl, Lucien. *How Natives Think (Les Fonctions Mentales Dans Les Sociétés Inférieures)*. Trans. Lilian A. Clare. London: George Allen & Unwin, 1926.

Liggett, P. A. "A Study in Modernism: Exploring the Relationship of T. S. Eliot and Virginia Woolf." *Yeats Eliot Review* 9.4: 165–168.

Litz, A. Walton, ed. *Eliot in His Time*. Princeton, NJ: Princeton UP, 1973.

Lobb, Edward, ed. *Words in Time: New Essays on Eliot's* Four Quartets. London: Athlone P, 1993.

Longenbach, James. "Guarding the Hornèd Gates: History and Interpretation in the Early Poetry of T. S. Eliot." *ELH* 52 (1985): 503–527.

———. *Modernist Poetics of History: Pound, Eliot, and the Sense of the Past.* Princeton: Princeton UP, 1987.

MacDiarmid, Laurie. "'Torture and Delight': T. S. Eliot's Love Song for St. Sebastian." *Arizona Quarterly* 57.2 (Summer 2001): 77–92.

Manganaro, Marc. "'Beating a Drum in a Jungle': T. S. Eliot on the Artist as 'Primitive'." *Modern Language Quarterly* 47.4 (1986): 393–421.

———. *Myth, Rhetoric, and the Voice of Authority: A Critique of Frazer, Eliot, Frye, and Campbell.* New Haven: Yale UP, 1992.

March, Richard and Tambimuttu, eds. *T. S. Eliot: A symposium.* Freeport, NY: Books for Libraries P, 1968.

Marett, R. R. "Is Taboo a Negative Magic?" *Anthropological Essays Presented to Edward Burnett Tylor.* Oxford: Clarendon P, 1907. 219–234.

———. *The Threshold of Religion.* New York: MacMillan, 1914.

Matthews, T. S. *Great Tom: Notes Towards the Definition of T. S. Eliot.* New York: Harper and Row, 1973.

Mayer, John T. *T. S. Eliot's Silent Voices.* New York: Oxford UP, 1989.

McCombie, Frank. Rev. of *The American T. S. Eliot: A Study of the Early Writings,* by E. Sigg and *T. S. Eliot: A Voice Descanting,* ed. S. Bagchee. *Notes and Queries* 38.3 (September 1991): 409–412.

Medcalf, Stephen. "The Shaman's Secret Heart." *Times Literary Supplement* 2 Oct. 1992: 10–12.

Menand, Louis and Sanford Schwartz. "T. S. Eliot on Durkheim: A New Attribution." *Modern Philology* 79.3 (February 1982): 309–315.

Menand, Louis. *Discovering Modernism: T. S. Eliot and his Context.* New York: Oxford UP, 1987.

———. "T. S. Eliot After His Time." *Raritan* 8.2 (Fall 1988): 88–102.

Michaels, Walter Benn. "Philosophy in Kinkanja: Eliot's Pragmatism." *Glyph* 8 (1981): 170–202.

Miller, James E., Jr. "T. S. Eliot's 'Uranian Muse': The Verdenal Letters." *ANQ* 11.4 (Fall 98): 4–21.

———. *T. S. Eliot's Personal Waste Land.* University Park: The Pennsylvania State UP, 1977.

Milosz, Czeslaw. *The Witness of Poetry.* Cambridge, MA: Harvard UP, 1983.

Müller, Max. *Natural Religion.* 1889. New York: AMS Press, 1975.

Murphy, Russell Elliot. "Demeaning Eliot: The Future of Literary Studies." *Yeats Eliot Review* 11.2: 46–47.

Nietzsche, Friedrich. *The Birth of Tragedy and The Case of Wagner.* 1886. Trans. Walter Kaufmann. New York: Random House, 1967.

O'Barr, Jean F., Deborah Pope and Mary Wyer, eds. *Ties that Bind: Essays on Mothering and Patriarchy.* Chicago: The U of Chicago P, 1990.

Olney, James. *T. S. Eliot: Essays from the* Southern Review. Oxford: Clarendon P, 1988.

Oser, Lee. *T. S. Eliot and American Poetry.* Columbia and London: U of Missouri Press, 1998.

Ovid. *Metamorphoses.* Trans. Rolfe Humphries. Bloomington: Indiana UP, 1961.

Ozick, Cynthia. "Eliot at 101." *The New Yorker* 20 Nov. 1989: 119–154.

Palmer, Marja. *Men and Women in T. S. Eliot's Early Poetry.* Lund, Sweden: Lund UP, 1996.

Pater, Walter. "Leonardo da Vinci." 1869. *Selected Writings of Walter Pater.* Ed. Harold Bloom. New York: Signet, 1974. 31–51.

Pearlman, Mickey, ed. *The Anna Book: Searching for Anna in Literary History.* Westport, CT: Greenwood P, 1992.

Perl, Jeffrey. *Skepticism and Modern Enmity: Before and After Eliot.* Baltimore: Johns Hopkins UP, 1989.

Petronius. *The Saytricon.* Trans. J. P. Sullivan. Middlesex: Penguin, 1986.

Philippe, Charles-Louis. *Bubu of Monparnasse.* Intro. Alan Ross. New York: Roy Publishers, 1953.

Phillips, William. "Eliot Today." *Partisan Review* 57.2 (1990): 178–180.

Pickering, W. S. F., ed. *Durkheim on Religion: A Selection of Readings with Bibliographies.* London: Routledge & Kegan Paul, 1975.

Pinkney, Tony. *Women in the Poetry of T. S. Eliot.* London: MacMillan, 1984.

Pound, Ezra. "Prefatio Aut Cimicium Tumulus." 1933. *Selected Prose 1909–1965.* Ed. and Intro. William Cookson. New York: New Directions, 1973. 389–400.

Reid, Captain Mayne. *The Boy Hunters.* London: George Routledge and Sons, n. d.

Rich, Adrienne. *Of Woman Born: Motherhood as Experience and Institution.* 1976. New York: Norton, 1986.

Ricks, Beatrice. *T. S. Eliot: A Bibliography of Secondary Works.* Metuchen, NJ: The Scarecrow P, 1980.

Riquelme, J. P. "The Modernist Essay: The Case of T. S. Eliot—Poet as Critic." *The Southern Review* 21.4 (Autumn 1985): 1024–1032.

Riviere, Joan. "Womanliness as Masquerade." *Formations of Fantasy.* Eds. Victor Burgin, James Donald, and Cora Kaplan. London: Methuen, 1986. 35–44.

Roberson, Susan L. "T. S. Eliot's Symbolical Woman: From Temptress to Priestess." *Midwest Quarterly* 27.4(1986): 476–486.

Roby, Kinley E., ed. *Critical Essays on T. S. Eliot: The Sweeney Motif.* Boston: G. K. Hall & Co., 1985.

Romney, Jonathan. "Tom and Viv." Review. *New Statesman and Society* 18 Mar. 1994: 50–51. *Expanded Academic Index ASAP.* Online. 24 Sept. 1996.

Rose, Jacqueline. *Sexuality in the Field of Vision.* London: Verso, 1986.

Said, Edward. "Representing the Colonized: Anthropology's Interlocutors." *Critical Inquiry* 15.2 (Winter 1989): 205–225.

Sandelowski, Margarete J. "Failures of Volition: Female Agency and Infertility in Historical Perspective." *Ties That Bind: Essays on Mothering and Patriarchy.* Eds. Jean F. O'Barr, Deborah Pope, and Mary Wyer. Chicago: U of Chicago P, 1990. 35–59.

Schneidau, Herbert N. *Waking Giants: The Presence of the Past in Modernism.* New York: Oxford UP, 1991.

Schuchard, Ronald. "Eliot and the Horrific Moment." *T. S. Eliot: Essays from the Southern Review.* Ed. James Olney. Oxford: Clarendon P, 1988. 191–204.

———. *Eliot's Dark Angel: Intersections of Life and Art.* New York: Oxford UP, 1999.

Schwartz, Sanford. *The Matrix of Modernism: Pound, Eliot, and Early Twentieth-Century Thought.* Princeton: Princeton UP, 1985.

Seaton, James. "Old Enemies, New Allies." *Journal of Popular Culture* 25.1 (Summer 1991): 149–155.

Sencourt, Robert. *T. S. Eliot: A Memoir,* ed. Donald Adamson. New York: Dodd, Mead and Co., 1971.

Seymour-Jones, Carole. *Painted Shadow: The Life of Vivienne Eliot, First Wife of T. S. Eliot, and the Long-Suppressed Truth About Her Influence on His Genius.* New York: Doubleday, 2002.

Shusterman, Richard. *T. S. Eliot and the Philosophy of Criticism.* London: Duckworth, 1988.

Sigg, Eric. *The American T. S. Eliot: A Study of the Early Writings.* Cambridge: Cambridge UP, 1989.

Silverman, Kaja. *Male Subjectivity at the Margins.* New York: Routledge, 1992.

Skaff, William. *The Philosophy of T. S. Eliot: From Skepticism to A Surrealist Poetic.* Philadelphia: U of Pennsylvania P, 1986.

Smith, Lee. "Memory and Desire." *The Village Voice* 18 Jun 1996: 63+. Online. ProQuest. 26 Aug 2002.

Sparks, Elisa Kay. "Old Father Nile: T. S. Eliot and Harold Bloom on the Creative Process as Spontaneous Generation." *Engendering the Word: Feminist Essays in Psychosexual Poetics.* Ed. Temma F. Berg. Urbana, IL: U of Illinois P, 1989. 51–80.

Spender, Stephen. *T. S. Eliot.* New York: Viking, 1976.

Springsted, Eric O. "The Religious Basis of Culture: T. S. Eliot and Simone Weil." *Religious Studies* 25.1 (1989): 105–116.

Spurr, David. *Conflicts in Consciousness.* Urbana: U of Illinois P, 1984.

Sullivan, C. W., III. "Ann of Ages." *The Anna Book: Searching for Anna in Literary History.* Ed. Mickey Pearlman. Westport, CT: Greenwood P, 1992. 9–15.

Surrette, Leon. *The Birth of Modernism: Ezra Pound, T. S. Eliot, W. B. Yeats, and the Occult.* Montreal & Kingston: McGill-Queen's UP, 1993.

Thormählen, Marianne, ed. *T. S. Eliot at the Turn of the Century.* Sweden: Lund UP, 1994.

Tom and Viv. Dir. Brian Gilbert. Wr. Michael Hastings and Adrian Hodges. Perf. Willem Dafoe, Miranda Richardson. Miramax, 1994.

Tourneur, Cyril. *The Revenger's Tragedy.* Ed. Brian Gibbons. New York: Hill and Wang, 1967.

Tratnor, Michael. *Modernism and Mass Politics: Joyce, Woolf, Eliot, Yeats.* Stanford, CA: Stanford UP, 1995.

Tylor, Edward B. *Primitive Culture.* 1871. 2 vols. 6th ed. London: John Murray, 1920.

Underhill, Evelyn. *Mysticism.* 1911. New York: E. P. Dutton, 1961.

Unger, Leonard. *Eliot's Compound Ghost: Influence and Confluence.* University Park: The Pennsylvania State UP, 1981.

Vendler, Helen. "T. S. Eliot." *Time* 8 June 1998: 111–112.

Virgil. *The Aeneid.* Trans C. H. Sisson. Manchester: Carcanet P, 1986.

Warner, Marina. *Alone of All her Sex: The Myth and the Cult of the Virgin Mary.* New York: Vintage Books, 1983.

Weinberg, Kerry. "The Women of Eliot and Baudelaire: The Boredom, the Horror and the Glory." *Modern Language Studies* 14.3 (1984): 31–42.

Welter, Barbara. "The Cult of True Womanhood: 1820–1860." *The American Family in Social-Historical Perspective.* Ed. Michael Gordon. New York: St. Martin's, 1973. 224–250.

Weston, Jessie L. *From Ritual to Romance.* 1920. Princeton, NJ: Princeton UP, 1993.

Wiznitzer, Eileen. "Legends of Lil: The repressed thematic center of *The Waste Land.*" *The Female Imagination & the Modernist Aesthetic.* Eds. Sandra M. Gilbert and Susan Gubar. New York: Gordon and Breach Science Publishers, 1986. 87–102.

Index